THE CAMBRIDGE COMPANION TO WORLD LITERATURE

The *Cambridge Companion to World Literature* introduces the significant ideas and practices of world literary studies. It provides a lucid and accessible account of the fundamental issues and concepts in world literature, including the problems of imagining the totality of literature; comparing literary works across histories, cultures and languages; and understanding how literary production is affected by forces such as imperialism and globalization. The essays demonstrate how detailed critical engagements with particular literary texts call forth differing conceptions of world literature and, conversely, how theories of world literature shape our practices of reading. Subjects covered include cosmopolitanism, transnationalism, internationalism, scale and systems, sociological criticism, translation, scripts, and orality. This book also includes original analyses of genres and forms, ranging from tragedy to the novel and graphic fiction, lyric poetry to the short story and world cinema.

Ben Etherington is Senior Lecturer in the School of Humanities and Communication Arts and a member of the Writing and Society Research Centre at Western Sydney University. His monograph *Literary Primitivism* (2018) argues for a global conception of primitivism as a utopian reaction to the apotheosis of European imperialism. He is currently a Chief Investigator on the three-year Australian Research Council project *Other Worlds*, for which he is working with eminent Australian writers, including Alexis Wright and J. M. Coetzee, to explore the idiosyncratic ways in which writers create literary worlds. He is also known as a public commentator on universities and Australian literature.

Jarad Zimbler is Senior Lecturer in English Literature at the University of Birmingham, and Marie Skłodowska-Curie Global Fellow at the University of Illinois at Chicago. His previous publications bring together a range of approaches, from narratology and stylistics, to book history and the sociology of literature. His first monograph, *J. M. Coetzee and the Politics of Style* (2014), was shortlisted for the 2016 University English Book Prize. In his new research project, Literary Communities and Literary Worlds, he examines several mid-twentieth-century authors who moved from one literary field to another, and who reshaped their practices in response to their new literary environments.

T0381666

THE CAMBRIDGE COMPANION TO
WORLD LITERATURE

EDITED BY

BEN ETHERINGTON
Western Sydney University

JARAD ZIMBLER
University of Birmingham

CAMBRIDGE
UNIVERSITY PRESS

CAMBRIDGE
UNIVERSITY PRESS

University Printing House, Cambridge CB2 8BS, United Kingdom

One Liberty Plaza, 20th Floor, New York, NY 10006, USA

477 Williamstown Road, Port Melbourne, VIC 3207, Australia

314–321, 3rd Floor, Plot 3, Splendor Forum, Jasola District Centre,
New Delhi – 110025, India

79 Anson Road, #06–04/06, Singapore 079906

Cambridge University Press is part of the University of Cambridge.

It furthers the University's mission by disseminating knowledge in the pursuit of
education, learning, and research at the highest international levels of excellence.

www.cambridge.org
Information on this title: www.cambridge.org/9781108471374
DOI: 10.1017/9781108613354

© Cambridge University Press 2018

First published 2018

Printed in the United States of America by Sheridan Books, Inc.

A catalogue record for this publication is available from the British Library.

Library of Congress Cataloging-in-Publication Data
NAMES: Etherington, Ben, editor. | Zimbler, Jarad, 1980– editor.
TITLE: The Cambridge companion to world literature / edited by Ben Etherington,
University of Western Sydney ; Jarad Zimbler, University of Birmingham.
DESCRIPTION: Cambridge, United Kingdom; New York, NY : Cambridge University Press,
2018. | Includes index.
IDENTIFIERS: LCCN 2018011112 | ISBN 9781108471374
SUBJECTS: LCSH: Literature – History and criticism.
CLASSIFICATION: LCC PN523 .C36 2018 | DDC 809–dc23
LC record available at https://lccn.loc.gov/2018011112

ISBN 978-1-108-47137-4 Hardback
ISBN 978-1-108-45784-2 Paperback

CONTENTS

CONTENTS

PART II: PRACTICES

FIGURES

CONTRIBUTORS

CHRIS ANDREWS is a translator, scholar, and poet. He lectures at Western Sydney University. His translations include Roberto Bolaño's *By Night in Chile* (2003) and César Aira's *The Lime Tree* (2017). His monograph *Roberto Bolaño's Fiction: An Expanding Universe* was published by Columbia in 2014. He is currently working on potential literature within and beyond the Oulipo.

ANNA BERNARD is Senior Lecturer in English and Comparative Literature at King's College London. She is the author of *Rhetorics of Belonging: Nation, Narration, and Israel/Palestine* (2013), and has co-edited *What Postcolonial Theory Doesn't Say* (2015) and *Debating Orientalism* (2013). Her current book project, 'International Solidarity and Culture', considers the uses of literature and film in major international solidarity movements after 1975.

TIMOTHY BRENNAN is the Samuel Russell Chair in the Humanities at the University of Minnesota and the author of foundational essays in postcolonial theory. His early study on the role of US book markets and taste cultures in the making of 'world literature' can be found in *At Home in the World: Cosmopolitanism Now* (1997). His essays on intellectuals, imperial culture, and the politics of popular music have appeared in numerous publications, including *The Nation*, the *Times Literary Supplement*, *New Left Review*, *Critical Inquiry*, and the *London Review of Books*. He is the author most recently of the first of a two-volume study, *Borrowed Light: Vico, Hegel and the Colonies*, which traces the emergence of anti-colonial thought in Europe. He is currently at work on an intellectual biography of Edward W. Said.

BEN ETHERINGTON is Senior Lecturer in English in the School of Humanities and Communication Arts, and a member of the Writing and Society Research Centre at Western Sydney University. His work focuses on the relationship between literature and decolonization. His recent book, *Literary Primitivism*, argues that primitivism was a vexed utopian project adopted most vigorously by colonized artists. His current project traces the emergence of a creole poetics in the Caribbean in the period between the end of slavery and its flourishing at the time of political independence.

KEYA GANGULY is Professor in the Department of Cultural Studies and Comparative Literature at the University of Minnesota. Her research interests include film, postcolonial criticism, Critical Theory of the Frankfurt School, and the sociology of culture. She is the author of *States of Exception: Everyday Life and Postcolonial Identity* (2001) and *Cinema, Emergence, and the Films of Satyajit Ray* (2010). She was Senior Editor of *Cultural Critique* from 1998 to 2010, and is currently finishing a book on the revolutionary utopianism of the Indian nationalist Aurobindo Ghose.

LIZ GUNNER is Visiting Research Professor in the School of Languages at the University of Johannesburg. She is also a Professorial Research Associate at the School of Oriental and African Studies, University of London. She has written extensively on Zulu oral literature and more broadly on the role of verbal art in political and literary culture in southern Africa. Her present work covers cultures of performance, media, and the intersection of oral and written literary art. Her publications include the edited *Politics and Performance: Theatre, Poetry and Song in Southern Africa* (1994), *The Man of Heaven and the Beautiful Ones of God* (2002), the co-edited *Power, Marginality and African Oral Literature* (2008) and the co-edited *Radio in Africa: Publics, Cultures, Communities* (2012). Her book *Radio Soundings: South Africa and the Black Modern* is forthcoming with Cambridge University Press.

STEFAN HELGESSON is Professor of English at Stockholm University. His work has considered the relationship between postcolonial studies and comparative literature as they have collided within the purview of world literature, and includes the recent *Institutions of World Literature* (2015), which he co-edited. His first monograph was on Gordimer, Ndebele, and Coetzee, and his second book, *Transnationalism in Southern African Literature* (Routledge, 2009), theorized regional literary fields and networks. He currently leads the six-year Swedish research programme "Cosmopolitan and Vernacular Dynamics in World Literatures".

NEIL LAZARUS is Professor of English and Comparative Literary Studies at the University of Warwick. A prominent thinker in postcolonial literary studies, he has also been a key contributor in debates on world literature, particularly through his work with the Warwick Research Collective, whose collectively authored *Combined and Uneven Development: Towards a New Theory of World-Literature* appeared in 2015. Previous books include *The Postcolonial Unconscious* (2011) and *Nationalism and Cultural Practice in the Postcolonial World* (1999). He is currently working on a monograph entitled *Into Our Labours: Work and Literary Form in World-Literature*.

BORIS MASLOV is Associate Professor of Comparative Literature at the University of Chicago. He is a founding member of the Historical Poetics Working Group, and has played a significant role in recovering the work of A. N. Veselovsky for comparative literary study. His research centres on Archaic Greek poetry and its reception, as well as on imperial/Byzantine Greek and Russian literatures. He is the author of *Pindar and the Emergence of Literature* (2015), and co-editor of *Persistent Forms: Explorations in Historical Poetics* (2016). He is currently working on a book that traces the history and afterlife of Ancient Greek ethical and socio-political vocabulary.

SOWON S. PARK is Assistant Professor in English and Comparative Literature at the University of California, Santa Barbara. She has held faculty positions at Oxford and Ewha (Seoul), visiting fellowships at Zentrum für Literatur- und Kulturforschung Berlin and University of California, San Diego, and was the Alice Tong Sze Research Fellow at Cambridge. Her publications include a special issue of *The Journal of World Literature*, 'The Chinese Scriptworld', the Oxford Bibliographies entry on 'World Literature' (with J. Habjan), and 'The Unknown Masterpiece: On Pak Kyongni's *Land* and World Literature'. Her current work is on the relationship between cognitive neuroscience and literature.

SHITAL PRAVINCHANDRA is Lecturer in Comparative Literature and Culture at Queen Mary University of London. She has published articles in *Cultural Critique*, *Interventions* and *New Literary History* and is currently completing her first monograph, *Same Difference: Postcolonial Studies in the Age of Life Science*. Her new project considers the short story and world literature, exploring the popularity of this genre in South Asian regional-language literatures, particularly Hindi and Gujarati, in contrast to the dominance of the novel in Anglophone South Asian writing.

ATO QUAYSON is University Professor and Director of the Centre for Diaspora and Transnational Studies at the University of Toronto. He is the general editor of the *Cambridge Journal of Postcolonial Literary Inquiry*, and is also the editor of the *Cambridge History of Postcolonial Literature*. He has published widely on African and postcolonial literature and theory, postmodernism, magical realism, representations of disability, and urban studies. He has also published articles and book chapters on transnationalism and diasporic writing, including the recent monograph *Oxford St., Accra: Urban Evolution, Street Life and Itineraries of the Transnational* (2014). He is at present completing a new book on postcolonial tragedy.

CHARLOTTA SALMI, formerly a British Academy Postdoctoral Research Fellow at the University of Birmingham, has recently taken up a lectureship in Postcolonial and Global Literature at Queen Mary University of London. She is completing her first monograph, *Bordering the World in Post-Partition Literature*, whilst working on a new project, which considers violent textualities in graphic literature from the Middle East and South Asia. More broadly, her research is concerned with conflict narratives, popular resistance literature, narratology, and cultures of reading.

JARAD ZIMBLER is Senior Lecturer in English Literature at the University of Birmingham, and Marie Skłodowska-Curie Global Fellow at the University of Illinois at Chicago. His previous publications, which include the monograph

J. M. Coetzee and the Politics of Style (2014), bring together a range of approaches, from narratology and stylistics to book history and the sociology of literature. In his new research project, Literary Communities and Literary Worlds, he examines several mid-twentieth-century authors who moved from one literary field to another, and who reshaped their practices in response to their new literary environments.

ACKNOWLEDGEMENTS

The editors and contributors would like to thank all of those who have helped bring this volume to fruition, especially the commissioning editor at Cambridge University Press, Ray Ryan, and his assistant, Edgar Mendez, for their support and encouragement; the many anonymous readers, both of the original proposal and of individual chapters, who helped ensure that our perspectives on an impossibly large subject were less partial than they would otherwise have been; and, finally, Xu Bing, Rachel Bower, Christos Hadjiyiannis, Vandad Jalili, Darren Jorgensen, Madeleine Kelly, Michelle Kelly, Arvind Krishna Mehrotra, Masako Ogawa, Benita Parry, Sean Pryor, Nicola Sayers, Maria Suriano, Marilena Triandifillou, Phoebe Tucker, and Tim Wright – their generosity, which has taken various forms, is deeply appreciated.

CHRONOLOGY

As we explain in our Introduction, the history of world literature is the history of notions of literary totality. A simple list of significant literary works and their dates of publication would not be a chronology of world literature but a version of world literary history produced in accordance with one such notion. With this in mind, the following is a timeline of conceptions of literary totality, particularly those that have had the ambition of putting the verbal arts of all human communities on a comparative footing. As far as possible, we have tried to restrict entries to works where this ambition is explicit. These include texts focused on poetics and aesthetics that entertain speculations on the totality of literary activity, as well as signal anthologies that aim to cover a range of literary writings. We have made these selections in the awareness of our own limitations (which are linguistic, as much as disciplinary), and of the fact that those conceiving of the literary world tend to locate themselves at its centre. Something of this tendency is reflected in the telescoping nature of the timeline, whose spans grow smaller as they approach closer to our own moment, though this should also be taken to reflect the gathering pace of what now gets called globalization, as well as the attrition to which all verbal arts of the human domain are exposed.

We begin with the earliest works mentioned in this volume rather than with any putative origin for world literature, giving their titles in the language of composition (albeit in Roman script) in order to capture the linguistic diversity of the history of thinking about literary totality. Alongside the timeline of notable conceptualizations of world literature in the left-hand column (which includes theoretical texts discussed in this volume), we have plotted events of other kinds in the right-hand column: the appearance of key technologies and institutions of production, dissemination, and evaluation; and of specific literary works discussed by our contributors, and others related to them. This will enable readers to see the historical relations between the ideas of totality that this *Companion* introduces and the literary practices and materials by which they have been made possible and conditioned.

This chronology aims neither to promote a clearly defined canon of texts, nor to provide a comprehensive overview of the evolution of a single idea or theory. It is no more and no less than a guide to using this *Companion*, and a helpful starting point from which readers – and student readers in particular – might begin to chart further explorations of this topic. In this respect, it will be especially valuable when used in conjunction with the recommended scholarly texts listed under Further Reading at the end of the volume.

Date	Ideas of Literary Totality	Practices, Institutions, and Technologies
900–301 BCE		Development of Hebrew and Aramaic writing systems in the Middle East (*c.* ninth century BCE)
		Persian postal system is established; Homer's *Iliad* and *Odyssey* are transcribed (*c.* sixth century BCE)
		Pindar, *Epinikia* (498–444 BCE)
		Sophocles, *Oedipus Tyrranus* (*c.* 429 BCE)
		Vālmīki's *Rāmāyaṇa* is compiled (*c.* 400–200 BCE)
		Twenty-four-letter Ionic Greek alphabet is adopted (*c.* 400 BCE)
	Aristotle, *Poetics* (*c.* 335 BCE)	Vyāsa's *Mahābhārata* is transcribed (*c.* 350 BCE)
300–1 BCE		Library of Alexandria is founded (*c.* 290 BCE)
		Livius Andronicus, *Odusia* (*c.* 220 BCE)
	Nātya Sāstra, which is later attributed to Bharata Muni, begins to take shape (*c.* second century BCE)	Improvements are made in the production of parchment, as the supply of papyrus begins to dwindle across the Mediterranean (second century BCE)
		Tibullus, *Liber Primus* (*c.* 29–26 BCE)
0–299	Ban Gu, 'Yiwen zhi' (*c.* 50–90) Quintilian, *Institutio Oratoria* (*c.* 93–96)	
		Paper comes into general use across Chinese cosmopolis (*c.* third century)

Date	Ideas of Literary Totality	Practices, Institutions, and Technologies
300–599		Development of Ge'ez script in East Africa (*c.* fourth century)
		Chinese Regular Script becomes dominant throughout Chinese cosmopolis; Kālidāsa, *Śākuntala* (*c.* fifth century)
		Xiao Tong directs compilation of *Wen xuan* (*c.* 520–530)
	Liu Xie, *Wenxin diaolong* (*c.* 510–526)	Use of quill pens spreads throughout Europe (sixth century)
600–999	al-Mufaḍḍal al-Ḍābbī, *al-Mufaḍḍaliyyāt* (*c.* 762–784)	Emergence of Bhakti movement in South Asia; standardization of modern Arabic script (*c.* seventh century)
	Ānandavardhana, *Dhvanyāloka* (*c.* 850)	
	Ibn al-Muʿtazz, *Kitāb al-Badīʿ* (*c.* 887)	
1000–1299		Modern standardized form of Devanāgāri in widespread use in Northern India (*c.* eleventh century)
		Murasaki Shikibu, *Genji monogatari* (*c.* 1008)
		Commercial printing becomes widespread across Chinese cosmopolis (*c.* 1100)
	Niẓāmī ʿArūḍī Samarqandī, *Chahār Maqāla* (*c.* 1155)	*Sīrat Banī Hilāl* is composed; knowledge and use of paper spreads from China through the Middle East to Europe (*c.* twelfth century)
	Ibn Rushd, *Talkhīṣ Kitāb al-Shiʾr* (*c.* 1150–1190)	
		Sunjata epic is composed (*c.* thirteenth century)
1300–1499	Dante, *De vulgari eloquentia* (*c.* 1302–1305)	Maximus Planudes, *Anthologia Graeca* (1301)
	Ibn Khaldūn, *Muqaddimah* (1377)	First printing press developed by Gutenberg in Europe (*c.* 1440)
		Proclamation of *Hunminjeongeum*, establishing Hangul script in Korea (1446)
		Kabir is active (*c.* fifteenth century)
1500–1699	Lodovico Castelvetro, *Poetica d'Aristotele vulgarizzata e sposta* (1570)	Luís de Camões, *Os Lusíadas* (1572)
	Philip Sidney, *An Apology for Poetry* (1595)	Globe Theatre is founded (1599)
		William Shakespeare, *Othello* (1603)

Date	Ideas of Literary Totality	Practices, Institutions, and Technologies
	Henry Reynolds, *Mythomystes* (1632)	Miguel de Cervantes, *Don Quijote* (1605)
	Nicolas Boileau-Despréaux, *L'Art poétique* (1674)	'Ajamī script spreads through Africa (c. seventeenth century)
1700–1799	Giambattista Vico, *Principi di una scienza nuova* (1725)	Father Ximénez transcribes the Mayan epic *Popul Vuh* (c. 1701)
	August Ludwig von Schlözer uses the term 'Weltlitteratur' in *Isländische Litteratur und Geschichte* (1773)	Mwengo bin Athuman, *Utendi wa Tambuka* (c. 1728)
		Hong DaeYong, *Damheon yeongi* (1765)
	Johan Gottfried von Herder, *Briefe zu Beförderung der Humanität* (1797)	
1800–1849		Johann Wolfgang von Goethe, *West-östlicher Divan* (1819)
		Ntsikana, 'Ulo Thixo omkhulu' (c. 1815–1821)
	Karl Rosenkranz, *Handbuch einer allgemeinen Geschichte der Poesie* (1832)	Glasgow Missionary Society publishes Xhosa orthography (1824)
	Philarète Chasles delivers lectures on 'La Littérature étrangère comparée' in Paris (1835)	Rodolphe Töpffer, *Histoire de Monsieur Jabot* (1833)
	Johann Peter Eckermann, *Gespräche mit Goethe* (1836)	
	Karl Marx and Friedrich Engels, *Manifest der Kommunistischen Partei* (1848)	Industrialization of paper production (begins c. 1840s)
		Edgar Allan Poe, 'The Black Cat' (1843)
1850–1899	Johannes Scherr, *Allgemeine Geschichte der Literatur von den ältesten Zeiten bis auf die Gegenwart* (1851)	Sigismund Wilhelm Koelle, *Polyglotta Africana* (1854)
	First volume of *Alden's Cyclopedia of Universal Literature* (1885)	First commercial typewriters become available (1874)
	Hugo von Meltzl, 'Vorläufige Aufgaben der vergleichenden Literatur' (1887)	Hugo von Meltzl and Sámuel Brassai found the journal *Acta Comparationis Litterarum Universarum* (1877)
	Trübner's American and Oriental Literary Record (1889)	David Gestetner patents his Cyclostyle stylus (1881)
	James Frazer, *The Golden Bough* (1890)	Knut Hamsun, *Sult* (1890)
		Lumière brothers screen their first motion picture, *Sortie des Usines Lumière à Lyon*; Richard F. Outcault's strip *Hogan's Alley* begins (1895)
	Alexander Veselovsky, 'Tri glavy iz istoricheskoi poetiki' (1899)	

Date	Ideas of Literary Totality	Practices, Institutions, and Technologies
1900–1919	Benedetto Croce, *Estetica come scienza dell'espressione e linguistica generale* (1902)	First Pan-African Conference, in London (1900) Nobel Prize in Literature is established (1901) Prix Goncourt is established (1903) Prix Femina is established (1904)
	Rabindranath Tagore, 'Visva-Sahitya' (1907) Richard Moulton, *World Literature and its Place in General Culture* (1911)	
		Dadasaheb Phalke (dir), *Raja Harishchandra*; Rabindranath Tagore the first non-European to win the Nobel Prize in Literature (1913)
		Vladimir Mayakovsky, 'Poslushayte!'; Grand Prix du Roman de l'Académie française is established (1914)
	Maxim Gorky, 'Vsemirnaia literatura' (1919)	Vsemirnaia Literatura publishing house launched by Maxim Gorky in Petrograd (1918)
1920–1939	György Lukács, *Die Theorie des Romans* (1920)	PEN International is founded (1921)
	Zheng Zhenduo, 'Wenxue de tongyi guan' (1922)	
	John Macy, *The Story of the World's Literature* (1925)	
	Vladimir Propp, *Morfologija skazki* (1928)	Adoption of standard dialect and orthography for Swahili (1928)
	Mikhail Bakhtin, *Problemy tvorchestva Dostoevskogo* (1929)	Zaria Translation Bureau is founded (1930)
	Bruno Jasieński (ed.), *Literature of the World Revolution*, (1931–1932)	Index Translationum is established (1932)
	Giacomo Prampolini, *Storia universale della letteratura* (1932–1938) Philo Buck (ed.), *An Anthology of World Literature*; Kobayashi Hideo, 'Bungakkai no konran' (1934)	
	Walter Benjamin, 'Das Kunstwerk im Zeitalter seiner technischen Reproduzierbarkeit' (1936)	World Congress of Universal Documentation (1937)

Date	Ideas of Literary Totality	Practices, Institutions, and Technologies
	Ford Madox Ford, *The March of Literature: From Confucius to Modern Times* (1938)	J. L. Borges, 'La biblioteca total'; Stalin Prize is established (1939)
1940–1959		Stefan Heym, *Hostages* (1942)
	Qian Zhongshu, *Tan yi lu* (1948)	Founding of *Présence africaine* (1947)
	J. L. Borges, 'El escritor argentino y la tradición' (1951)	World Congress of Intellectuals in Defense of Peace; Aimé Césaire, *Soleil cou coupé* (1948)
	Erich Auerbach, 'Philologie der Weltliteratur' (1952)	Congress for Cultural Freedom is founded (1950)
	Calvin S. Brown, 'Debased Standards in World Literature Courses' (1953)	Alejo Carpentier, *Los pasos perdidos* (1953)
	S. H. Steinberg (ed.), *Cassell's Encyclopedia of World Literature* (1954)	Vladimir Nabokov, *Lolita* (1955)
	Maynard Mack (ed.), *The Norton Anthology of World Masterpieces*; József Reményi, *World Literatures* (1956)	Congress of Black Writers and Artists (1956)
	Raymond Queneau (ed.), *Histoire des littératures* (1955–1958); Roman Jakobson, 'Closing Statement: Linguistics and Poetics' (1958)	
1960–1969	Paul Celan, 'Der Meridian' (1961)	Mimeo revolution begins (*c.* 1960s)
	René Etiemble, 'Faut-il réviser la notion de *Weltliteratur*?'; first volume of Krishna Chaitanya's ten-volume *History of World Literature* published (1964)	Grand prix littéraire de l'Afrique noire is established; *Transition/ Ch'indaba* is founded (1961)
		José Craveirinha, *Xigubo* (1964)
	Nikolai Konrad, *Zapad i Vostok* (1966)	World Festival of Black Arts, in Dakar (1966)
	Jerome Rothenberg, *Technicians of the Sacred: A Range of Poetries from Africa, America, Asia, Europe and Oceania* (1968)	Booker Prize established; Ayi Kwei Armah, *The Beautyful Ones Are Not Yet Born* (1968)
1970–1979	Martin Seymour-Smith, *Guide to Modern World Literature* (1973)	Software-based word processing becomes widely available (1970s)
	Immanuel Wallerstein, *The Modern World-System, Vol. 1*; S. S. Prawer, *Karl Marx and World Literature* (1974)	Keiji Nakazawa, *Hadashi no Gen* (1973/1974)
		Barry Feinberg (ed.), *Poets to the People* (1974)
	Dionýz Ďurišin, *Teória literárnej komparatistiky* (1975)	Wole Soyinka, *Death and the King's Horseman* (1975)

Date	Ideas of Literary Totality	Practices, Institutions, and Technologies
	Paik Nak-chung, *Minjok munhak kwa segye munhak*; Nelson Goodman, *Ways of Worldmaking* (1978)	Premio Miguel de Cervantes is established (1976) Satjayit Ray, *Shatranj Ke Khilari* (1977)
1980–1989		Bridget Aldacara et al. (eds.) *Nicaragua in Revolution* (1980)
	Edward Said, *The World, the Text, and the Critic*; first volume of *Istorija vsemirnoj literatury v devjati tomach* published (1983) Fredric Jameson, 'Third-World Literature in the Era of Multinational Capitalism' (1986)	César Aira, *Ema, la cautiva* (1981) Abdelwahab Elmessiri (ed.), *The Palestinian Wedding* (1982) Wiesław Myśliwski, *Kamień na kamieniu* (1984) Commonwealth Writers' Prize is established (1987) Prémio Camões is established (1988) Public commercial use of the Internet begins (1989)
1990–1999	Itamar Even-Zohar, *Polysystem Studies* (1990) Sarah Lawall, *Reading World Literature* (1994) Timothy Brennan, *At Home in the World: Cosmopolitanism Now* (1997) Pascale Casanova, *La République mondiale des lettres*; Johan Heilbron, 'Towards a Sociology of Translation: Book Translations as a Cultural World-System' (1999)	Parlement international des écrivains is founded (1993) Sergey Brin and Larry Page register google.com (1997)
2000–2009	Franco Moretti, 'Conjectures on World Literature' (2000) Peter Singer, *One World: The Ethics of Globalization* (2002) David Damrosch, *What is World Literature?* (2003) Christopher Prendergast (ed.), *Debating World Literature*; David Damrosch et al. (eds.), *The Longman Anthology of World Literature*; Edward Said, *Humanism and Democratic Criticism* (2004)	Caine Prize is established; Marjane Satrapi, *Persepolis* (2000) Roberto Bolaño, 'El viaje de Álvaro Rousselot'; Franz Kafka Prize is established (2001) Ajay Navaria, *Paṭkathā aur anya Kahāniyāṁ* (2006)

Date	Ideas of Literary Totality	Practices, Institutions, and Technologies
2010–	Sheldon Pollock, *The Language of the Gods in the World of Men*; Michel Le Bris, Jean Rouad et al., 'Pour une littérature-monde en français' (2007) Emily Apter, *Against World Literature* (2013) WReC, *Combined and Uneven Development*; Alexander Beecroft, *An Ecology of World Literature* (2015) Aamir Mufti, *Forget English!* (2016)	J. M. Coetzee, *Summertime* (2009) Arvind Krishna Mehrotra, *Songs of Kabir*; S. Anand, Srividya Natarajan, Durgabai Vyam and Subhash Vyam, *Bhimayana* (2011)

BEN ETHERINGTON
AND
JARAD ZIMBLER

Introduction

World literature can arrive on your doorstep in any number of guises. Always seeming to come from afar, it may present itself as an adventurer, displaying the exotic spoils of distant lands; as a missionary, professing universal values; as a commercial traveller, peddling the wares of a global market; or even as a broadband technician, offering instant worldwide connectivity. In spite of their differences in costume and itinerary, and in the goods and services they deliver, each of these figures attests to a world in which human societies are connected. If the first few come with a whiff of Victoriana, they do so as a reminder that, even in our day, world literature travels by routes established in the moments of industrialization and imperialism.

This is all by way of saying that writers, scholars, critics, and students may well share reasons for grappling with the question of world literature, including the facts of existence in a globalized economy, but this does not mean that they are always speaking about the same thing. For some, world literature means exotic literature, verbal art of the world beyond their own; and, given the dominance of North American and European academic and literary institutions, such usage typically refers to literature produced beyond 'the West'. For others, world literature means a universal canon of master-pieces: the proverbial best that has been thought and said across histories and cultures. For still others, world literature consists of innumerable works that travel globally, exposing themselves to readers in new places and languages and taking part in the flows of transcultural interaction and exchange. In their contemporary manifestations, such notions inevitably take us into the web of the global market. World literature, some therefore insist, compels us to reflect on the ways in which works are caught up in an unequal world-system made up of highly developed centres and underdeveloped peripheries.

These differences in understanding are not simply matters of choice, because the manner in which world literature appears depends very much on the address at which it finds us, and where it is supposed to begin.

It certainly makes a difference how we interpret the two concepts of which world literature is compounded, but we need to keep in mind that these are both fluid and highly capacious, and act upon one another in such a way as to ensure that the meaning of *world literature* is irreducible to its constituent elements. If we wish to say what world literature is, we must also be prepared to think through fundamental questions concerning the shifting relationship between literature and the social world in which it is produced and experienced. These questions animate and give purpose to world literary studies, whose objective is nothing less than conceptualizing the entire sphere of literary activity. In view of these considerations, we cannot hope through this *Companion* to reach some kind of negotiated compromise between positions, for what we face is a *problematic*, not a stable object of study.[1]

World Literature as a Totality

As a starting point for confronting this problematic – and for exploring the conceptual frameworks implicated in conceiving *world literature*, as well as the ideological environments they entail – we suggest beginning with the following working definition of the term: the verbal arts of the human domain considered as a whole. This is admittedly very broad, and seemingly tautological, since verbal arts are usually deemed human by definition. It does, however, capture a constant aspect of *world* that we believe is important. There is a tendency today to think of *world* as being closely related to, or indeed much the same as *planet* or *globe*; to treat it as a synonym, in other words, for the spatial extension of the earth. But 'world' is both more and less than this. If we are able to speak of multiple planets, this is because 'planet' does no more than describe a certain kind of object, one of the celestial wanderers that ancient astronomers could distinguish from fixed points of the night sky. It is only by a later deduction that earth itself comes to be placed in the same category. As for 'globe', any planet can be one of these, and the number of globes in the universe approaches infinity.

The term world, however, tends to attach specifically to the domain of the human; where it does not – the animal world, the world of fashion, and so forth – it typically requires modification. It is also a temporal as much as a spatial concept. Indeed, the word originates from a sense both of the particularity of humanity's experience, and of the here and now, rather than the far and distant. It is one of a number of cognates belonging to Germanic languages – *Welt* (German), *wereld* (Dutch), *värld* (Swedish), *verden* (Danish) – that trace their roots to a nominal compound meaning something like 'age of man'.[2] Their meanings thus come to include: the material world; humanity's present, temporal state of existence; earthly things, or temporal possessions; an age; a person's conditions of life; the course of human affairs.[3] These meanings are extended in the kinds of compounds that Germanic languages delight in, all related to humans existing in secular time. In Old English, these include Aelfric's *weorold-cræft*, meaning a secular art; and Bede's *weoruld-gewritu*, meaning secular or profane literature. In Modern English, the sense lingers in the adjective 'worldly'.

If, in our time, we tend to confuse 'world' with 'planet' and 'globe', this reveals something about the current state of the imagination: humanity has subjugated the planet to its needs to the extent that we now unconsciously mistake the (human) world for the earth itself; at the same time, we conflate the world with globe because we tend to forget that, like the word human, world is an emphatic concept, being at once descriptive and qualitative. (An 'inhuman world' is an oxymoron; it has lost the qualities that make it a world.) It is therefore no coincidence that the surge of scholarly interest in 'world literature' over the last twenty years, a surge that has given rise to this *Companion*, has coincided with the popularity of 'globalization' and 'transnationalism', terms now used across disciplines in the social sciences and humanities. For many contemporary critics 'world literature' is simply shorthand for 'literature and globalization studies'.[4] They believe that the field's purpose is to reflect on the relationship between literature, however conceived, and the planetary expansion of capitalism, with its attendant forms of communication, market exchange, and statecraft.

This recent scholarship has been extensively discussed and picked over, and the chapters of this volume engage with it from a variety of angles.[5] There is no need, therefore, to tell the whole story again. However, it is worth remarking that the concerns of contemporary world literature studies have arisen largely from the exigencies of our present, and hardly encompass the numerous ways in which 'world literature' had been conceived previously. The influential work of Franco Moretti, Pascale Casanova, and David Damrosch should neither be passed over nor overemphasized. Without doubt, these scholars made distinctive contributions in conceptualizing the systems and processes by which literature moves through the world. Yet what is more striking today is that interventions in comparative literary sociology (Casanova's 'republic of letters'), translation studies (Damrosch's 'mode of circulation and reading'), and what would come to be called the digital humanities (Moretti's 'distant reading') were perceived as significant *qua* theories of 'world literature'. Above all, this testifies to the atmosphere of literary studies at the turn of the millennium. The apparently sudden promulgation of world literature as a field of *research* (displacing the term's

predominant usage as a banner for 'literatures of the world') was not insti-
gated solely by these scholars; rather, their efforts reflected a renewed appe-
tite for addressing the question of literary *totality*. In a 'rapidly globalizing'
world, it was felt that literary studies too would need to adopt 'one world'
thinking.[6]

We will say more shortly about literary totality, but it is helpful, first, to
consider the kinds of conceptual genealogies used by scholars in the new
world literary studies to frame their collective project. In general, they have
zeroed in on passages in which the formation of world literature appears as
the inevitable consequence of 'globalization' thought of in the *longue durée*.
For instance, critics treat as foundational fragmentary comments by Johann
Wolfgang von Goethe on '*Weltliteratur*' that concern the intensification of
high-level exchanges between cultures, especially in an industrializing
Europe, and they routinely cite a speculative aside from Karl Marx and
Friedrich Engels in the *Communist Manifesto* that mentions the term
Weltliteratur in connection with the rise of international markets. This outline of the concept's trajectory – one born of the growing awareness of the
impact of the expanding world-economy on literary communities – supplies
the form into which the variety of subsequent uses of 'world literature' are
then inserted as detail.

However, if we think of the term *Weltliteratur* as one conceptual manifestation of a question germane for literary communities across history –
what is literary totality? – a broader set of reflections and methodological
possibilities come into view. To take one example, the nineteenth-century
Russian philologist Alexander Veselovsky developed a critical approach he
called 'historical poetics' which looked to trans-historically attested formal
practices in order to speculate on deep relations between the morphologies of
verbal art and social processes. Veselovsky made use of the term world
literature when he was an exchange student in Berlin, but he has been absent
from the scholarly discussion, no doubt because of the field's current transnational predilections and conceptual strictures.[7]

The notion of 'totality' itself has a certain theoretical hue, bestowed by the
tradition of dialectical thought in particular. We use it here in a relatively
neutral sense to denote 'that which is concerned with the total'. Whether
articulated in terms of a 'domain', 'sphere', 'realm', 'ecology', 'zone', or,
indeed, 'world', totality brings to the fore the dynamic relationship between
parts and whole; that is, the ways in which the interrelations and interactions
of particulars cumulatively constitute a single intelligible entity. Totality in
this sense is not the same as the *universal*, which includes all that has existed,
currently exists, and might possibly exist, and which we might call the
totality of totalities, but instead denotes the always active configuration of

every particular at any given point. With this in mind, we might stop to formulate a second iteration of our definition of world literature: *the totality of verbal art.*

This iteration is offered with the proviso that any given framework may limit the set 'verbal art' in ways that restrict the number and the kinds of works that could be considered as world literature. Inevitably, these restrictions have to do with questions of value. This is especially apparent in the case of the canonical view of world literature, for which a basic criterion is that admissible works be acknowledged as great across many (if not all) cultures. The number of elements comprising the totality therefore becomes relatively small, but since greatness can be achieved regardless of where and when the work was made (at least in theory), the use of the term 'world literature' is justified in these instances. This also helps to explain something important about the other part of our definition: 'verbal art' is at once expansive, pointing beyond the printed text and received notions of what counts as properly 'literary', but also restrictive, insofar as it connotes works that are subjected to judgements of quality.

Making World Literature

'World Literature has to be made; it cannot simply be found', Chris Andrews remarks in this volume, echoing the formulation of Stefan Helgesson and Pieter Vermeulen:[8] 'As readers, students and teachers of world literature, we construct literary worlds by discerning relations at a range of scales.' Those coming to this field for the first time will find themselves faced with very different constructions of literary worlds, involving scales that often are incommensurate. One efficient way of sizing up any given theory of world literature is to ask how it conceives of i) the discrete elements of literary totality; ii) the nature of the movement and interaction of these elements; and, iii) the composite whole that these elements cumulatively constitute, as well as the temporal logic they assume.[9]

We might consider three recent accounts by way of demonstration. Alexander Beecroft proposes a trans-historical model of world literature for which the discrete elements are acts of verbal art across human history, and the nature of their circulation and interaction is determined by the socio-linguistic 'biome' in which they exist (local, national, cosmopolitan, global, and so forth). World literature thus consists of a meta-ecology of co-existing biomes.[10] The Warwick Research Collective proposes a materialist model for which the discrete elements are all literary works produced in the modern world-economy. These elements are shaped by their location within and interaction with this world-economy, one which is constitutively marked by uneven and combined development. World literature thus is rendered 'the literature of the modern world-system'.[11] Pheng Cheah proposes a normative conception of world literature for which the discrete elements are literary works which strive to establish a different temporal existence, and hence a different sense of totality, to that which globalization prescribes. These acts of temporalization project into ideal alternate worlds, and do not so much interact with as purposively disrupt the world created by global capitalism; thus, world literature is that which the fallen, globalized world necessitates.[12]

Clearly, each of these accounts offers a radically different conception of literary totality. They disagree on almost everything: how literary totality is related to the broader social totality; whether it consists of specifically literary elements; whether it is particular to the modern capitalist era; whether its existence is real or ideal. They also entail very different kinds of literary critical practice, although, in truth, criticism itself has often seemed secondary when it has come to thinking about world literature, with literary works frequently serving merely as illustrative examples. World literature can sometimes seem to be only one more battle-ground on which to renew enduring conflicts between materialism, phenomenology, historicism, anti-humanism, empiricism, and so forth. It is, however, a concept older than many current theoretical approaches, and the concern with literary totality is much older still, as Timothy Brennan explains in this volume. Whatever the reasons for its current popularity, the term brings with it a semantic halo, especially from humanist traditions, of fruitful literary exchange and a world-historical archive of human achievement. As such, the critical debate is also a battle for the term's soul: to redefine world literature is to commandeer literary ideals (or to disenchant them). The tensions we repeatedly encounter between different conceptions of world literature ultimately have to do with the direction in which literary studies itself is travelling.

The purpose of this *Companion* is not to advocate for any particular model of the totality of verbal arts, but to enable readers to navigate the diversity of approaches to world literature so that they themselves might wield the critical possibilities these make available. If the tendency has been to *debate* world literature, this volume is committed above all to *doing* world literature. It is committed, in other words, to exploring the totality of verbal arts through engagements with literary materials. *World literature* will be deemed a necessary concept or category only if it proves vital to understanding actual literary practices. In this respect, there is no reason for us to feign neutrality, especially since several theories of world literature place criticism itself out of court. The essays in this *Companion* attest to an overriding conviction that literary materials provide the best evidence of their worlds, both those which they constitute and those which shape them. This is a *Companion*, then, to world literary criticism.

We will shortly explain the organization of the volume in more detail; but before we do, we will take our bearings from a literary work. We do this to make tangible what world literary criticism demands as well as to introduce some of the ways in which familiar theorizations of world literature can be brought to bear in practice.

The Location of Cosmopolitanism

Some poems are born global, it would seem. The one we will read in a moment certainly gives that impression. It comes from *Songs of Kabir* (2011), a volume of translations by the Allahabad-based poet Arvind Krishna Mehrotra, which was published by New York Review Books in its 'nyrb Classics' series.

The choice to translate Kabir – the most celebrated of India's medieval *bhakti* poets – immediately brings Mehrotra into the ambit of several conceptions of world literature.[13] For Kabir has taken his place among those heroic figures of early modern demotic literatures (Dante, Boccaccio, Chaucer) whose works have attained the status of classics alongside the sacred and secular masterpieces of the ancient world. An anti-clerical mystic caught up in the cultural struggles of northern India in the late fifteenth century, Kabir nevertheless seems to address universal problems and values. Moreover, his oeuvre, and not only his stature, is very much the product of processes of translation and circulation, both within and beyond South Asia. There is no authentic text or set of texts we might identify with Kabir, who was in all likelihood unlettered; there is even some disagreement about the language in which he composed (probably 'the ancient composite idiom known as Hindui: the language of the bazaar');[14] but the poems, songs and sayings he uttered in public have found a place in the canon of great books through centuries of oral transmission in several dialects, of transcription in a number of different literary traditions, and of translation into a great many South Asian languages, as well as into languages such as Italian, French, German, English, Polish, and Russian. And with each moment of diffusion, his reputation, and the richness of his oeuvre seem to have been enhanced, not least because he has been taken up and translated by other significant poets, including Rabindranath Tagore, Ezra Pound, and Czesław Miłosz. Such headline acts did much to circulate Kabir's name in and out of the hypercentral language of English,[15] but it was the philologically rigorous translations of the French scholar Charlotte Vaudeville, produced in the postwar period, that enshrined Kabir in the metropolitan Academy, that laboratory of global prestige.[16]

In his introduction to *Songs of Kabir*, Mehrotra makes clear his debt to these metropolitan traditions of translation. This is in keeping with a long-standing and durable cosmopolitan disposition. Mehrotra has insisted for some time that the progress of his career depended on taking 'bearings from distant stars';[17] and, in a 2014 essay responding to the notion of world literature, he celebrated the 'globe-encircling stride' of three fellow Indian poet-translators.[18] These commitments do not find purchase only in his decision to offer another English-language rendering of Kabir. On the contrary, in his own practice as poet and translator, Mehrotra signals and amplifies the expansive cosmopolitanism of his source. The following is his translation of a *pada* – a short rhymed poem or lyric – found in several of the manuscripts of the 'western' tradition:[19]

> *Though only death has baffled him*
> *he owns the universe, the stars …*
> – Tom Paulin, 'Chorus'
>
> 'Me shogun.'
> 'Me bigwig.'
> 'Me the chief's son.
> I make the rules here.'
>
> It's a load of crap.
> Laughing, skipping,
> Tumbling, they're all
> Headed for Deathville.
>
> It takes only the blink
> Of an eye, says Kabir,
> For a king to be
> Separated from his kingdom.[20]

From its epigraph, the poem juxtaposes the human world with the unknowable expanse with which death confronts us. 'Death,' says Vaudeville, 'appears to be at the core of Kabir's thought. He speaks about it in the most vivid and blunt manner, using a variety of images and symbols mostly borrowed from popular tradition and direct, matter-of-fact observation.'[21] This characterization holds for Mehrotra's choices: 'Laughing, skipping, / Tumbling, they're all / Headed for Deathville' is a matter-of-fact if playful reminder of humanity's common end. But the poem is not simply about death; it is about the transience and boundedness of human dominion, and thus the world, a familiar figure for which is offered in the final word, *kingdom*.

Lest the theme's universality elude us, Mehrotra provides a prompt in his choice of epigraph. The lines he selects from Tom Paulin's poem follow its opening distich: 'There are many wonders on this earth / and man has made the most of them'.[22] Taken together, the four lines key us into a concern with the challenge mortality presents to universalizing human endeavour. It is not incidental that Paulin himself is offering a version of lines from Sophocles's *Antigone*. The original likewise is concerned with the extent and scope of human power, and the limits imposed by death.[23] The epigraph thus links Kabir (and Mehrotra) with another figure of world classics, and Mehrotra (and Kabir) with a contemporary Northern Irish poet-translator working in English, weaving a web that starts to encircle the world spatially and temporally. It also intimates a shared Indo-European linguistic and even cultural heritage. In a note which follows the poem, Mehrotra makes such connections explicit, informing us that the figuring of an instant in time as a 'blink/ Of an eye' (*palak*, पलक) 'goes back 3,500 years and occurs universally. It is there in the *Rig Veda* and the *Ramayana*, in Sophocles and Euripides, and in the Armenian oral epic *Sassountsy David'*.[24]

Mehrotra's translational practice and poetics seem to enact this world-encircling paratextual framing. His lexical choices carry Kabir over into not just another linguistic-cultural domain, but another time. *Bigwig, load of crap, headed* and *Deathville*, and contractions such as *they're* and *it's* are somewhat idiomatic and colloquial, ensuring a sense of near-contemporaneity. They also seem to avoid imbuing the verse with any detail that would require specific regional knowledge. There is no linguistic marker of the poem's subcontinental origins (even the poet's name can be traced to Arabic rather than Indic roots). As for the versification, the lines may not scan as regular feet, but they are all short (three to five syllables) and grouped neatly into quatrains; and in the first two stanzas, line-breaks correspond with syntax. There is nothing very unusual about this structure. In fact, the poem could be read as a modified Shakespearean sonnet, with Kabir's maxim coming at the turn, and the epigraph serving as a pre-emptive couplet. At the same time, the line-break on 'blink', which renders time also as space, exploits techniques associated with imagism, conjuring Pound, another of Kabir's translators. This will be approachable fare for readers schooled in the strategies of twentieth-century free verse.

In a number of ways then, Mehrotra seems to assert the universality of Kabir through the cosmopolitanism of his own practice. The poem's theme, its paratexts and allusions, and even its language and prosody apparently perform a kind of de-localization; something all the more pronounced when we consider the circumstances of its publication. It would be easy to advance the claim that Mehrotra exemplifies a world literature consisting of innumerable works that travel and circulate globally, taking part in the free flow of transcultural interaction and exchange; or to treat him more sceptically, by focusing on how, writing from a semi-peripheral position in the world republic of letters, he lays claim in various ways to a metropolitan inheritance and its associated symbolic capital. Another perspective might see the poem's unusual mixture of sources and literary styles as testimony to asynchronous orders of experience bearing the pressures of an unequal global system. Whichever framework we adopt, the poem appears as the manifestation of the literary totality wrought by globalization to which it transparently attests. Kabir's maxims are updated and made available to the modern English-speaking citizen of the world ('it only takes a tweet for an autocrat's stocks to tumble').

The preceding paragraphs give some flavour of world literary themes and approaches that might be brought to bear when reading a poem such as Mehrotra's, although these certainly do not exhaust or put an end to interpretative possibilities. Thus far, we have loosely characterized the poem's language as colloquial and contemporary, but this is only partially true of the first stanza. Here, the syntax of the first three sentences evoke a pidgin (a contact language usually devised for purposes of trade).[25] The phrase 'chief's son' seems to allude in particular to the stereotyped form of American Indian Pidgin English, popularized from the 1930s onwards in radio, film, and television westerns.[26] The other predicates of the first stanza – *shogun*, *bigwig* – may not originate in America, but both words are associated, like *chief*, with a kind of outmoded, even antiquated form of authority. Japan's shogunate was abolished in 1867; and, since male wigs were unfashionable by the end of the eighteenth century, *bigwig* was used in a satirical, comic, or derogatory sense almost from the outset. A thoroughgoing and derisive scepticism about claims to power, towards which the remainder of the poem will push, is already lodged in the lexis and syntax of these opening lines. They evoke situations of agonistic encounter between different cultures, and the clichés these produce. As Mehrotra explains in his introduction, Kabir was himself the product of an encounter (and conflict) between Hinduism and Islam, and the way in which the poem articulates, shapes, and satirizes these claims to power are relevant to Mehrotra's own situation, as a poet writing in English in the lingering aftermath of British imperialism.

There are other ways in which the poem resists a blithely cosmopolitan reading. One of these can be followed if we return to the theme of death. *Deathville* is a fairly hokey figuration of humanity's end as some kind of townlet or suburban neighbourhood; a fitting way to terminate a stanza in which worldly actions and activities are viewed as the antics of a parading troupe of clowns and acrobats. The phrase translates *jamapuri*, which means, literally, the town or city of Yama, the god of death and the underworld.[27] Other translators have preferred the sombre and sonorous 'City of Death', or the more matter-of-fact 'Death City'.[28] Why Deathville?

The OED informs us that '-ville' is chiefly associated with American collo-quial speech, especially of the 1930s through to the 1960s. The *Dictionary of American Slang* confirms that, from the mid-fifties to the mid-sixties, the suffix was 'in wide bop and cool use', often designating a place or a state as uninteresting, as in '*Dullsville*', '*Hicksville*', and '*squaresville*'.[29] *Deathville*, then, is a means of mocking death, and also of associating Kabir with the countercultural charge of a particular place and period, and even a particular poetry, that of the Beats, whose own preferences were for a language of the everyday and, no less important, one which drew much of its vocabulary from African-American Vernacular English.[30]

'Deathville' coheres with the stanza's opening line – 'It's a load of crap' – which is similarly associated with mid-century American colloquial uses. (Mehrotra is also borrowing from Philip Larkin, who likewise uses the phrase when evoking the imaginative worlds of American popular fictions.)[31] More broadly, it is consistent with Mehrotra's practice across his career and, indeed, with the practice of the Indian poet Arun Kolatkar, responsible for translating other key figures of the *bhakti* movement. Of Kolatkar, Mehrotra writes: 'gangster films, cartoon strips and blues had shaped his sense of the English language and he felt closer to the American idiom, particularly Black American speech, than to British English'.[32] Mehrotra is by no means identical with Kolatkar, but they share an interest in the Beats, an investment in American speech, as well as the intuition that there are real parallels between *bhakti* poetry and blues, notably that 'each speaks in the idiom of the street'.[33]

As it happens, Kolatkar is one of three authors Mehrotra identifies with the 'globe-encircling stride'. The other two are Toru Dutt and A. K. Ramanujan. All three were Indian poet-translators, which is in fact the central point of his argument: that there is a peculiarly Indian way of translating the past. In this light, it is worth returning to Mehrotra's remarks on his foreign influences, this time quoted in full:

> In 1964, the year Nehru died, the year V. S. Naipaul's *An Area of Darkness* was published, I was sitting in darkness's heart, in a bungalow in Allahabad, in a railway waiting room in Bilaspur, and as scores of Indian poets – from Henry Derozio to Srinavas Rayaprol – had done before me, I was taking my bearings from distant stars. The two I took mine from were e. e. cummings and Kahlil Gibran.[34]

It is striking that, before Mehrotra gets to his distant stars he locates himself not just in a year, but in a specific moment of Indian political history and diasporic literary history. He also locates himself in specific places which localize the horizon of his cosmopolitanism, so that, in the very act of seeking guidance from elsewhere, Mehrotra aligns himself most clearly with a tradition of Anglophone Indian poets stretching back to the nineteenth century. The significance of staking out this tradition, moreover, cannot be understood without also understanding the particular position-takings within the Indian literary field, which have been sub-tended, at least since the 1950s, by arguments about the value of English as a literary language, and of literary models which seem to be imported from abroad. In fact, the character of these arguments is crucial to appreciating the aesthetic logic which underlies the preference for translating the *bhakti* poets over Sanskrit texts, as much as it underlies a preference for a counter-cultural American idiom.

So, whilst seeming to celebrate unfettered and borderless cosmopolitanism, Mehrotra is in fact describing materials and practices characteristic of a literary community in which he himself is embedded. He re-assimilates a North-Indian syncretism inherent to the Kabir tradition, and in so doing rescues that which is alive in Kabir's verse from a global dispersion that had threatened to render it either as a philological specimen or the conduit of bland truisms. 'Me Shogun' draws on literary materials thrown up by an interconnected global totality, but does so in order to testify to the nonsynchronous presence of the Kabirian sensibility in a political environment marked by humourless religious nationalism. Mehrotra's Kabir is thus caught up in aesthetic currents peculiar to the Indian literary situation and South Asian politics, and the constraints and dynamics inherent in local and localized literary materials. If we cannot, or could not, see this straightaway – if we were tempted to mistake Mehrotra's surface cosmopolitanisms and his literary world for that transnationalism celebrated recently by scholars in the United States and Europe – this suggests the pitfalls of any critical or pedagogical practice that takes for granted the meaning, and indeed existence, of world literature.

Worlds and Practices

World literature has to be made, but its constituent elements are not inert components that can be fixed into place. The literary materials out of which we construct literary worlds are themselves alive, because they too are made. For this reason, the essays in this volume are attentive above all to the relationship between literary crafts or practices, and the worlds into which they extend. They demonstrate how detailed critical engagements with literary materials call forth conceptions of totality and, conversely, how contentions regarding literary totality entail certain critical commitments.

The chapters in Part I, 'Worlds', set out from the latter perspective. They raise general problems of conceptualization and interrogate some of the major frameworks and theorists in the field in order to consider how certain models of world literature arrange our attention and disposition towards particular literary acts. The chapters in Part II, 'Practices', work from particular genres, techniques, modes, and forms out to the configurations and networks of literary traditions and worldly institutions that these set into motion. They also reflect on the kinds of worldmaking undertaken by particular practices.

In the *Companion*'s opening chapter, Timothy Brennan gives an overview of world literature and cosmopolitanism which shows that the intellectual traditions behind both are double-sided. He pushes against the inclinations of scholars to treat hegemonic forms of cosmopolitanism as instances of a pluralism without prejudice, and to take world literature as a colloquy of those writers with easy access to metropolitan centres. For Brennan, Herder, not Goethe, is the key progenitor of *Weltliteratur* as an anti-imperial ideal, and internationalism, not transnationalism, is the mode of this world literature's cosmopolitanism. He calls for a 'sociological hermeneutic' that 'captures the affiliative networks of authors choosing, strategizing, carving out a space in a hostile commercial environment of circles, schools, and class fractions', and intimates the outcome of such an approach in addressing the work of Alejo Carpentier.

Anna Bernard's discussion of nation and transnationalism follows suit, identifying affiliative international networks of anti-colonial writers working within discrete national contexts. She looks to the poetry anthologies that arose in connection with anti-colonial struggles in Palestine, South Africa, and Nicaragua, and that were circulated through movements of international solidarity, to draw attention to the interlinking of national liberation movements. The choice between nation and transnationalism is thus revealed as a bad one, and Bernard is able to call into question the assumption that world literary studies entails the transcendence of the former. Ben Etherington, whose essay considers the epistemological and critical challenges that scale poses for conceptions of world literature, highlights the antagonistic relation between literary and economic value. He argues that the circumstances of globalization have compelled 'world literature' to become a negative concept. Therefore, rather than mapping networks, mega-data and interconnections, the onus is on world literary studies to seek out latent solidarities of localism across literary cultures and works that are united in their opposition to the economization of social life. He reads works by Aimé Césaire as poetic enactments of such an alternate meridian for world literature.

Jarad Zimbler's chapter takes up the question of what a world literary sociological hermeneutic might involve, especially if it were to set out from Pierre Bourdieu's notion of the literary field. This framework has been adapted in several studies of world literature, and Zimbler undertakes an immanent critique of the most prominent amongst them, Pascale Casanova's. He considers the literary practices and publication histories of two writers, Vladimir Nabokov and Stefan Heym, who moved from one literary field to another, as a way of exploring how literary relationality is established, and how it comes to define those horizons of possibility that shape a work's effects and meanings. The critical engagement with socio-logical questions is carried over into Stefan Helgesson's chapter on world literature as translation, which merges Casanova's transnational institu-tional analysis with Beecroft's typologies of circulation in order to under-stand the variegated life of translated texts as they unfold in an uneven global linguistic system. Looking first at the 'scarcely translated' work of the nationally celebrated Mozambican poet José Craveirinha, Helgesson shows how even a single poem can get caught up simultaneously in different ecologies of circulation, each bringing quite different actors into play. He then discusses the ways in which J. M. Coetzee's work anticipates its trans-lated versions, demonstrating, conversely, that assumptions about the stabi-lity of a source text are undermined when its compositional horizon already includes those 'textual zones' into which it might extend.

The circulatory ecologies with which Helgesson is concerned are deter-mined by the reach and movement of particular languages. Sowon Park's chapter on 'scriptworlds' shows that attending to the media in which these languages are transcribed produces, over and again, a different literary cartography. Scripts frequently cluster together several languages, revealing intermediate arenas and networks of interaction. Moreover, as Park explains, they condition 'the form, structure and even mode or genre' of literary works, as well as our psycho-affective relation to literary language. In thinking about how script worlds interact, Park looks to Xu Bing, whose inter-script experiments exploit the semantic and aesthetic expectations attaching to different scripts. Liz Gunner's chapter addresses an even larger lacuna in world literary studies: oral literature. The inclusion of verbal art that is publicly performed and somatically rendered requires the field funda-mentally to rethink its models, not only by reflecting diachronically on the periods in human history in which verbal art was predominantly oral, but also by understanding the complex ways in which oral forms persist, circu-late through new technologies, and interact with the world of print. Gunner considers first the case of the West African epic *Sunjata*, and then the genre of praise poetry across the African continent. A world literature that encompasses orality throws up challenges for comparison and demands quite different forms of expertise and data collection than those methodologies centred on print archives and their digital doppelgangers.

In the first of our 'Practices' chapters, Boris Maslov outlines one route into the kinds of comparison that Gunner demands. Drawing on Veselovsky's historical poetics, Russian formalism, and structural linguistics, Maslov's account of the lyric evokes a literary totality that is universally expansive. His chapter moves across the millennia, and between lyric poems in several ancient and modern languages, offering a trans-historical analysis of instances of the odic, elegiac, and epigrammatic modes. He thereby brings attention to the (non-teleological) ways in which literary forms and poetic principles recur across cultures and histories. Ato Quayson's discussion of tragedy conjures a similarly vast world. Quayson also understands literary totality as trans-historical and transcontinental, though he sees the basis for comparison less in literary forms and principles and more in what he describes as the 'ethico-cognitive' underpinnings of literary production. In the case of tragedy, these have to do with a desire to enact and experience suffering, and it is here that Quayson finds grounds for comparing tragedies by Sophocles, William Shakespeare, and Wole Soyinka.

The particular works Maslov and Quayson address may suggest a canon of literary classics, but the world each brings into view is much more extensive, both spatially and temporally. In other chapters in Part II, the forms addressed tend to open out into a totality whose elements are circumscribed by the modern world economy. Of these, the novel, often considered the paradigmatic literary form of capitalist modernity, has been pre-eminent in the recent theoretical debates. Neil Lazarus's approach to the novel begins by arguing that the insinuation of commodity production into all aspects of social life has produced the conditions for the 'full *worlding* of capital', and that literary production across all human societies has thus had to contend, since the nineteenth century, with a unified, though uneven world-system. Lazarus argues that this predicament calls for comparative methods that look to analogous 'generative situations' of literary works. In this vein, he gives detailed readings of Ayi Kwei Armah's *The Beautyful Ones Are Not Yet Born* and Wiesław Myśliwski's *Stone Upon Stone* as novels that thematize labour, and which register, through *form*, the character of the world-system as it is experienced in particular situations.

Charlotta Salmi's account of the graphic narrative considers the emergence of varieties of 'sequential art'. From the outset, these were products of 'crossover and cultural exchange' fostered by European imperialism and colonial expansion; and comics today seem exemplary instances of cultural goods on a global market, especially in view of the apparent ease with which images can circulate across linguistic boundaries. But Salmi explores other ways in which graphic narrative exists as a 'transnational form' through detailed readings of three texts. The first – Keiji Nakazawa's ground-breaking manga *Barefoot Gen* – has been extensively translated, adapted, and circulated, and thus provides evidence of the kind of world literary text theorized by Damrosch; whilst Marjane Satrapi's *Persepolis* and Anand, Natarajan, and the Vyams' *Bhimayana* express what Edward Said describes as 'worldliness'. Like Salmi, Shital Pravinchandra questions the tendency of world literature scholars to privilege the novel. In her chapter on the short story, she notes that the form's brevity should make it more readily available for circulation and consumption than the novel, and also that particular short stories are frequently relied upon to ensure diverse regional representation in anthologies. Yet the short story is largely absent from theoretical debates. As a form that frequently plays a key role in 'peripheral' nations, the short story calls for an approach that is oriented to the conditions of production elsewhere than in the metropolitan centres of Europe and the United States. Surveying several such contexts, Pravinchandra comes to focus on metafictional and intertextual strategies in Dalit short fiction, and in the work of Ajay Navaria in particular.

The *Companion*'s penultimate chapter considers world cinema, a form which also exists within the fold of the economy of the modern world-system. Keya Ganguly turns to debates about world cinema in order to interrogate the theoretical premises of much recent world literature scholarship. Although she affirms the importance of integrating 'a materialist understanding of culture under capitalism with an interrogation of art forms', she is sceptical about the systems-based theories that have been so influential in world literature. She calls for a dialectical criticism that moves away from reductively contextual readings, and engages with the world-historical contradictions sedimented in the form and technique of art works. Her careful analysis of Satyajit Ray's *The Chess Players* brings into view the particular importance of temporality as a necessary element both of the world with which works are concerned, and the ways in which narrative functions.

Our volume is brought to a close by Chris Andrews, who returns to the question of translation, but from the perspective of someone who has been centrally involved in carrying over into the English-speaking world the work of Roberto Bolaño, the Chilean writer frequently cited as exemplary of contemporary world literature. Andrews's experience allows him to describe in concrete terms the many 'valves' that regulate the flow of literary works, and to remind us that the networks which sustain translation often consist of a relatively small number of people, and can be fragile. It is therefore always possible that, when 'circulating works reach a dead end', sometimes through incomprehension or ignorance rather than bad faith, the network might become a labyrinth which 'entraps as well as connects'. This insight is developed in careful readings of the ways in which Bolaño, Jorge Luis Borges, and César Aira themselves engage, through their practice, with the valves of world literature.

As will be clear from the foregoing synopses, the chapters in this volume neither pursue a single approach, nor pretend to cover all possible theories, histories, or literary forms that might be considered within the remit of world literature. The regions and cultures addressed through particular works and authors are only a fraction of those making up the human world as it currently exists, let alone of those that have existed previously; and, with more space, we might well have solicited chapters on literary experimentation, the Internet and digital practices, life writing, literature and the Anthropocene, script-writing and adaptation, and any number of further subjects. Our brief is not to cover world literature from every angle, but to show that each engagement with world literature brings into play different possible angles. We hope that the following essays will give readers the basis to think for themselves in world-literary terms about other authorships, cultures, geographies, histories, genres, and media.

Notes

1. In saying this, we mean something different from Franco Moretti's well-known contention that world literature is a 'problem'. Moretti was alluding to the methodological challenges that arise when world literature is approached as the sum of all literary texts, not the problematic of conceptualizing 'world literature' itself. F. Moretti, 'Conjectures on World Literature', *New Left Review*, 1 (2000), 54–68 (p. 55).
2. Vladimir Orel postulates a proto-Germanic compound formed of *wiraz* (man, hero) and *aldiz* (age, nourishment, period of growth), in his *Handbook of Germanic Etymology* (Leiden: Brill, 2003), p. 462.
3. J. Bosworth and T. N. Toller, *Anglo-Saxon Dictionary* (Oxford: Clarendon Press, 1898), p. 1193–1194.
4. A critical appraisal of the relation between world literature and globalization studies is found in E. Hayot, 'World Literature and Globalization', in T. D'haen, D. Damrosch, D. Kadir (eds.), *The Routledge Companion to World Literature* (London: Routledge, 2012), pp. 223–231.
5. Theo D'haen provides a concise synopsis of recent debates and their prehistory in *The Routledge Concise History of World Literature* (London: Routledge, 2012).
6. Peter Singer made signal use of the term 'one world' in a lecture series delivered in 2000, later published as: *One World. The Ethics of Globalization* (New Haven: Yale University Press, 2002). Aamir Mufti recently has argued that the genealogy of such 'one world thinking' can be traced to the 'classical phase of modern

Orientalism'. *Forget English! Orientalisms and World Literatures* (Cambridge: Harvard University Press, 2016), p. 19.

7. A. N. Veselovksy, 'Envisioning World Literature in 1863: From the Reports on a Mission Abroad', B. Maslov (ed. and intro.), J. Flaherty (trans.), *PMLA*, 128.2 (2013), 439–451. For more on Veselovsky, see Maslov's chapter in this volume.

8. S. Helgesson and P. Vermeulen, 'Introduction: World Literature in the Making', in Helgesson and Vermeulen (eds.), *Institutions of World Literature: Writing, Translation, Markets* (New York: Routledge, 2016), pp. 1–22 (p. 1).

9. For Eric Hayot also, 'totality' presents a helpful means of abstracting from and comparing the various conflicting meanings assigned to 'world' in recent scholarship, though his own purpose is to prepare the ground for a method of analysis focused on the worlds made by literary works, and how these relate to the world at large. 'On Literary Worlds', *Modern Language Quarterly*, 72.2 (2011), 129–161.

10. A. Beecroft, *An Ecology of World Literature: From Antiquity to the Present Day* (London: Verso, 2015).

11. Warwick Research Collective, *Combined and Uneven Development: Towards a New Theory of World-Literature* (Liverpool: Liverpool University Press, 2015), p. 15.

12. P. Cheah, *What is a World? On Postcolonial Literature as World Literature* (Durham, NC: Duke University Press, 2016). Cheah's distinction between 'world' and 'globe' is similar to our own, though it is made en route to advocating an ethical approach.

13. The *bhakti* movement – principally a religious, devotional movement – emerged on the subcontinent in the seventh century CE. The poets associated with this movement, who are also revered as saintly figures, are notable for refusing the monopoly of the priestly class, as well as of the priestly language, Sanskrit.

14. C. Vaudeville, *A Weaver Named Kabir* (Oxford: Oxford University Press, 1993), p. 121.

15. Tagore's *One Hundred Poems of Kabir*, based on a Bangla translation by Kshiti Mohan Sen, was published in 1915, two years after Tagore had become the first non-European to win the Nobel Prize in Literature, and eight years after he had presented his views on what he called *visva sahitya*; a phrase which recent translators have taken to mean 'world literature', but which might just as easily be translated 'universal arts'. Tagore's enthusiasm for Kabir sparked the interest of other English-language poets, including Ezra Pound and, later, Robert Bly.

16. Kabir, *Kabīr granthāvāli (dohā)*, C. Vaudeville (ed. and trans.) (Pondichéry: Institut Français d'Indologie, 1957); Kabir, *Kabīr*, Vol. I, C. Vaudeville (ed. and trans.) (Oxford: Clarendon Press, 1974).

17. A. K. Mehrotra, 'Introduction', *A History of Indian Literature in English* (New York: Columbia University Press, 2003), p. 26.

18. A. K. Mehrotra, 'Translating the Indian Past: The Poets' Experience', *Journal of Commonwealth Literature*, 49.3 (2014), 427–439.

19. There are three principal traditions in which Kabir has been transmitted: the Bijak, or eastern tradition; the Rajasthani, or western tradition; and the Adi Granth, or Sikh sacred text.

20. A. K. Mehrotra, *Songs of Kabir* (New York: New York Review Books, 2011), p. 67. Mehrotra translates the version included as *pada* 3.53 in Mata

Prasad Gupta's *Kabir Granthavali* (Allahabad, 1969). This is *pada* 263 in *The Millennium Kabir Vani*, W. M. Callewaert et al. (eds.) (New Delhi, 2000), p. 370.

21. Vaudeville, *Kabīr*, p. 147.

22. T. Paulin, *The Road to Inver: Translations, Versions, Imitations* (London: Faber and Faber, 2004), p. 17.

23. See: Sophocles, *Antigone*, R. C. Jebb (trans.) (Bristol: Bristol Classical Press, 2004), pp. 69–77.

24. Mehrotra, *Songs of Kabir*, pp. 66–67.

25. See J. Holm, *An Introduction to Pidgins and Creoles* (Cambridge: Cambridge University Press, 2000), pp. 4–6.

26. *Chief* is used to mean 'the headman or ruler of a clan' from the late sixteenth century, particularly as a 'jocular name (modelled on the speech of American Indians) given to a person of authority or importance'. *Oxford English Dictionary*, 'chief', *n*, II.b.

27. *Jamapuri* is a transliteration of the word that appears in various manuscripts as जमपुरि, जंमपुरि or जंपुरि. See Callewaert et al., p. 370.

28. See, for example, the versions of KG2 179 by Vaudeville in *A Weaver Named Kabir*, p. 226; and by S. Singh and L. Hess, *The Bijak of Kabir* (Oxford: Oxford University Press, 2002), pp. 54–55. In his own version of the *pada*, Mehrotra again translates *jamapuri* as Deathville.

29. H. Wentworth and S. B. Flexner (eds.), *Dictionary of American Slang*, 2nd supplemented edition (New York: Thomas Y. Crowell Company, 1975), p. 625. Italics in original.

30. Rosemarie Ostler, who associates the proliferation of '–ville' explicitly with the Beats, explains that their 'group vernacular' was 'largely a version of hipster slang spoken by African-American musicians and bebop fans in 1950s New York'. *Dewdroppers, Waldos, and Slackers: A Decade-by-Decade Guide to the Vanishing Vocabulary of the Twentieth Century* (Oxford: Oxford University Press, 2003), pp. 112–113.

31. P. Larkin, 'A Study of Reading Habits', *Collected Poems*, Anthony Thwaite (ed.) (London: Faber and Faber, 1988), p. 131.

32. A. K. Mehrotra, 'Death of a Poet', in Arun Kolatkar, *Collected Poems in English*, A. K. Mehrotra (ed.) (Highreen: Bloodaxe Books, 2010), pp. 12–40 (p. 29).

33. Mehrotra, 'Death of a Poet', p. 30. The contact with the Beats also had a personal dimension. Kolatkar met Allen Ginsberg in 1962, as did his publisher, Ashok Shahane, who was the first to publish Ginsberg's 'September on Jessore Road', which he printed and distributed in Bombay in 1971.

34. Mehrotra, 'Introduction', p. 26.

PART I

Worlds

I

TIMOTHY BRENNAN

Cosmopolitanism and World Literature

Simply to entertain the idea of world literature is already to be cosmopolitan, it would seem. How else might global humanity find itself on the same page, except by adopting cosmopolitanism's openness to difference? As soon as the view implicit in this question is accepted, the totality of literature becomes a kind of family romance: national bigotries and taste preferences – plaguing relations between countries in other areas – are overcome when writers around the world have more in common with each other than with their own compatriots, and speak the lingua franca of the imagination.

But this is only how it seems, for cosmopolitanism in history is far from straightforward. In Greek antiquity, the notion of *cosmopolis* was more about absorbing other nations than understanding them. The idea became pronounced in the wake of Alexander's conquests, when Stoic philosophers sought to knit together the natural and social orders, thereby giving divine sanction to the Greek nobility of mind as it was being spread on a spear-point to the 'barbarian' world. Take a second historical example: the great inter-war Italian theorist Antonio Gramsci, a revolutionary who studied philology at the University of Turin, saw cosmopolitanism as the natural outlook of a centralizing and incorporative Catholic Church. He pointed out that in the early centuries of the first millennium, the Church had stepped into the shoes of the Roman Empire by taking over its role of disarticulating local cultures and languages across Europe in the name of an 'imperial-universal' based on the authority of Rome and the (now hieratic) language of Latin.

The remarkable late-eighteenth-century philosopher of language, cognition, and world history, Johann Gottfried Herder, was equally hesitant. 'Universal love for humanity, for all nations, and even enemies' too often goes hand-in-hand, he observed, with repression at home.[1] He saw cosmopolitanism as a 'pretext for exporting one's own values abroad or a justification for slavishly imitating other nations at the cost of one's free-dom and independence'.[2] In the end, he thought, the position was hypocrit-ical. As a call to arms, cosmopolitanism suspiciously surged into academic and media circles just after the fall of the Berlin Wall when the last impediments to the American Century were removed. That fact alone should make us think again about any natural affinity between a healthy respect for cultural differences and a unified vision of global literature – particularly in view of such cultural conflicts between political and economic systems as the conquest of Eastern by Western Europe in the continuing Cold War. To what degree, we might ask, does such a unified vision rely on a redemptive notion of the literary imagination itself? One that places the intellectual – typically more mobile than the shopkeeper or field hand – as the hero of the story?

On the other hand, why denigrate the urbane, the worldly, and the multilingual? Cosmopolitans are hard to dislike if, as most intellectuals do, one lives in cities, travels widely, is familiar with the culture of others, has no particular preferences when sampling them, and has no obvious racial or ethnic prejudices. At this level, cosmopolitanism is difficult to resist, and one should applaud its basic decency. A critical stance towards it becomes necessary only when we look at its uses in recent literary and political theory. While this body of work draws on this general sense, it frequently deploys it in a more partial, temporally bounded way.[3] Let me quote an example of how cosmopolitanism currently gets framed in metropolitan settings: the refusal to be a member of any group or cause 'smaller than all humanity, and in particular, the specifically political ones of city, empire, kingdom, or state'.[4] This is accompanied by the corollary that embracing such an ethos 'undermines established authority'. Taken together, these comments waver between vagueness and intentional double entendre. It is hard to see, for example, how the refusal to be a member of any group smaller than that of all humanity could ever find meaningful political expression. For if there is no affiliative constituency, there can be no demands, and therefore no alternative vision. How, then, can this cosmopolitanism undermine authority?

In the cosmopolitan debates of recent years, ambiguity of this sort is put to use in such a way as to allow readers to confuse the internationalism of workers' organizations or the postwar decolonization movements of Africa and Asia with a cosmopolitan ethos of upwardly mobile professors and frequent-flying businessmen.[5] The ethical force of a history of commitment, danger, and militancy can in this way be appropriated by mainstream liberal sentiment, and so appear to derive from similar energies or to have similar ends. This is not to say that cosmopolitanism is a uniquely Western or metropolitan concept. Its appeals to tolerance and cross-cultural appreciation are found in the Vedas, the *Analects* of Confucius, the Mayan *Popol Vuh*, and the work of modern liberation intellectuals like Rabindranath Tagore. But the majority of scholarly attention and by far the most systematic theorizations of cosmopolitanism have occurred in Europe and the United

States where, in the last three decades, they have succeeded in muffling its uneasy relationship with an imperial centre bred of past conquests. China may have re-emerged as a world power, but it does not express its global authority otherwise than in the language and norms established by the European empires. Globally applicable international law and state systems derive ultimately from earlier Western *force majeure*. And the same can be said of calendars, customs, technical standards, weights, measures, Hollywood, and the English language in which I am now writing.

If cosmopolitanism's double-sidedness makes one hesitate before establishing any easy parallels with world literature, the same is true from the other direction. For, given that most scholars trace the modern understanding of world literature to Goethe's *Conversations with Eckermann* (1836), it matters that Goethe saw in that concept a way of discovering the quirks and prejudices of one's own nation through the eyes of foreigners.[6] Put more bluntly, world literature was an idea that required foreigners. By contrast, cosmopolitanism – which admirably devotes itself to sampling diverse cultural riches and repudiating parochialism – does not presuppose national differences in this way. It wants rather to transcend them, or believes it already has done so in a world characterized by easy access to transportation, the Internet, and smart phones – a technological terrain that has produced de facto, and without conscious planning, a common world culture that obviates national citizenship. But contradictions are not pure negatives. Each half of the assumed homology between 'world literature' and 'cosmopolitanism' can be construed differently, and the result will be progressive or regressive depending on the actors and the situations to which one appeals.

Most students likely will have the impression that world literature is of very recent provenance, prompted by postcolonial critiques of first-world canons and the welcome curricular revisions within English and European language departments trying to be less provincial. This version of the field – the one found in some of the inaugural texts and anthologies announcing the concept's revival – is based on the idea that sampling the world's literary riches, from Nahuatl to Tagalog, is essentially an act of art appreciation, and one without priority, programme, or context. Its middlebrow aura, and lack of interest in conceptual analysis, was from the start challenged by a consciously left-materialist understanding of world literature that arose at the same time, and which offered a return to literary sociology. (I am thinking particularly of Franco Moretti, the Warwick Research Collective, and Pascale Casanova.) Here one found a deliberate reversal of literary theory's obsessions in the 1970s and 1980s with language and 'discourse'. World literature in this second guise was less about expanding the number of texts to be read than proposing a counter-formalist style of reading based on institutional histories, the relation of literature to the global political economy, macro-readings of book markets, computer-generated mappings of the representations of space in novels, and so on. Curiously, though, its emphasis was not on *critique* (which had once been the riposte of literary sociology to formalism – as in Henri Lefebvre, Raymond Williams, Lucien Goldmann, and Jean-Paul Sartre) but on impersonal systems, a sociology without authors, the decoupling of taste from political economy, and a literary landscape without writers, critics, or reviewers. Its models were taken not from the literary materialism made available from earlier traditions of philology, with their emphasis on the intricacies of a socially inflected form, but from non-literary sources such as economic historians and systems theorists.

Despite its vigour and expertise, this two-pronged initiative (oscillating between the poles of readerliness and system) foreclosed other vital traditions of world literature. All sides might agree that world literature as such is not new, but there has been sharp disagreement about whose past to use. Greece has always been the first research stop. But apart from its dubious cosmopolitanism (which I have already remarked), we find our way back to Greece so frequently in such discussions only because its achievements were preserved by al-Ma'mun in ninth-century Baghdad, whereas the genius of the Persians, Chaldeans, Babylonians, and Copts was lost to history, often by means of the deliberate destruction of their writing by invaders.[7] Such examples are often forgotten, as is the transformation of modern Chinese letters undertaken by the efforts of Lu Xun's translation team in the 1920s, which was part of a conscious effort to bring China's writing into a world community of letters by turning classics from Russia, France, the United States, Poland, and elsewhere into vernacular Mandarin.[8] To take an even less well-known example, a number of younger scholars have begun to draw our attention to the significant Soviet republic of letters launched in the interwar years under the influences of the communist internationals and an already well-developed native Soviet philology.[9] The decolonizing ethos of the Soviet experiment – the first major material and military (not simply ethical) challenge to the dominance of the European empires – had the result of moving beyond the feel-good optic of Goethe in recognizing, and in some cases inspiring, vast regional centres of literary authority and circulation: Persia in the near East, revolutionary Cuba in Latin America, and Bengal in South Asia (not least in the lyrical texts supplied by Bengali poets and musicians to the popular film music of 'Hindi' cinema).

Nevertheless, world literature in its current form should be applauded for its meticulous attention, however belated, to forgotten pioneers. To take a representative case, *The Routledge Companion to World Literature* (2012) resourcefully discovers such relatively obscure trailblazers as Dionýz Ďurišin, Qiang Zhongshu, and Hugo Meltzl.[10] What the list implies is fair enough – that we have settled for received canons while ignoring the accomplishments of scholars who were strange or unfashionable. But the rectification says very little about the more important philosophical principles and political outlooks that ultimately determine scholarly invisibility. We might think here, for example, of celebrated writers and intellectuals in their own spheres who fall outside the patterns of Western taste formation on the basis of their political non-compliance. For instance, Paik Nak-Chung – author of the important collection *National Literature and World Literature* (1978) and, more recently, *The Division System in Crisis* (2011) – has been neglected as much for the 'foreignness' of his political emphases as for his language and location.[11] Paik's sensitivity to form and method resists any facile overstatement of high modernism's productive relationship to the politics of the periphery, foregrounding instead the role of social movements in the taste cultures of the Cold War, with its legacy of a divided Korea. He outlines a compelling 'double mission' (in his words) of adapting to, while also overcoming, modernity in a nation artificially and coercively divided by the United States – a project, therefore, of great relevance to any contemporary challenge to cosmopolitanism's indifference to national integrity.

Similarly, as Galin Tihanov has explained – and to continue this theme of neglected political *beliefs* rather than only neglected races or languages – the Central European exiles who voluntarily left the West for the Soviet Union (rather than the other way around) are nowhere to be found in the archival digging for which world literature often congratulates itself.[12] Figures like Belá Balázs, Bruno Jasienski, and György Lukács evoked a home which corresponded not to a place of origin or native land but to solidarities and visions from which they were nevertheless exiled precisely because they broke with an obstinate liberal discourse. Their diaspora took them to an Eastern European centre, which for most literary critics of the Euro-American mainstream registers hardly at all. They fled repression at home (in France and Hungary), and yet were treated in their adopted country of the Soviet Union as politically suspect fellow-travellers, neither here nor there: true, but unwilling, cosmopolitans. On both counts, what makes them vital to an alternate theorization of cosmopolitanism and world literature has made them invisible within the liberal paradigm: they do not fit the Romantic model of the individual genius beset by *Heimweh,* who uses pain and dislocation to sharpen his critical vision. Their paradigm has no name, for theirs was a story of forced cosmopolitanism as a tragic substitute for the internationalism that was their aim.

A true break with English-department parochialism would demand a more forthright challenge to Anglo-American literary modernism itself, encumbered as it is by notions of Western urbanity, ethical transgression, linguistic revolution, and a cosmopolitan sublime based on the figure of expatriates like Joseph Conrad, F. Scott Fitzgerald, or Samuel Beckett; or the heroic third-world literary migrants to New York, announced with American fanfare as the immigrant capital of the world. To break this doxa is easier said than done, of course, but an enticing option can be found in a tradition of dissident philology that is not so much invisible as hiding in the light, nestled between the extremes of individual form and system.

Take one of its earliest and most influential figures, Herder, the true founder of world literature in its European guise. And then, in turn, the thinkers upon whom Herder relied for his ideas about the family of nations and the relativism of cultural values, notions so central to his colloquial take on the cosmopolitan ideal. These he took from *The New Science* (1744) by the Neapolitan rhetorician Giambattista Vico; and Vico, the grand polymath and student of antiquities, had almost certainly read the astounding *Muqaddimah* (1377), written in Tunis by the medieval historian and sociologist, Ibn Khaldūn. This fourteenth-century cosmopolitan masterpiece treats literature, poetics, and literary theory in a world-historical mode; indeed, it uses literary theory to create an original historical sociology of comparative cultural value.[13] The 1,200-page manuscript, divided into seven books, is in every respect a work of philology in the modern, here non-technical, sense of being a science of interpretive competence based on the recovery of the historical past through texts. Its central concept, *assabiyya* ('group feeling' or 'social solidarity'), is precisely about moving past a tribalism based on 'bonds of blood' to a society based on alliances and like-mindedness.

World literature lately has instead banked on Goethe, but this seems mistaken. According to John K. Noyes, he did not see the importance of the idea of world literature until learning about it 'from the young Herder during the short period of their intense friendship in Strasbourg'.[14] Then again, why should it matter whether Herder or Goethe developed the concept? Simply put, because of the different intellectual traditions within which each worked, and the less Olympian, profoundly more social and egalitarian direction in which Herder took world literature. Herder speaks of a common humanity in a world of cultural differences, whereas for Goethe *Weltliteratur* is really about the creative process and artistic genius in a world of market forces.

As one reads Goethe's surprisingly sparse reflections on world literature, their limitations become apparent. Even though we learn of his love of Serbian poetry and Chinese novels, or of his cycle of poems inspired by the medieval Persian poet Hafiz (*Westöstliche Divan*, 1819), most of his comments on world literature were in aid of a colloquy among a small circle of artists in England, France, and Germany. At the time he had been drawn into an exchange on world literature with the imperially minded Thomas Carlyle, for whose translation of Schiller he wrote an introduction. He was therefore mostly preoccupied with the new means of communication that were making it easier for authors to be in contact; with the futility of opposing market influences and the need to take advantage of them; and with the practical problem-solving benefits of literature (what is 'true' is also 'useful', he stresses). His was a sort of team-Europe concept, both far from and less than a cosmic vision.[15]

Apart from being more radically egalitarian, Herder's thinking was more sustained on the matter of literature and cosmopolitanism in its non-imperial sense, delving with great originality into the origins of language, the ethnocentricity of taste, the common character of human beings, the manner in which civilizations are varied, and the impediments to thinking posed by what Vico called 'the conceit of nations' and the 'conceit of the scholars'.[16] Far from being a cultural nationalist, as some have painted him, Herder excoriates the bumptious universal judgements of Europe, its 'facile or grandiose generalities', by stressing cultural incommensurabilities and the contingencies of period and place.[17] What is more, quite unlike Goethe, he believed that the world's peoples solve their own problems on their own terms – a notion taken wholesale from Vico's harsh diagnosis of colonial conquest in *The New Science*. Without temporizing, Herder refers to the imperial project as 'the grand European sponging enterprise' and writes bitterly about 'human beings [who] have been forced, through a process of conversion or civilization, into mines, treadmills and depravity'.[18] '*Women* are [part of the] people', he declared.[19] His politics and literary theory, we might say, were of a piece. Goethe went so far as to distrust Herder's use of the term *Humanität*, for its progressivist delusions, and thought that Herder threatened 'the particularity of cultural phenomena by subsuming them *a priori* under a pre-existing logically derived schema', a now mainstream sentiment heard in more than a few keynote lectures on the contemporary conference circuit.[20] Goethe's outlook, in other words, fits more comfortably than Herder's with the liberal ideal of aesthetic freedom, which wishes to liberate aesthetic work from geopolitical determinations, and to 'stick up' for peripheral literatures on the grounds that they too are capable of rising to the high levels of metropolitan experimental modernism.

By contrast, the more historically alert sense of world literature that we get from the lineage of Khaldūn, Vico, and Herder – and the same can be said of their intellectual descendants, Erich Auerbach and Edward Said – responds to just-completed or newly threatened wars (the Arabic conquest of the Berbers, World War II, the 1967 war in Palestine). It is an effort to preserve culture in the face of barbarous extremes and foster amity among nations. But for thinkers in this Vichian lineage, unlike many in the current field, the ideals of cosmopolitanism and world literature have more to do with methods and philosophical positions than with adding authors to canons or broadening representation for languages or ethnicities. Cosmopolitanism is positive for them only when not confused with an actually realized rejection of national polities or a Pax Americana masquerading as global citizenship, just as world literature is valuable only insofar as it is not confused with a body of texts that might ontologically *be* a cosmopolitan world republic of letters.

We can see the degree to which cosmopolitanism is ambiguous by noting that it too is a response to war, although in a different way from that of world literature in the Herderian sense. For we might understand it not necessarily as a bid for dialogue with others or a solidarity across cultures in the face of a collapse of polities, the threat of invasion, and the mobility of peoples (often in the form of the flight of refugees following regional catastrophes), but as a weapon of war itself, and a mode of expanding war into new cultural territory. Here one might consider the sort of cosmopolitanism that is the natural reflex of an imperial centre (like ancient Greece and the Church, with which I began), an identification of one's national values with the aspirations of the world that it is busy assimilating: not cynically or with conscious malice, but unreflectively under the weight of norms so ubiquitous as to be invisible. We confront here structures of taste-formation institutionalized as a result of the imperial encounters of the past, which many of the current debates in world literature underplay – structures that materially develop out of book markets, the techno-fixations of digital distribution, circulation of American styles via film and television, the presence abroad of military personnel, missionaries, tourists, and real estate speculators.

The traditions of dissident philology are large and significant, not ephemeral. As one example, Nikolai Konrad's *The West and the East (Zapad I Vostok)* argues that literary paradigms historically have moved from East to West by way of Italy's longstanding maritime trade with the Levant, where Europe was renewed by returning to classical texts via Arabic learning. Or take S. S. Prawer's remarkable *Karl Marx and World Literature*, which gives a sense of the worldliness and literary ground of Marx's sociological imagination.[21] Interestingly, Khaldūn issues a methodological warning against the errors of historical reporting, cautioning against the misuse of figurative language for the purpose of concealing motives, and against the perpetually ironic state of mind that cannot decide or choose.[22] This has profound implications for the status of literary modernism in third-world literature, since it implies a counter-modernist aesthetic of witness and testimony. Given that a similar argument can be found after Khaldūn in Vico, Hegel, and twentieth-century Marxist thinkers, a suspicion towards the misuses of irony might be said to form the basis of a broad peripheral aesthetics.

The idea of world literature in recent academic writing, even though I am suggesting it misses the emphases found in its Herderian origins, can be traced to the interventions, very much against the stream, of the young Edward Said. He, of course (unlike Konrad or Paik), is *not* excluded from the canon of world literature theorists. But his insights have been distorted, often due to an ignorance of the way in which he inherits Vico. Even a Goethean world literature is the product, not of the US academy of the last decade, but of Fritz Strich's seminal book in 1949. And it was Auerbach's 1952 dedicatory essay in honour of Strich ('Philology and *Weltliteratur*') that Said translated with his then wife Maire (née Jaanus, an Estonian and native speaker of German) in 1967, at a time when the profession had lost touch in most ways with philology, opting for a counter-historical school of formalist close-reading known as 'New Criticism' in its more old-fashioned guise and 'deconstruction' in its avant-garde articulation. In different but complementary ways, both paradigms stood against everything that philology represented: the authority of authorship, historical context, and the possibility of an accurate interpretation based on documentary evidence and care for the integrity of the text.

It is true that Said, the great instigator of the world literature concept in the contemporary university settings of Europe and the United States, highlighted Goethe rather than Herder. And yet his emphasis was not so much on Goethe as on philology. *That* was the polemical intent (unpolemically delivered) in this translation, which is to say in this indirect manner of address at a time when theory declared authorship a dead letter, spoke of discursive regimes, and argued that readers create the text's meaning decoupled from the writer's intention. Even in these early days, Said was trying to reorient the field of comparative literature by taking it out of the sterile system-thinking of Left-Bank theory into a more humane, unspecialized love of literature as a disordered, arbitrary, and always partial set of textual encounters. There, the Goethean idea lay dormant, waiting for its time during a long poststructuralist lull, only to be disinterred by others more recently on the edge of Said's orbit, but without his philological commitments.

It is important that the translators (Edward and Maire) – in a nod, perhaps, to Herder's view that our native languages are the ones we find most alive with meaning and nuance – declined to translate the term *Weltliteratur*.

To have done so, they argue, would have been to 'betray the rather unique traditions of the German word'.[23] They give to Goethe, in fact, a Herderian gloss, arguing that he coined the term with the intention of capturing the idea of 'universal literature, or literature which expresses *Humanität*'. It is not to be understood as a 'collection of world classics or great books' but as a concert among all the literature produced by man about man'. And then, decisively, they reach the crucial point: 'into this complex of meanings flows another stream, this one deriving from Herder, Grimm, the Schlegels, and especially in Auerbach's case, Giambattista Vico'. This 'general tradition of German philology,' they continue, inaugurated historicism and vastly expanded the idea of philology to include not just textual matters of grammar, etymology, or authentic authorship but 'all, or most of, human verbal activity'.[24]

Philology is, they stress, the highest form of historical study, treating as it does all contingent truths at their 'most basic level', producing, thereby, a 'dialectical' rather than monadic conception of human activity.[25] Literature is political because it is historical, and because it is not limited to fiction or other genres of the imagination such as the novel, poetry, or drama. Auerbach's essay takes an untranslated quotation from Augustine as its epigraph: 'Some part of discovery is knowing what you are looking for.' What appears to be wholly invented, this suggests, is actually determined by a prior direction, an instinctive urge to solve problems – an argument that shapes the form of the imagination, which is tethered to the localities and vagaries of authorial experience.

The case for seeing world literature as more than a collection of world classics is most persuasive when considering masterpieces not found on the standard world-lit reading lists of American undergraduate courses. Alejo Carpentier's *The Lost Steps* (*Los Pasos Perdidos*, 1953) – thought by some to be the greatest of all Latin American novels – is helpful when considering the stakes of seeing world literature as an approach routed through philology, rather than as an actual corpus of texts.[26] Like the real ale and soft cheeses that, despite the claims of globalization, never survive export, certain world-historical themes are difficult to translate as they move from periphery to centre. The novel's story of an intellectually paralysed composer who flees the pretensions of the Parisian demi-monde and New York nightlife to live among villagers in the heart of a South American jungle is almost perfectly fashioned to be misunderstood, as Carpentier well knew. The composer, whose creativity has dried up, is looking for his next meal. Having written a thesis on the origins of primitive music, he gets a museum curator to send him on a mission to collect rare instruments and thus to provide definitive evidence that music began as an imitation of the calls of birds. Thinking he might collect the research funds more simply by palming off on the museum some old instruments found in a bric-à-brac shop on the outskirts of Caracas, he nevertheless sees the project through. When he witnesses the dirge of a shaman in the remotest part of the jungle, he understands that music derives not from mimesis, but ritual. His thesis had been wrong. Music is the soul-call of a people without power over nature. Inspired by the insight, he throws himself into finishing his sonata with a burst of inspiration, but runs out of paper. He returns briefly to the capital in order to buy the paper, but is then unable to find his way back. In Carpentier's words: 'My hero travels on the Orinoco to the point of the roots of all life, but when he wants to revisit them, he can't. He's lost the portal to authentic existence.'[27]

This theme of authenticity at first seems quaint. Everyone knows that nothing authentic exists, that everything is a copy of everything else, and that only tourists or nostalgia-mongers settle for myths of the noble savage. Carpentier, though, foresaw these objections: 'it would be absolutely vain to attempt an interpretation of America in whatever region, without taking into account the fact of an intact nature, the sort of nature that the Europeans have left behind and have been unable to experience for at least three centuries'.[28] In a nod to what today we would call the theory of uneven and combined development, he remarks that 'all of the stages of civilization known to humans throughout history can be witnessed *in the present* in the American continent [...] It is altogether possible there to *evade time*.'[29] To critique Carpentier's novel for its romantic notions about authenticity would be to overlook its self-criticism, particularly the way it sends up metropolitan attitudes. The protagonist is a sighing underachiever who plods through life bored by his own aestheticized observations, and his city friends are even more reprehensible. Out of touch with the enduring indigenous communities that are just next door in countries like Venezuela and Brazil, and having never lived the extremes of dictatorship routinely experienced by Latin American intellectuals, American critics tend to miss that Carpentier's invocation of authenticity is not a return to El Dorado but a portrait of class exasperation: it is about the vanity of civilizational niceties outside polite society, and the possibility that intellectuals do not simply observe poverty from an Archimedean viewpoint, but identify with it and become a part of its project.

The Vichian tradition swings the pendulum away from textual pieties and towards a reckoning with competing interests, wilful aesthetic foreclosures, and situated rivalries and agendas. Working within it, one is forced to reckon with the worldliness of authors and authorship – nasty editors, bought reviewers, the cronyism and snobbery of academic publishing, stultifying commercial taste-markets, etc. – all of which seem in our own time very much under erasure in an era of surface reading/distant reading, as well as in its other: the 'happy family' of world literature and its appeal to more catholic readers. In the former tendency, it is proposed not only that the author is dead but that the text itself no longer needs to be interpreted, that determining meaning is beside the point, and that we should be caught up instead with the ontology of the text or work itself, and the aesthetic experience of a reading untethered from its significance – literature as a mechanico-natural unfolding. Along with the unsubtle belletrism of the Euro-American academic mainstream and its principal institutions (such as the Modern Languages Association), this view closes its eyes to authors and to literary authority as intention and will.

For just that reason, the philological emphases of Khaldūn, Vico, Herder, and Said seem especially vital today. One could well argue that Raymond Williams's devotion to the work of V. N. Volosinov and Lucien Goldmann, Walter Benjamin's distinction between information and narration in 'The Storyteller', and Sartre's portrait of the author as manipulator and persuader in *What is Literature?* are all firmly in this tradition, and at odds with recent trends. They represent, one might say, the misplaced sociological hermeneutic of world literature. One longs for a different literary sociology that captures the affiliative networks of authors choosing, strategizing, carving out a space in a hostile commercial environment of circles, schools, and class fractions, as Raymond Williams so brilliantly explores in his under-studied masterpiece, *The Sociology of Culture*.[30] It would be in the spirit of that book to confront such little-asked questions today as the fate of reading in an environment of social media; of the degree to which the digital media pre-empt choice (just as CDs replaced vinyl records in a corporate *coup de main*); of the slavish homologies between anti-philological trends in literary study and these very technological determinates. We would be driven more in the direction of Régis Debray's mediologies, with their exciting linkages between socialism and the printed word and, in turn, between the digital and the neoliberal. It would allow us to see that being contemporary is not necessarily about employing new technologies, but about critically unpacking them according to a humanist calculus inherited from a mode of critical thinking whose contents certainly have changed, but not its form.

The impression that capitalism tends to contain and co-opt everything is ubiquitous these days. So it appears to many that nothing lies outside the embrace of capital, which can turn every idea, however subversive initially, into a marketing device. But is that true? Are there not, in fact, unspeakable opinions that determine who gets published? And, if published, reviewed? And, if reviewed, given pride of place on the graduate seminar reading lists? The alternative to the present understanding of world literature is to reinstate a critical encounter with conflicting movements, antagonistic constituencies, hostile theories, discordant practices, unequal access, mutual epistemological incomprehension, and historically situated openings or foreclosures – in other words, the real world of peoples and texts. It is to reject what at times has seemed in world literature circles to be on offer: either an ensemble of books confected of an aesthetic dream of universal uplift, or a faceless network of systemic determinants whose 'materialism' makes literary trends appear as unconscious as volcanic eruptions or the migration of birds.

Notes

1. J. G. Herder, *J. G. Herder on Social and Political Culture*, F. M. Barnard (ed. and trans.) (Cambridge: Cambridge University Press, 1969), p. 200.
2. S. Muthu, *Enlightenment against Empire* (Princeton: Princeton University Press, 2003), p. 226.
3. See T. Brennan, *At Home in the World: Cosmopolitanism Now* (Cambridge, MA: Harvard University Press, 1997); and 'Cosmo-Theory', *South Atlantic Quarterly*, 100.3 (2001), 659–692.
4. This quotation and the one that follows are taken from J. Ingram, *Radical Cosmopolitics: The Ethics and Politics of Democratic Universalism* (New York: Columbia University Press, 2013), pp. 7, 67.
5. For more on this distinction, see T. Brennan, 'Cosmopolitanism and Internationalism', *New Left Review*, 7 (2001), 75–84.
6. J. W. Goethe, *Conversations with Eckermann*, J. Oxenford (trans.) (San Francisco: North Point, 1984), p. 135.
7. Ibn Khaldūn, *The Muqaddimah: An Introduction to History*, N. J. Dawood (ed.), F. Rozenthal (trans.) (Princeton: Princeton University Press, 2015), p. 10.
8. See Daniel Dooghan's innovative work along these lines: 'Old Tales, Untold: Lu Xun against World Literature', *Journal of Modern Literature in Chinese*, 16.1 (2017), 31–64.
9. See, for instance, the work of Monica Popescu, Sandeep Banerjee, Rossen Djagalov, Auritro Majumder, and Marla Zubel.
10. T. D'haen, D. Damrosch, D. Kadir (eds.), *The Routledge Companion to World Literature* (New York: Routledge, 2012).
11. N-C. Paik, *The Division System in Crisis: Essays on Contemporary Korea* (Berkeley: University of California, 2011), pp. 53–67. See also N-C. Paik, 'The Reunification Movement and Literature', in Kenneth M. Wells (ed.), *South Korea's Minjung Movement: The Culture and Politics of Dissidence* (Manoa: University of Hawaii at Manoa, Center for Korean Studies, 1995); N-C. Paik, 'The Two Cultures Problem and Renewal of the Humanities', *Inter-Asia Cultural Studies*, 11.4 (2010), 524–30.
12. G. Tihanov, 'Narratives of Exile: Cosmopolitanism beyond the Liberal Imagination', in N. Glick Schiller and A. Irving (eds.), *Whose Cosmopolitanism? Critical Perspectives, Relationalities and Discontents* (Oxford: Berghahn, 2015), pp. 141–159.
13. Khaldūn's achievement was known to the erudite in Vico's time. It had been prominently discussed by Jean Bodin (1576) and Jean-Baptiste Chardin (1680),

and had appeared in French translation at the end of the seventeenth century, a few decades before the first edition of Vico's *New Science* (although it is unclear how well Vico knew French). Vico, however, does not cite him, perhaps because Khaldūn was Muslim and the Inquisition in Naples at the time was vigorous.

14. J. K. Noyes, 'Writing the Dialectical Structure of the Subject: Goethe on World Literature and World Citizenship', *Seminar: A Journal of Germanic Studies*, 51.2 (2015), 100–114 (p. 100).

15. See F. Strich, *Goethe and World Literature* (London: Routledge and Kegan Paul, 1949), p. 350.

16. G. Vico, *The New Science of Giambattista Vico*, T. G. Bergin and M. H. Fisch (trans.) (Ithaca: Cornell University Press, 1948), pp. 34, 27.

17. Muthu, *Enlightenment*, p. 215.

18. Muthu, *Enlightenment*, pp. 253, 230.

19. J. G. Herder, 'How Can Philosophy Become More Universal?' in M. N. Forster (ed.), *Philosophical Writings* (Cambridge: Cambridge University Press, 2002), p. 26.

20. For a fuller account of this relationship, see Noyes, 'Writing the Dialectical Structure', pp. 101, 107.

21. N. I. Konrad, *Zapad i Vostok: Stat'i* (Moscow: Nauka, 1966); S. S. Prawer, *Karl Marx and World Literature* (Oxford: Oxford University Press, 1976).

22. Khaldūn, *Muqaddimah*, p. 7.

23. E. Auerbach, 'Philology and *Weltliteratur*', M. Said and E. Said (trans.), *Centennial Review*, 13.1 (1969), 1–17 (p. 1).

24. Ibid., p. 1.

25. Ibid., p. 2.

26. A. Carpentier, *Los Pasos Perdidos* (Mexico D. F.: Edición y Distribución Ibero Americana de Publicaciones, 1953).

27. A. García-Carranza, *Bibliografía de Alejo Carpentier* (Havana: Editorial Letras Cubanas, 1984), p. 22. My translation.

28. V. L. Lemus (ed.), *Entrevistas: Alejo Carpentier* (Havana: Editorial Letras Cubanas, 1985), p. 29. My translation.

29. *Entrevistas*, p. 172 (Carpentier's emphasis). My translation.

30. R. Williams, *The Sociology of Culture* (Chicago: University of Chicago Press, 1978).

2

ANNA BERNARD*

Nation, Transnationalism, and Internationalism

Arguments over the definition, scope, and remit of world literature that have taken place since the term's resurgence at the turn of the present century have introduced fresh approaches and concepts, including the method of 'distant reading' and the view that globalized literary cultures constitute a single but unequal world-system.[1] At the same time, they have restaged debates from other disciplinary formations, including one of the most enduring disputes in postcolonial literary studies, which concerns the relative value of national and supranational literary-critical frameworks. The idea that texts from formerly colonized regions of the world should be read in terms of underlying national claims – as national allegories or as an expression of a 'national longing for form' – has long contended with a critical disposition that is more sceptical about the literary representation of anti-colonial and postcolonial nationhood.[2] The latter current, which is most closely associated with the work of Homi Bhabha and Gayatri Spivak, has championed texts that appear to endorse trans- or postnational outlooks through their articulation of post-independence disillusionment and their thematization of migration, diasporic identity, and cultural plurality.[3] This disagreement about the literary impact and significance of the idea of the nation has constituted a major fault line between the materialist and poststructuralist schools of postcolonial criticism.[4]

Contemporary scholarship on world literature has widened the purview of these debates to all literary fields, and has shifted the emphasis from the interpretation of individual texts to institutional questions about the relationship of national literatures to transnational genres, curricula, markets, and capital.[5] As 'world literature' has become a scholarly field in its own right, the positions regarding the significance of the nation have solidified and become recognizable. The idea of world literature is purported to be either a welcome cosmopolitan corrective to the insularity of national literatures or a market-driven packaging of cultural 'difference' that caters to the tastes of a metropolitan elite, obscuring national, local, and regional traditions of literary practice. Between these extremes, many critics assert the interdependence of national and transnational paradigms, but differ in how they explain this interdependence, in what they mean by 'transnational', and in how much importance they assign to each formation.

In what follows, I outline the principal ways in which recent theories of world literature have portrayed the national and transnational dimensions of literary texts and their interconnections. I contrast the interventions of scholars who have privileged transnational or global interpretations – by describing, for example, literature's capacity to imagine the planet, its usefulness as a means of negotiating cultural difference, or the cross-border mobility of particular texts – with criticism that has defended the need for national and local orientations within a global context of circulation and reception. While these approaches differ sharply in their attitudes to the nation – the first group assumes a fixed idea of the nation as exclusionary and repressive, the second takes a more flexible stance – none foregrounds the anti-colonial legacy of the nation as an ongoing social and political project that literature must help imagine into being. There is, however, another literary tradition that depends upon this view: that is, a revolutionary left internationalism. Its idea of world literature is motivated by a desire to connect discrete national struggles in a project of 'mutual liberation'.[6]

The second part of this chapter examines this paradigm, which has not received significant attention in contemporary world literature criticism, with reference to a selection of poetry anthologies that circulated within left international solidarity movements of the 1970s and 1980s, namely the Nicaragua solidarity campaign, the South African anti-apartheid struggle, and the Palestinian national movement. The anthology has long been a major vehicle for the circulation of world literature; likewise, these internationalist anthologies were aimed at readerships outside the texts' nations of origin and made use of a transnational genre of verse: the protest poem. Yet these particular anthologies crossed borders in pursuit of national outcomes: they sought to persuade potential allies elsewhere to support a national liberation struggle within the colonial or semi-colonial state. By turning to this material, I respond to renewed interest in the idea of literary internationalism, as expressed in the call by the literary magazine *n+1* for a restoration of the 'programmatically internationalist literature of the revolutionary left' that has been in decline since the 1960s.[7] Rather than seeking to transcend the nation, an internationalist world literature envisions an alliance of popular democratic national movements and nation states that seeks to transcend the colonial state and global empire. The anthologies I consider do not present the demand for a national literature as parochial or chauvinistic, but rather see it as part of an anti-imperialist commitment that is always already transnational, and that readers are enjoined to share. The tradition to which they belong thus demonstrates an historically specific and politically strategic way of conceiving the interdependence of national and transnational frames within the larger configuration of world literature.

Critical Debates

To date, few scholars of world literature have understood the transnational in terms of the 'programmatically' international.[8] As I have suggested, some critics instead celebrate world literature's supersession of the nation, which they depict as a regressive political form associated with ethnic conflict and imperial conquest. This kind of opposition is already present in the *Communist Manifesto*: 'National one-sidedness and narrow-mindedness become more and more impossible, and from the numerous national and local literatures, there arises a world literature.'[9] However, this suspicion of the nation must be seen in its historical context. Karl Marx and Friedrich Engels were 'rac[ing]', as Aijaz Ahmad notes, to finish the *Manifesto* before the outbreak of revolution across Europe in 1848, and they were concerned about the threat that cultural nationalism posed to the international solidarity of the proletariat.[10] At the present time, scholars who associate nationalism with narrow-mindedness tend to see cultural and ethnic nationalism and anti-colonial nationalism as synonymous, although the ideological positions of the latter have in fact been much more various, 'capable of drawing on rationalist, romantic, positivist, and irrationalist currents of thought all at the same time'.[11] In place of nation states, these scholars invoke a postnational world order, which they suggest might be prefigured or even advanced by a postnational world literature.

Gayatri Spivak's and Wai Chee Dimock's vocabularies for describing the supranational affiliations of literary texts promote this idea most explicitly. Spivak introduces the notion of 'planetarity' as a challenge to postcolonial studies' apparent failure to transcend 'mere nationalism over against colonialism'.[12] She emphasizes literature's capacity to foreground nationalism's strategic and moral limits and imagine a postnational order, which she contends is exhibited even in the work of anti-colonial nationalist thinkers like José Martí and W. E. B. DuBois.[13] Dimock, too, positions her notion of world literature as a rebuttal of 'the glaring inadequacy of a nation-based model in world politics', which she sees reflected in literary studies.[14] She is particularly scathing of the bracketing of American literature (and by implication, other national literatures) from the study of literature in general. Against such constraints, Dimock suggests an approach based on 'deep time', which locates American literature in a quasi-geological *longue durée* and allows for interpretation based on phenomena that are 'not reducible to capitalism'.[15] In her view, as in Spivak's, the transnational does not merely complicate the national: it is a weapon to be wielded against it.

Scholars who are more cautious about privileging supranational frameworks can broadly be divided into two groups. Those in the first group tend to view world literature as an appropriation of peripheral and semi-peripheral texts for metropolitan consumption, yet they are often equally sceptical about national literatures; those in the second give the nation a more substantial role in their accounts of how world literature should be understood. Emily Apter is widely associated with the first position. In place of a 'drive to anthologize and curricularize the world's cultural resources', she invokes the idea of 'untranslatability', which she contends is a 'deflationary gesture' intended to emphasize literature's diversity, fragmentation, and resistance to systematization.[16] As this summary suggests, Apter takes a deconstructionist approach: she defends the specificity of language and the singularity of literary texts and philosophical concepts rather than the idea of national literature, which has been a target of her previous work.[17]

By contrast, the most widely influential contemporary world literature scholars – Franco Moretti, David Damrosch, and Pascale Casanova – have resisted the dismissal of national literatures. Although Moretti closes his essay 'Conjectures on World Literature' with the declaration that world literature must be 'a thorn in the side, a permanent intellectual challenge to national literatures', he does not actually claim that world literature should supplant them. Instead, he presents these formations as different lenses for looking at the same set of texts: 'national literature, for people who see trees; world literature, for people who see waves'.[18] Damrosch shifts the focus from critical methodology to transmission. His definition of world literature as a group of texts that 'circulate beyond their culture of origin'[19] describes the process of transnational dissemination and reception as an 'elliptical refraction'[20] of national or proto-national 'traditions' and 'heritage'.[21] He thus locates the nation as a source of cultural and linguistic identity within a global network of artistic exchange and adaptation. Casanova offers a less harmonious model, in which literature is a site of contest between nations who see their cultural patrimony as 'a matter of foremost national interest'.[22] Casanova distinguishes, however, between the 'national conformism and conservatism' of the literary institutions of dominant countries and the 'building of the symbolic nation' in texts from 'emerging literary spaces', where literature becomes a 'weapon of combat and national resistance'.[23]

More recently, the Warwick Research Collective (WReC) has made a similar distinction between dominant and peripheral nations, arguing that the 'militantly idealist transcendentalism' of world literature scholarship that seeks to eclipse the nation can only be articulated from the privileged position of a resident of a dominant state.[24] WReC's definition of 'world-literature' as 'the literary registration of modernity under the sign of combined and uneven development'[25] makes it possible to situate literary responses to different national settings within a common frame of subjection and resistance to capitalism. However, while this model is ideologically compatible with the idea of an internationalist world literature, WReC does not offer a more specific vocabulary for analysing texts that expressly invoke a revolutionary internationalism, since, as the collective emphasizes, its purview is not limited to 'works that self-consciously define themselves in opposition to capitalist modernity'.[26]

An historical example of literary internationalism appears in the proletarian literature movement of the 1920s to the 1960s, which Michael Denning has argued 'was the first self-conscious attempt to create a world literature'.[27] The literary landscape of Third World internationalism builds on this legacy, and offers another way of conceiving the transnationalism of world literature that neither obviates the nation nor sees it primarily as a site of cultural heritage or inter-imperial competition. The internationalist anthologies of the 1970s and 1980s construe the nation as a political structure charged with representing the interests of all people within a given territory. Where this full democratic expression has yet to be realized, poetry becomes a medium for envisioning and demanding a new nation state whose citizens will participate equally in determining its future. The transnationalism of these anthologies emerges in their affirmation of the global nature of this struggle for the emancipation of the 'people', and in their use of an established world literary form to build imaginative links between congruent national movements and among their supporters.

International Solidarity and an Internationalist World Literature

Before turning to the internationalist anthologies that are my principal concern, it is worth contrasting them with the character and remit of the many contemporary anthologies of world literature. The profusion of the latter in the late 1990s and early 2000s was an early sign of world literature's revival. Norton produced an 'expanded edition' of its flagship anthology of Western 'world masterpieces' that included an equal number of pages of non-Western works (divided into 'Western' and 'global' volumes in subsequent editions), while other educational publishers including HarperCollins, Bedford, and

Longman published new collections which likewise sought a balance between European and non-European texts.[28] Generally, the editors of these volumes identify them as informative works designed for classroom use, offering various resources for teachers and students who may find texts from other parts of the world 'unfamiliar'.[29] The interpretive strategies they deploy include not only formal and thematic comparison but also attention to cultural and national difference and commonality,[30] positioning the collections as vehicles for apprehending 'cultural complexity'.[31] While editors name historical and geographical range as major criteria for their selection of texts,[32] they also cite institutional and qualitative criteria, including recognized merit beyond their cultures of origin and a 'compelling' reading experience.[33]

In their aspiration to expand their Anglophone readers' literary knowledge and cross-cultural competence, contemporary world literature anthologies share some of the assumptions of their predecessors. The world literature anthology first emerged in the late nineteenth century, when perpetual copyright was lifted in Britain and commercial publishers began to produce a range of anthologies for a domestic audience, including various collections of 'world literature'.[34] While these volumes included few non-Western texts, they similarly emphasized diversity, quality, historical significance, and the notion of 'representative voices'.[35] The history of the world literature anthology also includes volumes with an explicitly political outlook, such as *Literature of the World Revolution* (1931, later *International Literature*, 1932–1945), a periodical showcasing revolutionary and proletarian writing. Edited by Bruno Jasieński, and published in English and several other languages by the State Publishing House in Moscow, it sought to provide 'a comprehensive marxist analysis of the cultural life of all countries', including China, Egypt, and Brazil, as well as countries within the Soviet Union.[36] The anthologies of international solidarity movements belong to this latter tradition. Criteria for the selection of texts include political commitment, documentation and analysis of national movements, and, in some cases, defiance of aesthetic conventions as a sign of revolutionary consciousness.

The movements to which the anthologies I am interested in sought to contribute were a major focus for left international solidarity activists in the 1970s and 1980s, who saw them as a chance to pursue earlier anti-colonial struggles' unrealized visions of sovereignty and social equality. The Nicaraguan Sandinistas (*Frente Sandinista de Liberación Nacional*) came to prominence after their 1979 military victory over the dictatorship of Anastasio Somoza, whose family had ruled the country since 1936. Their name commemorated Augusto Sandino, the leader of the resistance to the United States' occupation of Nicaragua in the 1930s. Once in power, the

Sandinistas began to institute policies promoting land redistribution, mass literacy campaigns, mass organization of workers, and women's equality. While the international left championed the Sandinistas' 'revolutionary democracy',[37] their ideology made them a target of US foreign policy from 1981 onwards, when President Ronald Reagan's administration clandestinely began training and arming the anti-Sandinista Nicaraguan forces known as the Contras. Support for the Sandinista government thus became a way for US and British citizens to express opposition to Reagan and his close ally, the British prime minister Margaret Thatcher.[38]

The ongoing popular struggles against settler-colonial regimes in South Africa and Israel/Palestine also gained recognition among the metropolitan and international left during this period. Support for the South African anti-apartheid movement grew exponentially from the late 1970s onwards. This was partly in response to globally circulated images and accounts of the massacre of hundreds of students in Soweto in 1976 and the murder of the activist Steve Biko in police custody in 1977, which drew attention to the extreme levels of state violence used to defend white minority rule. Palestinian resistance to the Israeli state had gained international visibility, and some notoriety, in the late 1960s and early 1970s, when several Palestinian organizations carried out high-profile military campaigns and hostage takings in the Middle East and Europe. However, the massacre of thousands of Palestinian civilians in the Sabra and Shatila refugee camps in Beirut in September 1982, which was perpetrated by Lebanese Phalangist soldiers with the support of the Israeli army, led to greater support for the Palestinian cause, including the founding of organizations like the Palestine Solidarity Campaign in the UK and the November 29th Coalition (later the Palestine Solidarity Committee) in the United States.[39] In the cases of South Africa and Israel/Palestine in particular, international activists increasingly emphasized the regimes' human rights violations over the resistance movements' anti-colonial nationalism. Yet solidarity activism also took the form of a revolutionary internationalism that saw national liberation from colonial or (in Nicaragua) semi-colonial rule as a crucial intermediate step toward global liberation from capitalism, even as each movement's turn to less revolutionary forms of statism made this prospect seem increasingly remote.[40]

In keeping with an emphasis on national liberation, the anthologies produced within these movements offer a selection of texts from single national traditions and a defined historical period. This is generally the period of the resistance, although some collections also provide examples of earlier 'shibboleth texts', which are intended to demonstrate continuity between past and present literary expressions of the nation.[41] The anthologies' status as 'world literature' derives in part from their use of a vocabulary of revolutionary struggle with both national and transnational origins, which is offered as the main lens for interpreting the work. I will focus on three examples. *Nicaragua in Revolution: The Poets Speak* (1980), a bilingual collection, was published immediately after the Sandinistas' accession to power. It was edited by a group of activists from Nicaragua and the United States and appeared with a small US publisher, the Marxist Educational Press. *Poets to the People* (1974/1980), edited by the white South African activist and poet Barry Feinberg, appeared first with the London press Allen & Unwin – the publisher of Bertrand Russell and J. R. R. Tolkien – and subsequently in the London Heinemann African Writers series, as one of several South African poetry anthologies that the commissioning editor James Currey hoped would illustrate the political 'ferment' of the aftermath of the Soweto massacre.[42] *The Palestinian Wedding* (1982), a bilingual collection of Palestinian poetry edited and translated by the Egyptian literary critic Abdelwahab Elmessiri, was published a few months after the massacre at Sabra and Shatila. It was an expanded edition of an anthology Elmessiri had published in 1970 with an activist American publisher, the Free Palestine Press; the 1982 edition appeared with Three Continents Press, a specialist in African, Asian, and Middle Eastern literature and the US distributor of Heinemann's African and Arab titles. While single-author collections by the Palestinian poets Rashid Hussein, Fawaz Turki, and Mahmoud Darwish had appeared in English in the previous decade, Elmessiri's appears to be the only anthology of Palestinian poetry that was available in English at that time.[43]

While the poems in these anthologies were not necessarily composed with an international audience in mind, their selection by the editors asserts their relevance for readers outside the nation. Such conditions of production link literary internationalism to system-oriented definitions of world literature: the idea of an internationalist world literature extends beyond the form and content of individual works to include a process of selection, presentation, circulation, and reception, which, in this case, is geared toward the organizational needs of a political movement. *Nicaragua in Revolution* most explicitly asserts its relationship to the national struggle. The editors state their hope that the volume will make a practical contribution to pro-Sandinista activism on the first page: 'Our purpose was to create a book which would tell the story of the Nicaraguan people's struggle to free themselves from their oppressors and which, at the same time, would be of some use in organizing international solidarity campaigns.'[44] Their insistence on the poems' revolutionary aesthetics is reflected in their editorial decisions. Rather than presenting each work in its entirety, they gather extracts and short poems under thematic headings including 'The Tyranny', 'The Struggle Continues' (a direct translation of the slogan *la lucha continuala luta continua*), and 'March to Victory'. The editors claim that '[t]he result is *not an anthology of poems, but rather a poetic collage* in which one narrative voice breaks off and cedes to another, and in the process a collective poem of Nicaragua's century-long struggle for national liberation is written'.[45] This emphasis on collective authorship prefigures the artistic ideology of the neighbourhood poetry workshops (*talleres de poesía*) that the poet Ernesto Cardenal would establish as Minister of Culture after the revolution, which sought to democratize the writing of poetry as a shared national activity. The editors of *Nicaragua in Revolution* further argue that the style and political content of the poems must be seen as interdependent, in keeping with the workshops' controversial promotion of a poetry of commitment.[46]

Feinberg's introduction to the second edition of *Poets to the People* similarly names the struggle for a post-apartheid nation as the book's organizing principle, asserting that the selected poems were chosen on the basis of their 'compatibility' with the theme of opposition to apartheid.[47] While Feinberg's thematic focus on resistance to apartheid was shared by other contemporaneous collections, his understanding of poetry as 'an increasingly conscious component of revolutionary action'[48] departs from Robert Royston's emphasis, in a volume published six years previously by Heinemann, on South African poets' expression of the desire to be 'human, alive and free',[49] and from Michael Chapman and Achmat Dangor's subsequent effort to trace a longer history of 'distinctively black-orientated aesthetic development' that links post-Soweto poetry to earlier South African and African-American poetic traditions.[50] Meanwhile, *The Palestinian Wedding* offers the idea of a revolutionary aesthetics alongside other ways of understanding the poems' significance, demonstrating the 'ideological syncretism' of anti-colonial nationalisms noted above.[51] Elmessiri's introduction veers between pan-Arab nationalism, in its assertion that the Palestinian struggle must be understood in the context of regional politics, and a specifically Palestinian national consciousness, in his description of Palestinian poets as 'revolutionary artists' who must 'cast around for new words and forms'.[52] Elmessiri anticipates English-language readers' resistance to this aesthetic, urging them to keep an open mind: 'it is simply appropriate to ask the reader to bring the proper kind of expectations to bear upon this particular art form'.[53]

A number of the poets included would later be recognized well beyond their nations of origin and thus become 'world poets' in Damrosch's sense, among them Cardenal, Darwish, and Dennis Brutus. In the work by these poets that appears in the anthologies, however, both national and transnational resonances are grounded in the portrayal of the national struggle, which is historically specific, but also appeals to general principles, including political and economic equality and the right to national self-determination. Darwish names Palestine in the title of his early poem 'A Lover from Palestine' ('*Ashiq min Falastin*', 1966), which, as the poem itself suggests, is an 'elegy' (*marthiyati*)[54] for a beloved who is knowingly cast as both lover and nation. The poem begins by addressing a lover in language that is not obviously allegorical: 'Your eyes are a thorn in my heart / Inflicting pain, yet I cherish that thorn / And shield it from the wind'.[55] However, the lover gradually becomes more openly identified with Palestine, culminating in the incantatory address of the final stanza: 'Her eyes and the tattoo on her hands are Palestinian [*falastinit*] / Her name, Palestinian / Her dreams and sorrow, Palestinian / [...] Her birth and death, Palestinian'.[56] The poem also makes numerous references to national symbols and themes that would be familiar to a reader with some knowledge of the struggle (whether or not s/he can read the Arabic original): 'our tragedy' (*nakbana*), 'exile' (*manfa*), the 'earth' (*al-'ard*), 'youth' (*al-shabab*), and 'return' (the translator's addition).[57] It thus simultaneously affirms insider status for the reader who recognizes the references, and introduces a distinctive catalogue of national imagery for the reader who is encountering them for the first time. The use of the elegy and the love poem to frame this invocation of the nation might be read as a claim to shared human experience, but it also seeks to persuade the reader of the justice of the speaker's cause by identifying the national struggle with life, love, and finally, with poetry itself: 'I plant the Levantine borders / With poems that set eagles free / And in your name I have shouted at the enemy'.[58]

Brutus's and Cardenal's references to the nation similarly affirm the larger significance of the national resistance, with more explicit reference to its anti-imperialism. Feinberg opens his anthology (organized alphabetically by surname) with Brutus's early poem 'For a Dead African' (1956), which, as Brutus's own footnote explains, was written for John Nangoza Jebe, who had recently been killed by Port Elizabeth police. In addition to this statement of time and place, Brutus gives national meaning to Nangoza Jebe's death through an overtly liberationist vocabulary and vision. The poem anticipates the general trajectory of the anti-apartheid movement by predicting that the civil disobedience of the 1950s will give way to armed resistance, which the speaker claims will be victorious: 'Yet when the roll of those who died / to free our land is called, without surprise / the nameless unarmed ones will stand beside / the warriors who secured the final prize'.[59] This prediction of a turn to arms links the anti-apartheid movement to other anti-colonial struggles across Africa and Asia, few of which had yet run their course at the time the poem was written. By the time the poem appeared in Feinberg's anthology, many of them had, and so the poem takes on another meaning, declaring that South Africa too will be liberated from colonial rule. Like 'A Lover from Palestine', the poem has an elegiac quality, which is exaggerated by the negative syntax of the first two stanzas – 'We have no heroes and no wars / [...] We have no battles and no fights' – and the dirge-like effect created by the handling of metre and rhyme.[60] Yet, while Brutus shares Darwish's lament for a people that are defined by their subjugation, his use of a national 'we' envisions the nation not as a lover in need of rescue, but as a collective with its own capacity for resistance, which it invites the reader to endorse.

This narrative structure, in which an account of the case for resistance gives way to an anticipatory celebration of its future realization, also appears in the anthologized extracts from Cardenal's 'National Song' ('*Canto nacional*', 1972) in *Nicaragua in Revolution*. However, Cardenal provides much more detailed documentation and analysis of the struggle's motivations. The first extract rails at length against US intervention in Nicaragua in the early twentieth century, focusing on the Nicaraguan government's sale of the nation's land and institutions: 'the moneylenders have acquired the National Bank, and / the railroad, buying 51% of the shares for a / million dollars, and all that remains of the nation is its flag'.[61] Cardenal presents financial speculation as a form of imperial violence by using metaphors of physical violence to depict it: 'That was the plunder [*saqueo*] of the mafia of the bankers. / Like stickup men they held up [*asaltaron como pisteleros*] the national currency.'[62] At the same time, by naming this history of 'investment' as '*imperialismo*',[63] Cardenal designates it as a subject for a revolutionary national literature. In a subsequent extract, the speaker identifies the poem with the effort to create such a literature by alluding to its title: 'I am singing / a country yet to be born'. This claim is expressed more forthrightly in the original Spanish, which summons a nation that is going to be born: '*Yo canto / un país que va a nacer*'.[64] The poem envisions a national future of abundance and well-being, founded in more equal practices of agriculture, education, health care, and artistic expression: 'There is so much corn to be sown so many children to teach so many / sick to be cured so much love / to be had so much singing [*tanto canto*]'.[65]

The idea of an internationalist world literature that these poems exhibit is inseparable from their appearance in anthologies that present them as a part of a transnational cultural offensive on behalf of national movements. However, as these brief readings have suggested, it also emerges from the poems' common demand for a more just future, which is based in the nation but also seeks a wider audience. Each poem offers a rallying cry, from Darwish's invocation of the resistant poet-hero, to Brutus's encomium to protestors and soldiers, to Cardenal's call to his readers to 'tear down the wire fences, comrades, / break with the past, a past that was never ours'.[66] This open invitation to resist potentially includes the distant reader by negating the assumption of a categorical opposition between imperialist North and anti-imperialist South: '[w]hat must be resisted, rather, is capitalism, wherever it arises'.[67] The poetry's political and artistic value thus lies not in its crossing of cultural borders, but in its collective adversarial demand for a better world. Yet these texts represent a transient moment in the history of international solidarity with national liberation struggles; the Sandinistas would lose control of Nicaragua after a decade, and the dominant expression of North-South affiliation with South Africa and Palestine would give way to solidarity based on humanitarian feeling rather than ideological commitment. The internationalist imagination put forward by these texts comes to seem especially precarious, as forms of transnationalism that bypass the nation have proved more amenable to the current global order, and to current formulations of the idea of world literature.

Notes

* The work for this chapter was supported by a Research Fellowship from the Leverhulme Trust.

1. F. Moretti, 'Conjectures on World Literature', *New Left Review*, 1 (2000), 54–68; P. Casanova, *The World Republic of Letters*, M. B. DeBevoise (trans). (Cambridge, MA: Harvard University Press, 2004); Warwick Research Collective (WReC), *Combined and Uneven Development: Towards a New Theory of World-Literature* (Liverpool: Liverpool University Press, 2015).

2. F. Jameson, 'Third-World Literature in the Era of Multinational Capitalism', *Social Text*, 15 (1986), 65–88; T. Brennan, 'The National Longing for Form', in H. K. Bhabha (ed.), *Nation and Narration* (London: Routledge, 1990), pp. 44–70.

3. H. K. Bhabha, *The Location of Culture* (London: Routledge, 1994); G. Spivak, *Death of a Discipline* (New York: Columbia University Press, 2003).

4. C. Bartolovich, 'Global Capital and Transnationalism', in H. Schwarz and S. Ray (eds.), *A Companion to Postcolonial Studies* (Oxford: Wiley-Blackwell, 2000), p. 128.

5. See S. Helgesson and P. Vermeulen (eds.), *Institutions of World Literature: Writing, Translation, Markets* (Abingdon: Routledge, 2015).

6. S. Salaita, *Inter/Nationalism: Decolonizing Native America and Palestine* (Minneapolis: University of Minnesota Press, 2016), p. ix.

7. 'World Lite: What Is Global Literature?', *n+1*, 17 (2013), https://nplusonemag .com/issue-17/the-intellectual-situation/world-lite/.

8. 'World Lite', n. p. Exceptions include A. Ahmad, 'The Communist Manifesto and "World Literature"', *Social Scientist*, 28.7/8 (2000), 3–30; M. Denning, *Culture in the Age of Three Worlds* (London: Verso, 2004).

9. K. Marx and F. Engels, *The Communist Manifesto*, S. Moore and F. Engels (trans.) (1888) (Public Domain Books, n.d [1848]), p. 5. Kindle ebook.

10. Ahmad, 'The Communist Manifesto', pp. 15–16; see also P. Anderson, 'Internationalism: A Breviary', *New Left Review*, II.14 (2002), 9–11, https://newleftreview.org/II/14/perry-anderson-internationalism-a-breviary.

11. Anderson, 'Internationalism', p. 17.

12. Spivak, *Death*, p. 81.

13. Ibid., pp. 92–100.

14. W. C. Dimock, *Through Other Continents: American Literature across Deep Time* (Princeton: Princeton University Press, 2006), p. 2.

15. Ibid., p. 5.

16. E. Apter, *Against World Literature: On the Politics of Untranslatability* (London: Verso, 2013), p. 3.

17. E. Apter, *The Translation Zone: A New Comparative Literature* (Princeton: Princeton University Press, 2006).

18. Moretti, 'Conjectures', p. 68.

19. D. Damrosch, *What Is World Literature?* (Princeton: Princeton University Press, 2003), p. 3.

20. Ibid., p. 281.

21. Ibid., pp. 283, 298.

22. Casanova, *World Republic*, p. 34.

23. Ibid., pp. 191, 195–197.

24. WReC, *Combined and Uneven*, p. 42.

25. Ibid., p. 17.

26. Ibid., p. 20.

27. Denning, *Three Worlds*, pp. 53, 60.

28. M. Mack (ed.), *The Norton Anthology of World Masterpieces*, expanded edn. (New York: W. W. Norton, 1997); M. Caws and C. Prendergast (eds.), *The HarperCollins World Reader* (New York: HarperCollins, 1994); P. Davis et al. (eds.), *The Bedford Anthology of World Literature* (Boston: Bedford/St Martin's, 2004); D. Damrosch and D. Pike (eds.), *The Longman Anthology of World Literature*, 2nd edn. (London and New York: Pearson/Longman, 2009).

29. Davis, *Bedford*, p. xvi; Mack, *Norton*, p. xxv.

30. Davis, *Bedford*, p. xvi; Damrosch and Pike, *Longman*, pp. xx, xxiii; Mack, *Norton*, pp. xxv, xxvii.

31. S. Lawall, 'Anthologising "World Literature"', in T. D'haen, C. Dominguez, and M. R. Thomsen (eds.), *World Literature: A Reader* (Abingdon: Routledge, 2012), p. 255.

32. Mack, *Norton*, pp. xxiii–xxiv; Damrosch and Pike, *Longman*, p. xxi; Davis, *Bedford*, pp. v–vi.

33. Mack, *Norton*, p. xxiii; Damrosch and Pike, *Longman*, pp. xxi, xxiii.

34. Lawall, 'Anthologising', p. 241.

35. Ibid., p. 242.

36. *Literature of the World Revolution* (1931), back cover. For references to texts or writers from non-European countries (predominantly China), see O. Erdberg, 'Chinese Short Stories', 1.1 (1931), 28–45; 'To All Revolutionary Writers of the World', 1.2 (1931), 9; 'China' and 'Japan', 2.1 (1932), 126–131, Peng-Pai, 'Red Hai-feng', 2.2–3 (1932), 88–103. See also Denning, *Three Worlds,* p. 54.

37. K. Hoyt, *The Many Faces of Sandinista Democracy* (Athens: Ohio University Press, 1997), p. 1.

38. C. Smith, *Resisting Reagan: The U.S. Central America Peace Movement* (Chicago: University of Chicago Press, 1996); R. Gayton et al., *Central America: The Right to Live in Peace*, NALGO, 17–31 August 1988, p. 24.

39. On the US context, H. Obenzinger, 'Palestine Solidarity, Political Discourse, and the Peace Movement, 1982–1988', *The New Centennial Review*, 8.2 (2008) 233–252.

40. See Hoyt, *Many Faces*; P. Bond, *Elite Transition: From Apartheid to Neoliberalism in South Africa* (London: Pluto, 2014); R. Khalidi, *The Iron Cage: The Story of the Palestinian Struggle for Statehood* (London: Oneworld, 2007).

41. M. Mathijsen, qtd. in A. Beecroft, *An Ecology of World Literature: From Antiquity to the Present Day* (London: Verso, 2015), p. 228.

42. J. Currey, *Africa Writes Back: The African Writers Series and the Launch of African Literature* (Oxford: James Currey, 2008), p. 196.

43. F. Turki, *Poems from Exile* (Washington, DC: Free Palestine Press, 1975) and *Tel Zaatar Was the Hill of Thyme* (Washington, DC: Free Palestine Press, 1978); K. Boullata and M. Ghossein (eds.), *The World of Rashid Hussein, a Palestinian Poet in Exile* (Detroit: Association of Arab-American University Graduates, 1979); I. Wedde (ed.) and F. Tuqan (trans.), *Selected Poems: Mahmoud Darwish* (Cheshire: Carcanet, 1973); M. Darwish, *The Music of Human Flesh*, D. Johnson-Davies (trans.) (London: Heinemann, 1980).

44. B. Aldaraca et al. (eds.), *Nicaragua in Revolution: The Poets Speak* (Minneapolis,: Marxist Educational Press, 1980), p. i.

45. Ibid., p. 1.

46. J. Beverley and M. Zimmerman, *Literature and Politics in the Central American Revolutions* (Austin: University of Texas Press, 1990), pp. 96–101. For a related effort to democratize poetry writing in the South African context, see the anthologies by M. Mutloatse (ed.), *Forced Landing* (Johannesburg: Ravan Press, 2001 [1980]) and *Reconstruction* (Johannesburg: Ravan Press, 2001 [1981]).

47. B. Feinberg (ed.), *Poets to the People: South African Freedom Poems* (London: Heinemann, 1980), p. xii.

48. Ibid., p. xii.

49. R. Royston (ed.), *To Whom It May Concern: An Anthology of South African Poetry* (Johannesburg: Ad. Donker, 1973), p. 7.

50. M. Chapman and A. Dangor (eds.), *Voices from Within: Black Poetry from Southern Africa* (Johannesburg: Ad. Donker, 1982), p. 11.

51. Anderson, 'Internationalism', p. 17.

52. A. Elmessiri (ed.), *The Palestinian Wedding: A Bilingual Anthology of Contemporary Palestinian Resistance Poetry* (Washington, DC: Three Continents, 1982), pp. 1; 8.

53. Ibid., p. 10.

54. Ibid., pp. 120–121.

55. Ibid., p. 121.

56. Ibid., pp. 126–127.

57. Ibid., pp. 120–127. Elmessiri translates '*masarib illa al-beit*' (the path home) as 'the path of return to our home' (pp. 126–127).

58. Elmessiri, *The Palestinian Wedding*, p. 127.

59. Feinberg, *Poets to the People*, p. 19.

60. Ibid., p. 19.
61. Aldaraca et al., *Nicaragua in Revolution*, p. 29.
62. Ibid., pp. 26–27.
63. Ibid., p. 28.
64. Ibid., pp. 72–73.
65. Ibid., p. 73.
66. Ibid.
67. Bartolovich, 'Global Capital', p. 147.

3

BEN ETHERINGTON

Scales, Systems, and Meridians

It may even happen that, within a comparatively short period of time, only a limited number of literary languages will continue to exist, soon perhaps only one. If this were to come to pass, the idea of world literature would simultaneously be realized and destroyed. (Erich Auerbach)

There are two ways to lose oneself: walled segregation in the particular or dilution in the 'universal'. My conception of the universal is that of a universal enriched by all that is particular, a universal enriched by every particular: the deepening and coexistence of all particulars. (Aimé Césaire)

I find something – like language – immaterial yet earthly, terrestrial, something circular, returning upon itself by way of both poles and thereby – happily – even crossing the tropics (and tropes): I find . . . a *meridian*. (Paul Celan)

Do we have faith in world literature? Do we believe that such a thing exists? If we do, can we ever expect to make world literature an object of consciousness? Given its size – for, whatever it may be, world literature presumably is big – questions concerning its actuality and scale usually are posed in relation to knowledge, at least in recent times. '*How* can we know something so big?' has been the key question. The question of faith is different to that of knowledge, even if both can lead in the same direction. If we have faith in the existence of world literature, we can pursue an inquiry into its nature and analyse its constituent elements with the confidence that our efforts will bear fruit. Faith precedes knowledge; it could even be said to prepare the ground for knowledge insofar as it motivates those epistemological acts that will imbue the object with a specific content. Faith, though, does not depend on knowledge. Many people have faith in an absolute – God, human rights, communist society – and yet are reconciled to the fact that they will not be able to prove that it exists. In such situations we speak of a 'leap' of faith. The gap may never be bridged by empirical evidence, but believers refer all the same to concrete experiences of their faith. I have faith in human rights because I have seen people treat each other with compassion in spite of opposing material interests. I have faith in God because I have felt His benign presence during a crisis.

Is research into world literature similarly impelled by 'world literature experiences'? Presumably Wolfgang Johann von Goethe had an experience of this kind when he read Jean-Pierre Abel-Rémusat's translation of the Chinese novel *Iu-kiao-li*. He described a new and profound awareness of the connectedness of literary activity across diverse human cultures and histories.[1] What of the person who has had no such experiences, and professes no such faith? Do the efforts of world literature specialists cumulatively attest to the existence of world literature? Or are they the theologians of a collectively constructed illusion? Is the world literature sceptic more like a climate change denier or an atheist?

This chapter's brief is to introduce the question of the scale of world literature, a task one initially assumes will be a matter of ascertaining its 'relative or proportionate size or extent' (*Oxford English Dictionary*, 3.12.a). I begin by raising the question of faith, though, as there would seem to be little point in trying to get the measure of an object that no one believes exists. Granted, the existence of atoms and planets do not depend on one's faith in them, but 'world literature' is not a concept like an atom or a planet; or at least not necessarily. What I will argue in this chapter is that the question of the scale of world literature pivots on whether one regards the term as having an *ideal* or *empirical* referent.

Ideal and empirical conceptions of world literature are radically incommensurate, and so the very nature of the question of scale changes depending on one's conceptual disposition (something I am characterizing in terms of faith). Over the first two sections of this essay, I compare the way in which the problem of scale was dealt with in the humanist phase of world literature scholarship with the manner in which it has been construed by the new world literary studies. If, at first, this appears to pitch ideal/hermeneutic methodologies against empirical/positive ones, I show that even the most polemical of the empiricists have tended to gravitate to world literature's ideal aspect. In the third section, I explain that this is because, from the moment of its conceptual emergence, the ideal form of world literature has been pitched against its worldly condition of possibility – the hope of globe-spanning and mutually enriching intercultural exchange continually crashing against the uniform surface of globalizing capital. As a consequence, I argue, world literature is best conceived as a negative ideal of co-existing literary particularities. In the final section, I explore how we might go about getting the measure of this negative ideal by means of the revival of hermeneutic approaches to literary comparison on a world scale. I take as my starting point the idea of a literary meridian.

The Human Scale

Until recently, most conjectures on world literature proceeded from a leap of faith regarding literature's universality. When it came to transmuting this faith into a field of scholarly research, however, the scale of the task seemed to call for an impossible commitment of resources. When visiting Berlin in 1863, the young Alexander Veselovsky commented that 'world literary history as a field of scholarship [...] remains to be created', yet despaired that 'philological preparation alone would take dozens of years'.[2] He would go on to establish 'historical poetics', which transcended the problem of scale by positing deep continuities in literary genres and forms. Exploring particular instances of the way in which literary forms persist and adapt over time testifies to an enduring relationship between verbal art and human society.

Other world literary critics responded with different innovations. Erich Auerbach recommended that scholars start with a single 'organic inner part' of a literary work that can 'shed light in a radiating fashion'.[3] This *Ansatzpunkt* (beginning point), whose identification is a 'matter of intuition' (260), enables the critic to trace the movement, proliferation, and transformation of literary meaning over large temporal and geographical spans. By way of example, he imagines a project that would track interpretations of a single passage from Dante from the earliest commentaries up to the present (263). Committed to the ideal of *Weltliteratur* from early in his career, Edward Said developed a practice of 'contrapuntal reading' for his monumental study *Culture and Imperialism*: a capacious hermeneutic in which literary works are read not only with reference to their immediate literary culture and historical context, but also in relation to earlier and later works within the emergent imperial totality.[4] Said's attraction to counterpoint as both an internal and external structural analogy is a typical feature of world literature scholarship in its critical humanist phase. There is a loose, yet essential analogy between the construction of literary works and the relations they establish both with other works and with the world.

Literary interpretation, and the literary history it cumulatively traces, thus serves as a kind of secular-humanist *theology*. Auerbach calls it 'hermeneutical history writing'.[5] Frankly speculative interpretative methods were not only admissible, but world literature's condition of possibility. If literary works somehow encode the logic of world literary totality, one need not establish its *extent* ahead of undertaking particular world literary investigations. The critic does not expect to make the entirety of world literature an object of consciousness, but in seizing upon its radiating, polyphonic movement the *sense* of totality is developed and refined. Arvind Krishna Mehrotra thus speaks of literary totality as a 'living breathing thing, whose nervous system lets every part know if one part is touched'.[6]

What inspires the faith that literature inheres within the 'spiritual development of humanity in general'?[7] It is a commonplace in contemporary discussions to point out that world literature's conceptual emergence was coeval with the dawning realization that human communities across the globe were being integrated into a single world-system. It is remarked much less frequently that it was also coeval with a novel conception of literature. Stefan Hoesel-Uhlig has argued that the appeal of '*Weltliteratur*' arose not only from unprecedented circumstances in the world but also from a revolution in literature's concept; one which fused notions of aesthetic value with a literary history centred on canonical works.[8] Hoesel-Uhlig goes on to argue that Goethe's reflections lagged behind these developments. The *literatur* of his *Weltliteratur* more closely resembles the conception of literature *qua* 'letters' (script-based intellectual discourse in general), which was then in terminal decline. Thomas Carlyle, with whom Goethe corresponded, was much more *au courant*. For Carlyle, Hoesel-Uhlig summarizes, 'World-Literature' is a 'cosmopolitan archive whose selections would abstract from contingent localisms'. For his generation, this was an article of faith: 'Literature is fast becoming all in all to us; our Church, our Senate, our whole Social Constitution'.[9] The works that best nourished the faith took their place by dint of being world-historical acts of literary making. An account of world literature that attempted to take in the 'molten sea and wonder-bearing Chaos' of all verbal art would be the equivalent of a world history that treated a foot soldier as the equal of Napoleon.

It seems only inevitable that this once radical conception would calcify with its institutionalization. If the 1956 Norton anthology *World Masterpieces* is both the apogee and fossilization of Carlyle's 'World-Literature', a more symptomatic volume is Martin Seymour-Smith's autodidactic folly *Guide to Modern World Literature*. The book's 500,000 words take in an estimated 2,700 authors and 7,500 literary works, all of which Seymour-Smith feigns to have read.[10] That he clearly skimmed the great majority and cribbed others from national literary guides is beside the point. He *may as well* have read them, given that nearly all works of 'modern world literature' beyond the West inevitably fall short of the works of European modernism that are his gold-standard. 'Arabic poetry', he states, 'has changed in form over the past hundred years; its content has remained consistently dull'. Together, Cambodia, Laos, and Vietnam, whose modern literatures are 'exceedingly impoverished', need only a short paragraph.[11]

Seymour-Smith's guide demonstrates how briskly the literary world can be surveyed when filtered through an aesthetically prescriptive sensibility. This hypostatized humanism should not be mistaken for the critical humanist's faith in world literature. The speculative philological methods devised by the likes of Veselovsky, Auerbach, Leo Spitzer, and Said aimed to facilitate critical, work-centric investigations into a totality whose actuality and scope can be only notional at the point of entry. As the object of 'hermeneutic history writing', world literature is *produced* by acts of world-literary criticism. Crucially, those in this tradition were clear that their investigations were into an emergent totality, whose impetus was both intrinsic (fruitful literary intercourse) and extrinsic (the global integration of societies). To attempt definitively to establish its limit and scale would be a category error. In this mode, 'world literature' signals the progressive realization of an ideal concept, though a contradiction looms. If the extrinsic basis for world literature's emergence does not support its intrinsic humanistic architecture, its ideal form stands in opposition to its empirical condition of possibility.

System as an *A Priori*

I will explore this contradiction in detail in the next section. Before doing so, I want briefly to consider the way in which the tensions between literary ideals and global realities have permeated the new world literary studies, and the impact this has had on reckonings with world literature's scale. On the face of it, those responsible for the term's recent resurgence have turned decisively away from the precepts of the critical humanists. They have replaced their philological care and interpretative boldness with a different set of assumptions and methods. Most strikingly, the empirical existence of world literature is now largely taken for granted. With this, the question of scale has been rendered as a problem of spatial *extension*.[12] In order to delimit their object and to understand its modes of extension, scholars have looked to theories of global systems developed by social scientists, an area which gained new impetus in the 1990s. The external factors that precipitated this shift are obvious enough. Following the decline of Third World internationalism, the collapse of the Soviet bloc, Deng Xiaoping's market reforms in China, and the aggressive expansion of multinational companies blown by the favourable winds formed by the neoliberal restructuring of the social democratic state, an unimpeded vision of the all-consuming and systemic nature of capitalism has once again been possible; a clarity not experienced since the tumultuous era of 'Imperialism' a century ago. This time capital's universal ascendency has been called 'globalization', and the study of literature, it has been assumed, needs to adjust accordingly.

As often happens when scholarship is led by deduction, syllogisms have proliferated; most often, one or other variation of the following sequence: i) all human societies historically have produced literature; ii) all human societies have been assimilated into a single world-system; therefore iii) all literature is now world literature. This is the fallacy of four terms, in which a term is used in two distinct senses and yet treated as though it were same. The 'world-system' of globalizing capital is equivocated with the 'world' of 'world literature'. This occurs early in Franco Moretti's influential essay 'Conjectures on World Literature':

> I will borrow this initial hypothesis from the world-system school of economic history, for which international capitalism is a system that is simultaneously *one*, and *unequal* [...] *one* literature (*Weltliteratur*, singular, as in Goethe and Marx), or, perhaps better one world literary system (of inter-related literatures); but a system which is different from what Goethe and Marx had hoped for, because it's profoundly unequal.[13]

Moretti actually registers his slip from '*Weltliteratur*' to 'world literary system' but forges ahead regardless. The distinction between an emphatic concept (one that is both descriptive and prescriptive) and a flatly descriptive one presents no obstacle because he has no truck with its prescriptive side.

To strip world literature of its ideal dimension, Moretti famously targets close reading, which he disdains as 'a theological exercise' (57). What his polemic conceals is that philology and hermeneutics were precisely the tools that enabled the critical-humanists to move across vast textual and historical distances. Moretti's excitement about working with units of analysis other than whole texts ('devices, themes, tropes – or genres and systems') recycles Auerbach's *Ansatzpunkt* minus its speculative premise. The 'distant reading' he proposes in its place does not so much alter the scale of world literature as reconfigure our disposition towards it. World literature's hermeneutic leap of faith is transmuted into an empirical conjecture: 'a leap, a wager – a hypothesis' (55).

On the face of it, to posit world literature as an empirical object has the effect of disenchanting the literary works that constitute it. They become mere data, nodes in a network. But, as with all reversals subject to enlightenment's dialectic, the demythologizing impulse has been ghosted by its own implicit mythologizing; in this case, an unexamined faith in the systematicity of the data concerned. Moretti's penchant for evocative metaphors such as 'waves' and 'trees' to characterize world literary systems already betrays this *a priori* faith. Indeed, in view of the term's humanist baggage, it is curious that Moretti, and those similarly drawn to systems thinking and computational reading, should have wanted to retain the term 'world literature'. There is no self-evident reason why these emerging areas of research were not just called 'literature and globalization studies' and 'literary systematics'. It points to an underlying desire to hold onto the term's humanist halo.

For all the debate that 'distant reading' has provoked, the number of scholars in the new world literary studies who have adopted it as their method is negligible. Moretti's invocation of Immanuel Wallerstein's world-systems analysis was more propitious. World-systems theory understands the modern world-economy as being divided into an unequal tripartite system of core, periphery, and semi-periphery, and it has given impetus to a number of methodological projects within the new world literary studies. The most stridently Wallersteinian is that developed by the Warwick Research Collective, for whom 'world literature' *is* 'literature of the world-system'. Helpfully, they signal their debt to Wallerstein, and differentiate the object of their concern, by hyphenating it. Their reading practice is not distant, but, in the vein of Fredric Jameson's *The Political Unconscious*, symptomatic. They look to novels in which the 'literary registration of modernity' is the 'most dramatically highlighted'.[14] Though they profess to treat world-literature as an analytic, rather than an aesthetic concept, one wonders whether, during the encounter with works that dramatically highlight modernity's contradictions, some of the old aesthetic intuitions might not creep back in. Their readings testify to world literature experiences, only in the negative: aesthetic form uniquely registers the profound *wrongness* of global capitalism.

Other scholars have fused Wallerstein with Pierre Bourdieu's field-theory to theorize literary totality as a global system that synthesizes national literary 'fields'. Here, the unreadable totality of world literature is cognized by understanding the logic that draws literary actors into an international system of rivalry. Pascale Casanova, who pioneered this approach, makes use of the cartographical notion of the 'meridian' to characterize the gravitational force exerted by 'core' literary cultures. Just as the Greenwich meridian anchors relativities of time, so the literary meridians of Paris and, latterly, London and New York, anchor literary value.

This discussion of the empirical turn in world literary studies has been far from comprehensive. A fuller account would have to consider the role that systems-based models, such as that of Itamar Even-Zohar, have played in world literary translation studies. I have pointed only to some of the more salient interventions to demonstrate that, in spite of its empiricist provocations, the new world literary studies have tended nevertheless to gravitate to the suggestive figure, the agile trope, the telling moment of mistranslation, the style or form that powerfully embodies the worldly forces which condition its materialization. Even as vocabularies have been purged of faith, the non-synchronous enchantment of literature yet has lured scholars into acts of interpretation.

World Literature as a Negative Ideal

Returning now to the question of faith, I have been arguing that the recent empirical turn entailed a dialectical reversal. Where faith in literature as world-historical making previously had been the basis for investigating its particular modes of totalization within and across human communities, now an *a priori* certainty regarding the world's systemic unity circumscribed investigations into the literary. Left behind was the paradox, gestured to earlier, that lay at the heart of the critical humanists' ideal of world literature. Auerbach saw this as a self-annihilating dialectic: the intensification of intercultural exchange attended a global process of 'standardization' that threatened to render void the distinction between cultures. Thus, 'the idea of world literature would simultaneously be realized and destroyed'.[15] This oft-quoted comment has bubbled beneath the surface of the new world literary studies but rarely have its implications been deliberated on. If world literature's passage from ideal to actuality is secured by the worlding of commodification, and the neoliberal state that legitimizes it, then world literature is inaugurated by forces that attack literature's very substance. The reason that world literature has not arrived in the hoped-for form is that literary practice opposes the logic that compels its globalization: the supremacy of exchange over use, consumerism over human need. This is not to suggest that, by dint of commodification and global circulation, literary value is eliminated at a stroke. Rather, that, as it is assimilated into market circuits, literary practice responds by insisting on its intrinsically expressive purpose.

This, too, needs to be understood dialectically. We noted earlier that world literature's conceptual birth was coeval with a novel, aesthetico-historical conception of literature. This reorientation was part of a broader diremption of value that was accelerating at the beginning of the nineteenth century; a process which Karl Marx would soon diagnose as the separation of value into 'use' and 'exchange'. The critical theorists Max Horkheimer and Theodor Adorno took this further, casting value's diremption under capitalism within a broader 'dialectic of enlightenment'.[16] They posited a deep correlation between the way in which capitalism assigns abstract value-ratios to non-identical objects (commodification) and a positivistic reason that seeks everywhere to group together non-identical things (classification). Art fights against commodification and classification by asserting the autonomy of its use value. If their appraisal is correct, then '*Weltliteratur*' has been a self-cannibalizing concept from the time that Goethe foresaw it; its speculative, ideal existence always already pitched against its worldly condition of possibility.

Seen from this vantage, it is clear that the new world literary studies has made the latter aspect – the worlding of capital – the arena for its investigations. This goes some way to explaining the tendency for scholars to cast literature in the mould of critical theory, with its core function becoming the critique of that which would destroy it. However, this leaves unasked the question of how literary actors and literary works have sought *positively* to realize world literature as a (negatively defined) ideal: how have they constructed their own forms and spheres of practice? Their own immanent literary worlds? In pursuing this question, we might find ourselves elaborating a neo-humanist world literature, for which 'world literature' serves as an article of faith; world literature as *those literary worlds brought about by the negation of literature's globalization.*

Such an anti-positivist strain of research recently has been gathering critical momentum, most conspicuously in monographs by Emily Apter and Pheng Cheah.[17] These studies push against empiricist transnationalism by invoking the literary as a kind of incommensurable alterity that holds open the promise of an Other to global capital. Their challenge to the empiricist tendencies, that is, finds its basis in a literary ontology. I would like to suggest a different point of departure; one that looks to the dialectic of literary materials and communities as they resist their commodification and integration into capitalist relations of production.

The statement on the universal and particular by Aimé Césaire that serves as the second epigraph to this essay presents one such *Ansatzpunkt*. His formulation of an ideal universalism that consists of the 'deepening and co-existence of all particulars' comes in a letter to Maurice Thorez in which he critiques the 'emaciated' universalism of the French Communist Party (PCF).[18] Césaire may not be discussing world literature, but his comments can help us to fashion a conception of it as the project of the particular within the empire of capital, whether in its colonial or globalizing phase. Here, the historical context of decolonization, which is the subtext for his break from the PCF, is key, for decolonization names the process by which the particular is to be deepened. This proposition might seem perverse given that formal decolonization i) subtended colonialism and globalization, and ii) was the process by which nearly all human societies came to adopt a single form, the nation state. We must keep in mind, though, that 'decolonization' itself shimmers between ideal and empirical. For the colonized, political sovereignty held the promise of recovering cultural particularities that had been suppressed under colonial rule.

World literature as the decolonial ideal of a totality of co-existing particulars also underlies Auerbach's essay on *Weltliteratur*. At one point he even addresses the emergent nations of the Third World directly:

I accept as inevitable that world culture is in the process of becoming standardized. But I do hope that my understanding of world literature will allow those nations that are in the midst of this fateful convergence to focus with greater precision on what is happening to them in these, their last productive moments of variety and difference, so that they can remain mindful of the process and make it part of their own mythologies.[19]

Auerbach and Césaire both know the dangers of parochialism (Césaire calls it 'walled segregation in the particular'), and this is not their objective. They are calling for a solidarity of localisms in the name of an alternative universal. A solidarity, it must be stressed, that is an *implicit* alignment of purpose. If scholars were to adjust their vision accordingly, what would be found is world literature as a patchwork of dogged non-synchronicity in which authors, readers, and audiences stubbornly dedicate themselves to literary forms and local fields in spite of their apparent structural redundancy. A world literature comprised of literary communities impelled by the ideal of meaningful civic sovereignty; a world literature for which a specific audience is a necessary condition of production; a world literature deeply ambivalent about questions of distribution and metropolitan reception. A world literature prone to abstruse statements, which itches to kick away the conceptual ladder of 'world literature' and get on with productive meaning making.

Of course, in a capitalist world-economy 'the local' is just as vexed as 'the global'. It too is relentlessly subject to systemic incorporation, such as with 'glocalization': the process by which global commodities and ideas are tailored to local markets and cultures. So let me be clear that I am not talking about unmediated conceptions of locality in the here and now, nor a sense of 'the local' that is restricted to geography. I am highlighting the tendency for the particular to become the locus of literary ideals under globalization; what Alexander Beecroft designates as the 'epichoric' sphere in his helpful typology of world-literary ecologies.[20] The ideal of co-existing epichoric literary cultures becomes both a project and an article of world-literary faith.

The Literary Meridian

Returning to this chapter's central brief – the matter of world literature's scale – the question arises: what is the scale of an ideal concept? How do we measure the ideal referent of world literature? We can hardly reach for the measuring tape, but that does not mean that these are impossible questions. There is a palpable difference of magnitude between that which is conjured by 'world literature' and, say, 'garden city'. We draw on empirical experiences when conceiving ideal notions, and world literature invariably invokes the question of totality. If world literature is a localizing project, it nevertheless calls for us to think about the forms and modes that enable the co-existence of literary particularities and localities. What, exactly, is a universal 'enriched by every particular'? Or does the concept of the universal itself dissolve into non-commensurate particularities?

Also, ideal concepts do not preclude empirical research. Are there meaningful patterns to be found in the formation of independent publishers, literary magazines, experimental poetry cliques, spoken word groups, autonomous translators, etc?[21] Or does literary localism necessarily preclude patterns? What are the modes of interaction between local literary ecologies, and on what basis, and towards what ends, do they take place? The picture that emerges certainly would not resemble the globe-spanning networks and nodes mapped by systems theory. Such investigations, though, would only show us the external traces of literary worlds that are always actively being forged through literary practices and experiences. A neo-humanist world literature of co-existing particularities can only be produced through intensive creative and hermeneutic practice.

To conclude this essay, I want briefly to explore what a world-literary hermeneutics conducted in this vein might involve. Earlier, we observed Casanova using the Greenwich meridian as an analogy for the power that accrues to 'core' literary cultures. This is the meridian of the literary world-system. I want to take as my *Ansatz* the possibility of a counter, neo-humanist literary meridian. Here we might turn to speculations on the meridian made by the poet Paul Celan in a well-known speech given in 1960. In Celan's cryptic ruminations, and that which radiates from them, we begin to perceive what it might take to reckon with the scale of world literature.

Conventionally, the meridian refers to the position of the sun when it reaches its highest point at noon. Geographically, it refers to that alignment of terrestrial locations where noon is experienced simultaneously (hence, the circles of longitude). In Celan's speech, though, 'meridian' does not refer to sunlight, but that which shines from the poem, and which guides us as we explore its meaning – an exploration undertaken 'in light of U-topia'.[22] Coming to the end of his speech, Celan proposes to undertake 'topos research' into the 'region' illuminated by this light. It is 'the place of my own origin' and also includes the places from which hail literary characters and works beloved of him. It cannot be found on a map, for 'these places [...] do not exist'. 'But', he continues, 'I know where [...] they would have to exist'.[23] This prompts Celan to make the comment that furnishes my third epigraph. The u-topian light is a '*meridian*' that is 'immaterial yet earthly [...] even crossing the tropics (or tropes)'. The meridian does not yield a map, but 'leads to encounter'. How are the connections between encounters made and put together?[24] We cannot think Celan's meridian without ourselves encountering and connecting literary works and literary places. Instead of glossing his earlier discussion of Georg Büchner, though, I want to test how his enigmatic comments might shed light elsewhere. I will start from the point on the meridian that Celan hints is the furthest from him: the literary tropics.

Aimé Césaire's collection, *Soleil Cou Coupé* (*Solar Throat Slashed*) was published in Paris in 1948 by an small modernist press. The poems in the volume were written over the course of the 1940s in Césaire's native Martinique. A key term that recurs throughout the volume is *demeure* ('dwelling'). As with the English 'dwelling', this is the noun form of a verb (*demeurer*). In three separate poems, Césaire exploits the word's capacity to pivot between noun and verb by making it the head term in an anaphoric series of (mostly) noun phrases whose adjectival component vacillates between action and object. The most sustained instance comes in 'Unmaking and Remaking the Sun'. The poem begins:

> dwelling made of not knowing which way to turn
> dwelling made of saber glitter
> dwelling made of cut necks
> dwelling made of rainstorms of the deluge
> dwelling made of male harmonicas
> dwelling made of green water and female ocarinas
> dwelling made of the fallen angel feathers
> dwelling made of the wisps of little laughs
> dwelling made of alarm bells
> dwelling made of animal skins and eyelids
> dwelling made of mustard seeds
> dwelling made of fan fingers
> dwelling made of mace
> dwelling made of rain of little eyelashes
> dwelling made of an epidemic of drums[25]

The opening line, which has the advantage of the reader's fresh mind, sets the scene, or, rather, unsettles it. This is not dwelling as repose, but dwelling as indecision and unstable stasis. The list that follows persistently subverts the syntax of representation: objects are mismatched to verbs and modifiers, verbal phrases are treated as nouns, and successive adjectival phrases contradict each other in such a way as to thwart the formation, even momentarily, of a single visual plane.

This is not to suggest that these lines are utterly random. Take the following pair as they appear in the French, '*demeure faite d'harminocas males / demeure faite d'eau verte et d'ocarinas femelles*'. The opposition of male and female correlates to that of modern and ancient instruments (ocarinas are small clay flutes, often formed in the shape of an animal) – binaries compounded by assonance and rhythmic parallelism. Nor is the semantic content indifferent. Certain classes of objects and actions recur – particularly bodily, meteorological, animalistic, sonic, cibarious, and fantastical – suggesting a consciousness impelled by certain desires. This is a dwelling full of natural forces, sensuality, and magic, intimating violence.

Césaire's technique of aphoristic manic-association is at least partly the result of his exposure to literary surrealism when he was a student in Paris in the 1930s. From the surrealists, he learned processes that were intended to break congealed associations and access otherwise repressed thoughts and ways of being. Two notions coined by André Breton succinctly capture this approach: the surreal image as 'exploding-fixed' and poetic procedure as 'objective-chance'.[26] The explosions of oxymoronic, self-contradictory or otherwise perverse linguistic effects are fixed into place by the shell of a syntax that maintains its formal integrity. The aim is to reach, by means of apparent chance, hidden 'objective' relations, both external and internal. Breton's concepts help us to identify the poetic procedure, but they do not determine meanings, which only come with the substantive content. The poem challenges us to think *this* dwelling as projected by a consciousness unleashed from conscious control.

After the above-cited dwelling sequence, the poem shifts to the first-person, with the 'I' posing a question to a 'we' before addressing, successively, a 'jailer', a 'beautiful angel', and then the 'jailer', again. In this section, the sense of conscious intention enters the poem, even if it is still hard to fathom what the poet-persona is up to. It is clear enough, though, that the lines stage an encounter. The poet-persona tells the jailer to look at his clenched eyes, which disgorge a 'swarm of cockroaches'. His anger yields a 'bouquet' of 'angel's odor' and a 'fistful of keys'. After a short prayer, the speaker tells the jailer that 'I am in / my dwelling in your face', before coming to a final statement:

> Dwelling made of your impotence of the power of my simple acts of the freedom of my spermatozoa dwelling black womb hung with a red curtain sole altar I may bless while watching the world explode at the choice of my silence (77, translation modified)

This dwelling is made of 'your impotence' (implicitly, though not necessarily, the 'jailer's'), of the speaker's simple acts, and of his sperm. Dwelling is then repeated, though this time without the anaphoric construction, suspending it exactly between verb and noun: it is a dwelling, but it is also the spermatozoa dwelling in the sacralized black womb. This final utterance of dwelling-making gives itself more readily to intentional paraphrase: it is a dwelling constituted by the jailer's impotence and by the speaker's free and sacred fertilization of a black womb.

At the time of *Soleil Cou Coupé*'s publication, Martinique was a semi-colonial society having just become an overseas department of France. Césaire was the leading figure of a cohort of black artists and intellectuals who forthrightly rejected the French colonial order as part of the explicit programme of 'négritude': a neo-Africanist movement begun by middle-class francophone students in Paris. Broadly, the artists of négritude attacked the normative whiteness of French colonialism and sought to recover an originary African selfhood. Seen against this backdrop, the final para-intentional utterance suggests an anti-colonial allegory: the jailer is the white colonizer made impotent by the negritudist's impregnation of the African ideal – an act that explodes colonial reality.

Such an allegorical reading is compelling, but sits in tension with the poem's aesthetic mode, which throws up the possibility of correspondence only immediately to withdraw from it. If one chooses an allegory of négritude over its surrealist counter-epistemology, it turns the poem into the kind of orderly statement that it is evidently working to dissolve. On the other hand, to characterize this as an intention only to meaninglessness would also be misguided. Césaire's poetics centre on utterance as gesture, so perhaps the key to its aesthetic will become apparent if we concentrate on the way that this poem performs the making of dwelling. Here the colonial situation is again unavoidable, but in a different way. By definition, all colonizing acts destroy dwellings and localities. In its imperialist phase of the later nineteenth and early twentieth centuries, when it was driven by what Joseph Schumpeter characterized as 'an objectless disposition' to 'forcible expansion',[27] European colonial powers were intent on destroying any final possibility of dwelling beyond the perimeter of their empires. Césaire was writing in the wake of a process whose logic sought to destroy not just this or that colonized people's dwelling but the possibility of non-colonial dwelling as such. It comes as no surprise, therefore, that to make a dwelling should be diverted from the spatial to memory, eroticism, animism, dreaming, magic, perversion, and, above all, confrontation.

In this respect, Césaire's poetics present the apogee of literary primitivism; an aesthetic mode whose history I can only point to here.[28] Primitivism was the artistic response to the extinguishment of space of the 'primitive', which is to say, the space of the non-colonial. Primitivist works attempted, thus, to reanimate the possibility of primitive experience; an aspiration fraught with contradictions, no doubt, but which was galvanized across the colonial world as the worlding of capital reached geographical saturation. I situate Césaire's work at the heart of this broader phenomenon, not for the sake of labels, but in order to argue for it as an early manifestation of world literature as a negative article of faith; a poetics that instantiates the primitive in a world that has banished it. This is a quintessential localism, where the local becomes the project of making a dwelling.

Why should we want to call this poetics of dwelling an expression of 'world literature'? Certainly not because it enlists surrealist poetic strategies that were circulating transnationally. The answer comes in cryptic form in 'Antipodal Dwelling':

> dwelling made of rumpled perfumes
> dwelling made of spangled sleep
> dwelling made of swelled chests stretched out of benumbed lizards
> strength lines me up on the shadowless meridian
>
> pythons crews of catastrophes denatured brothers of my longitude
>
> (151, translation modified)

Here, again, manic-association prepares the ground for the intervention of an intentional act. The incantation of a dwelling gives the speaker the strength to stand on the 'shadowless meridian', where he comes into longitudinal alignment with his 'denatured brothers'. Recall Celan: 'something circular, returning upon itself by way of both poles and thereby – happily – even crossing the tropics'. To make an antipodal dwelling is to unmake and remake a meridian. The light is the utopian possibility of once again making a dwelling in nature. It is a meridian of co-existing epichoric dwellings. The scale of this meridian cannot be determined, but we do know the scale of the destruction that has prompted it. It might be the outline of a world literature in which we can have faith.

Notes

1. See D. Purdy, 'Goethe, Rémusat, and the Chinese Novel: Translation and Circulation of World Literature', in T. O. Beebee (ed.), *German Literature as World Literature* (New York: Bloomsbury, 2014), pp. 43–61 (p. 43).
2. A. N. Veselovsky, 'Envisioning World Literature in 1863: From the Reports on a Mission Abroad', J. Flaherty and B. Maslov (trans.), *PMLA*, 128.2 (2013), 439–451 (p. 443).
3. E. Auerbach, 'The Philology of World Literature', in *Time, History, and Literature: Selected Essays of Erich Auerbach*, J. O. Newman (trans.)

(Princeton: Princeton University Press, 2014), p. 263. Rachel Bower has revived the notion of *Ansatzpunkt* in her recent *Epistolarity and World Literature, 1980–2010* (London: Palgrave Macmillan, 2017).

4. See B. Etherington, 'Said, Grainger and the Ethics of Polyphony', in N. Curthoys and D. Ganguly (eds.), *Edward Said: The Legacy of a Public Intellectual*, (Melbourne: Melbourne University Press, 2007), pp. 222–228.

5. Auerbach, 'Philology', p. 256.

6. Personal correspondence, June 2017.

7. Auerbach, 'Philology', p. 254.

8. S. Hoesel-Uhlig, 'Changing Fields: The Direction of Goethe's *Weltliteratur*', in Christopher C. Prendergast (ed.), *Debating World Literature* (London: Verso, 2004), pp. 26–53 (p. 48).

9. Cited in Hoesel-Uhlig, 'Changing Fields', p. 50.

10. See M. J. Marcuse, 'The New Guide to Modern World Literature by Martin Seymour-Smith', *Los Angeles Times*, 13 October 1985, http://articles.latimes .com/1985-10-13/books/bk-15771_1_world-literature.

11. M. Seymour-Smith, *Guide to Modern World Literature* (London: Wolfe, 1973), pp. 173, 380.

12. The turn to cartographical models as a basis for thinking about the scale of world literature has been critiqued by several scholars, with appeals then made to local dynamics and literature's own complex worldmaking. See, for example, N. Tanoukhi, 'The Scale of World Literature', *New Literary History*, 39.3 (2008), 599–617, and F. Orsini, 'The Multilingual Local in World Literature', *Comparative Literature*, 67. 4 (2015), 345–374.

13. F. Moretti, 'Conjectures on World Literature', *New Left Review*, I 2000, 54–68 (pp. 55–56).

14. Warwick Research Collective, *Combined and Uneven Development: Towards a New Theory of World-Literature* (Liverpool: Liverpool University Press, 2015), pp. 8, 15–16.

15. Auerbach, 'Philology', p. 254. Auerbach was not the only one drawn to para-doxical formulations at this time. A year earlier, Joseph Remenyi wrote of world literature as 'the glory of form in a malformed world [...] World literature is universal man sentenced to life and sentenced to death.' 'The Meaning of World Literature', *The Journal of Aesthetics and Art Criticism*, 9.3 (1951), 244–251 (p. 251).

16. T. W. Adorno and M. Horkheimer, *Dialectic of Enlightenment*, J. Cumming (trans.) (London: Verso, 1997).

17. E. Apter, *Against World Literature: On the Politics of Untranslatability* (London: Verso, 2013); P. Cheah, *What Is a World? On Postcolonial Literature as World Literature* (Durham: Duke University Press, 2016).

18. A. Césaire, 'Letter to Maurice Thorez', C. Jeffers (trans.), *Social Text*, 28.2 (2010), 144–152 (p. 152).

19. Auerbach, 'Philology', p. 257.

20. A. Beecroft, *An Ecology of World Literature: From Antiquity to the Present Day* (London: Verso Books, 2015).

21. An example of research in this direction is M. Brito, 'Small Presses and the Globalization of Poetry', in T. D'Haen, I. Goerlandt, and R. D. Sell (eds.),

Major Versus Minor? Languages and Literatures in a Globalized World (Amsterdam: John Benjamins, 2015), pp. 207–220.

22. P. Celan, 'The Meridian', in *Selected Poems and Prose*, J. Felstiner (trans.) (New York: Norton, 2001), p. 411. The quote that furnishes the epigraph is on p. 413.

23. Celan, 'The Meridian', p. 413.

24. The terms used to ask this question are inspired by Raymond Geuss, who suggests that the meridian serves as a figure for the way that poetry can '*put together*' distinct events without 'subsuming them under a single concept'. 'Celan's Meridian', *Boundary 2*, 33.3 (2006), 201–226 (p. 214).

25. A. Césaire, *Solar Throat Slashed: The Unexpurgated 1948 Edition*, A. James Arnold and C. Eshleman (trans.) (Middletown, CN: Wesleyan University Press, 2011), p. 75. (The French original is on the facing page.) Further references are in-text.

26. A. Breton, *Mad Love*, M. A. Caws (trans.) (Lincoln: University of Nebraska Press, 1988), pp. 19, 87.

27. Schumpeter was referring to the intensification of imperial competition as impelled by transnational finance. See N. Etherington, *Theories of Imperialism: War, Conquest and Capital* (London: Croom Helm, 1984), p. 152.

28. See B. Etherington, *Literary Primitivism* (Stanford: Stanford University Press, 2018).

4

JARAD ZIMBLER[*]

Literary Worlds and Literary Fields

When speaking of a literary world, we may not have in mind anything as large as the whole planet. Indeed, we may mean something as small as a particular community, in which all members participate in making literary works and their meanings. They may be novelists, poets, playwrights, or essayists, but they may also be editors, translators, or reviewers. In the same way, we might speak of the art world, the film world, or the worlds of journalism, law, or politics.[1] In fact, we could speak of any community whose members possess a set of related technical skills and pursue a set of related practices, and who are more visible to one another than to the broader public (knowing who belongs to the world is one marker of membership, though this is frequently given an institutional footing by guilds, clubs, professional associations, and regulatory bodies).

By describing such a community as a world we tend to impute to it values and rewards which differ from those of society at large. We might be less inclined to think of literary production as a domain unto itself if works were considered good or bad only on commercial grounds, such as volume of sales. But when questions of craft or beauty are deemed relevant to success, and when authors and other literary figures compete for literary prestige (chiefly the recognition of predecessors and peers), then the demands of the market and politics are somewhat vitiated, and a discrete literary world comes more clearly into view.

Pierre Bourdieu provides an especially compelling model of how such a world looks and functions.[2] In common with other sociologists, Bourdieu recognizes the labour of auxiliary institutions and agents (periodicals, publishers, prizes, and so on), and the importance of prestige, or symbolic capital. But his account of a 'relatively autonomous literary field' goes still further. In the world Bourdieu describes, writers craft their practices alongside and against one another. Struggling to find forms of expression that have not yet become passé or banal, and striving for distinction (to be different and to be recognized), they bring into being a field of relational position-takings, in which each work situates itself, via its craft or practice, in relation to all other works. The structure of this field is then necessarily modified by each new arrival, and a dynamic of generational conflict arises.

The fact that position-taking and thus relationality are achieved through craft is an especially important feature of Bourdieu's model. It means that, for authors as well as their auxiliaries and readers, the configuration of the field at any given moment determines which practices – which techniques, forms, genres, and themes – will seem distinctive, effective, and significant, rather than formulaic, outmoded, and irrelevant. The field of position-takings thus becomes a horizon of possibilities and expectations, its structure inviting certain interventions, and discouraging others. This has important consequences for literary scholars: any effort to understand the strategies of agents in the field, or the effects and meanings of their works, must attend to questions of craft, and reconstruct the space of positions-takings.

Such a demand, however, forces us to confront questions implicit whenever we posit the existence of a discrete literary world: where are its boundaries? What are the limits to autonomy, and to cooperative and competitive activity? What are the limits to relationality? How far can a literary community extend? Bourdieu's own account focuses entirely on French literary production.[3] Yet various literary institutions clearly have a transnational character; influential genres and techniques cross national boundaries; and, even without translation, works belong to multiple traditions. For these and other reasons, scholars such as Anna Boschetti, Gisèle Sapiro, and Pascale Casanova have sought to develop Bourdieu's model from a transnational perspective.[4]

Casanova's *The World Republic of Letters*, which describes a global field constituted of distinct national fields, remains the most thoroughgoing effort of this kind. It argues that, whilst competing as individuals, authors compete also as representatives of national traditions. Their success on the global stage generates value for themselves as well as for the literary cultures to which they are deemed to belong. When Elfriede Jelinek wins the Franz Kafka Prize and then the Nobel Prize, for example, the prestige of Austrian literature seems to increase; and, as a particular national field accumulates literary capital, it becomes more autonomous and thus better able to enforce its own conceptions of literary value – to say what counts as good or bad. As a result, literary capital ends up being unevenly distributed across the globe, concentrated in a few metropolitan centres (Paris, London, New York), where production is longstanding and intensive. Elsewhere, in the dominated peripheries, political and economic pressures are greater, and literary capital remains scarce. Moreover, since the most innovative practices of the most prestigious literary cultures will almost inevitably seem the most innovative practices of the world at large, the metropolitan fields also become sites of the literary present, of 'literary modernity', whereas the peripheries remain in the past, reduced to imitation and repetition.[5]

Casanova's account has generated a fair amount of controversy and criticism,[6] and is by no means the only attempt to explore global aspects of circulation, consecration, and reception.[7] Yet, what frequently goes missing in sociologically oriented research of this kind – whether focused on prizes, publication, translation, or educational curricula – is precisely the central insight of Bourdieu's model: that understanding a work in the moment of its emergence requires not only that we investigate networks of activity, and the mechanisms and hierarchies of prestige, but also that we analyse literary craft as relational practice. To this end, we cannot conflate value and meaning, as so often happens when literary community is thought in global terms.

For all its flaws, Casanova's study remains significant precisely because it retains an interest in literary form and interpretation. Indeed, the Preface to its English-language edition insists that the book theorizes the literary world in order to enable better understandings of works: 'This immense detour through transnational space has been undertaken for the sole purpose of proposing a new tool for reading and interpretation of literary texts that may be at once, and without any contradiction, internal (textual) and external (historical).'[8] The problem with this claim, however, is that it very closely resembles a remark of Bourdieu's own, that the 'notion of the field allows us to bypass the opposition between internal and external analysis without losing any of the benefits and exigencies of these two approaches'.[9] If Bourdieu is right, and a national field on its own suffices for understanding the contingencies of literary production, we might well ask: do we really need a 'detour through transnational space' to become better readers and inter-preters? Is a given work's space of relational position-takings – its horizon of expectation and possibility – necessarily global?

This chapter is centrally concerned with these very questions, which it seeks to answer by bringing Casanova into contact with two authors, Vladimir Nabokov (1899–1977) and Stefan Heym (1913–2001). Casanova's frame-work is thus subjected to immanent critique, not in order to target it, but as a way of exploring the limits and possibilities of a field-based approach to world literature (of which her study is only a single instance, albeit the most comprehensively articulated). If certain of her own version's shortcomings are exposed, this is a by-product of the chapter's method, rather than its principal aim, which is, instead, to indicate why we need to expand the ambit of Bourdieu's insights, and how we might do so. There are certainly good reasons for addressing relations between, and movements across, particular literary fields, but there are also more promising avenues than have hitherto been attempted.

My chosen authors speak directly to these matters, although they are admittedly odd companions. Nabokov, a figurehead of American post-modernism who was born Russian, and Heym, a dissident writer of the German Democratic Republic who lived for a while as an American, differed considerably on questions of politics and aesthetics, and whilst the former achieved global celebrity, the latter remains relatively obscure. However, they are united by a shared experience of multiple dislocations and migrations, which took them back and forth across Europe and the Atlantic during irruptions of international crises and armed conflicts. Nabokov left Russia after the 1917 revolution, and lived between Cambridge, Berlin, and Paris, before arriving in New York in 1940. By then, he was already widely celebrated as the author of nine Russian novels and several volumes of short stories. He had also recently completed his first English-language fiction. As for Heym, he too began his career in one domain before moving into another. His earliest poetic juvenilia had appeared in Germany and he continued to write for an émigré readership in Prague, and then in Chicago and New York. He may not have been as successful in his native tongue as Nabokov had been in Russian, but several German-language plays and short stories preceded his transition into English, which was fully accomplished in 1942 with the publication of the novel *Hostages*.

Nabokov and Heym therefore had in common not only the worldliness of exile, but also – and more importantly – the experience of leaving one literary field and attempting to gain entry to another.[10] Unlike most émigré authors, they chose to give up hard-won literary crafts in their first languages, as well as established networks and, to some extent, readerships. Clearly, their careers cannot be understood in terms of single national literary communities or traditions, or even single linguistic regions, and if a sense of 'transnational space' and its systemic relations is necessary for understanding the works of any twentieth-century authors, it must be necessary for understanding theirs.

At first glance, Nabokov seems the very paradigm of a dislocated cosmopolitan, whose career provides evidence of the dynamics of global success as Casanova describes them, and also supports one of her principal contentions: that Paris remained, into the latter half of the twentieth century, the centre of the literary world. It was in Paris that *Lolita* (1955) first appeared, brought out by Olympia Press, having been rejected by several American publishers; and the city could also claim some share in the success of Nabokov's earlier Russian fictions, since most of these were serialized in the Paris-based periodical *Sovremennye zapiski* (*Contemporary Annals*).

Not that we should confuse citizenship or location with membership of a field. Literary and geopolitical borders need not be aligned, and, regardless of his address, Nabokov remained part of the Russian émigré literary community so long as he wrote in Russian, published with émigré journals and presses, and was read, celebrated, and denigrated chiefly in émigré circles. Nevertheless, the relative autonomy and prestige of French literary culture was vital to Nabokov's later entry onto the world stage. Olympia, an English-language publisher, was hardly a bastion of French literary experimentalism, but its existence depended on a more permissive Parisian environment, and the novel's scandalous success could buy its author global notoriety only because literary and commercial capital were then more readily available to French- and English-language writers than to Russian ones. It is precisely for this reason that Casanova uses *Lolita* to illustrate her argument that, by accumulating prestige and powers of consecration, metropolitan literary centres come to preside over principles of aesthetic valuation, enabling them to determine which literary practices should be deemed innovative, and which passé.

But if *Lolita* reveals something about the structure of the literary world, does the literary world reveal anything about *Lolita*? If we route our analysis through the circuits of global prestige, does it help to make sense of *Lolita*'s meaning and distinctiveness, of its peculiar pleasures and challenges? Casanova offers no close reading of Nabokov's most famous novel, but her general approach is to divide literary practices between two camps: national-political practices, which tend to be identified with realism; and cosmopolitan-aesthetic practices, which tend to be identified with modernism – or at least a certain canon of modernist authors (Joyce, Kafka, Beckett). Whereas realism is treated as the characteristic mode of the peripheries, as well as of the global market, modernism is bound to the relatively autonomous spaces of metropolitan literary cultures.

A quadruple exile and self-proclaimed scourge of tendentious art, Nabokov fits all too neatly into the category of cosmopolitan anti-realist who disregarded the market, morality, and national belonging in order to celebrate aesthetic freedom. But, this identification concluded, have we travelled any further towards understanding the work, *Lolita*? Does setting Nabokov alongside Joyce, Kafka, and Beckett illuminate much about his novel, or the reasons it struck its first readers as distinctive, original, and important? The earliest reviews suggest not, for while these were frequently enthusiastic, the grounds of their praise had little to do with *Lolita*'s reflexivity, unreliability, anti-realism, or any other feature typically associated with modernism. Instead, American reviewers in particular celebrated Nabokov for dissolving 'moral absolutes in a sea of absurdity and passion';

for his comic technique and the 'force of his art'; and for the distinctiveness of his 'rich, raucous, exuberant style'.[11]

Of course, reviews do not mechanically register aesthetic effects. Reviewers have their own priorities and predilections, and are themselves caught up in struggles for prestige. Nevertheless, their reputations depend on the facility with which they issue the *mot juste*, and their judgements must draw upon and display a set of skills acquired through education, as well as practice. Precisely because they too belong to the field of literary production, and because they must demonstrate this proximity and familiarity as the basis for their evaluations, their knowing allusions to prominent works, authors, and genres, and their impressionistic descriptions of styles and practices, usefully (and often unwittingly) attest to key coordinates of a particular configuration of a field, as well as to the debates and aesthetic categories by which it is subtended. As such, when attempting to reconstruct a space of position-takings, an overview of contemporaneous critical pronouncements becomes a helpful starting point.[12]

With this in mind, we might note that reviewers of *Lolita* not only lavished praise on the vividness of 'a prose of spectacular vitality',[13] a prose 'flamboyant, free, liberated';[14] but also very frequently suggested that *Lolita*'s charm and potency had much to do with its 'remarkable ability to represent certain aspects of American life'.[15] This was the view of Lionel Trilling, amongst the best-known American critics of the time, and one shared by Paul Lauter, a future president of the American Studies Association, who wrote: 'the moral point of *Lolita* lies rather in what the recherché European discovers behind the billboards of America: purity of landscape beside depravity in motels'.[16] Indeed, it was precisely a sense of the novel's pleasure in traversing the 'wilderness of American motels, suburbs and progressive institutions' that led R. W. Flint to conclude: 'What makes the book "flame," [...] is first of all a love affair with the real America.'[17]

It seems, then, that *Lolita*'s earliest reviewers were struck more by its Americanness than by its modernism or cosmopolitanism. They were also beginning to think of Nabokov as an American author, a view he encouraged when explaining his novel's setting: 'I chose American motels instead of Swiss hotels or English inns only because I am trying to be an American writer and claim only the same rights that other American writers enjoy.'[18] For once, Nabokov was underselling (or over-ironizing) his achievement, since *Lolita* did far more than claim the rights to an American locale. Stepping back from the scene of its arrival, one is able to detect ways in which it anticipated and perhaps even initiated some of the prominent tropes of American fiction of the 1960s, not only in its treatment of sex and sexuality, but also in its fascination with the car and the road, the diner and motel, the suburb and country-club. It is striking, for example, that Jack Kerouac's *On the Road* – often identified as the originator of a new kind of American road novel – was itself not published until 1957.[19]

If *Lolita*'s themes therefore seem to connect Nabokov to the rising vanguard of American writers, one of his early readers believed not only that *Lolita* was 'an *American* novel'; but that it was 'probably the best fiction to come out of this country (so to speak) since Faulkner's burst in the thirties'.[20] The claim is remarkable, especially for elevating Nabokov above the most prominent novelists of the 1940s and 1950s, including John Steinbeck and Ernest Hemingway. In doing so, it also fills in the background against which the distinctive qualities of Nabokov's practice were thrown into relief. For if both Steinbeck and Hemingway were acknowledged masters of style, the relatively simple, idiomatic prose of the former, and the clipped, hypnotic, and elemental prose of latter became the yardsticks against which to measure the *flamboyant, free, vital, raucous, rich,* and *exuberant* prose of *Lolita*.

It is especially noteworthy that many early readers felt that *Lolita*'s singular style was attuned to its locale. Lauter observed that '*Lolita*'s humor, and its greatness, lies in Nabokov's ability to detonate American idiom against its own clichés'.[21] For Flint, the achievement of *Lolita*'s language was less a matter of parody than of profound affective force, creating an America 'where language and event make a seamless web of wonders, terrors, revelations and portents'. Indeed, Flint regarded Nabokov's English as 'an instrument for the wildest and most mysteriously fitting shifts of tone, the most cheerfully extraverted, slang-relishing, literate tomfoolery'.[22] Here, Nabokov's writing is magically matched to what it describes (*mysteriously fitting, seamless*), capable both of evoking the romantic America of sublime heights, expanses, and experiences (*wildness, mystery, wonders, revelations, portents*) and of recalling a down-home, folksy American past inexorably enmeshed with Mark Twain's rural south (*cheerful extraversion, slang-relishing, tomfoolery*).

Seen from the perspective of its contemporaneous critics, *Lolita* thus seems to embed itself in its setting linguistically and stylistically, as much as thematically. Of course, one has to be careful, since Nabokov's finely wrought prose had been remarked by his Russian readers too. Nevertheless, it appears that, transferred into English and transposed to the United States, his playful delight in words, phrases, and idioms, in repetitions of sound and sense, and in descriptive exhibitionism, was attributed a national character. Choosing American motels, in other words, may have set in motion the emergence of a literary practice experienced and recognized by readers as properly American. To ground such a claim comprehensively would require extensive analysis. Short of that, one might indicate a path of pursuit, by comparing a short passage from *Lolita* with a shorter one from *The Enchanter*, a novella originally composed in Russian in 1939 but published posthumously, in a translation by Dmitri Nabokov. This brings me onto the treacherous terrain of cross-linguistic comparison, where I will try for safety by focusing on features of narration.

Described by Nabokov as the 'prototype' of *Lolita, The Enchanter* likewise concerns a predatory middle-aged man fascinated by a pubescent girl.[23] In the following, this anonymous protagonist encounters for the first time the girl's middle-aged, widowed mother:

> He expected to find a sick, emaciated woman in an armchair, but instead was met by a tall, pale, broad-hipped lady, with a hairless wart near a nostril of her bulbous nose: one of the faces you describe without being able to say anything about the lips or the eyes because any mention of them – even this – would be an involuntary contradiction of their utter inconspicuousness.[24]

Here, in contrast, is the moment when Humbert Humbert first catches sight of Lolita's mother, the middle-aged Mrs Haze:

> Presently, the lady herself – sandals, maroon slacks, yellow silk blouse, squarish face, in that order – came down the steps, her index finger still tapping upon her cigarette.
>
> I think I had better describe her right away, to get it over with. The poor lady was in her middle thirties, she had a shiny forehead, plucked eyebrows and quite simple but not unattractive features of a type that may be defined as a weak solution of Marlene Dietrich. Patting her bronze-brown bun, she led me into the parlor.[25]

Certain family resemblances are apparent: archness of tone, acuity of vision (which seizes on warts in the first passage and plucked eyebrows in the second), and self-consciousness regarding the act of description. But where *The Enchanter*'s narrator sketches the woman's figure in outline before giving up entirely when confronted by features void of particularity (exhaustion is a feature of the subject and objection of narration), Humbert Humbert seems to relish identifying precisely that which is most generic about Charlotte Haze. His gaze, moreover, is cinematic, zooming in on her face after tracking her descent: an imitation film-narration matching the imitation film star, though in the kind of technicolour detail of which Dietrich herself was mostly deprived. Moreover, in spite of the narrator's desire to 'get it over with', the description continues well beyond the quoted passage, losing itself in an exuberant yet banal enthusiasm for cataloguing banality; and it is precisely this kind of delighted disgust that comes to seem characteristic of the novel's style, a horrified celebration of a life brought into being and at once emptied of meaning by films, magazines, and advertisements.

This does not prove that Nabokov set about consciously matching his prose to his subject matter, but it does explain the readiness of American readers to believe he had done so. It also explains their surprising lack of interest in non-American literary traditions. *Lolita*'s early readers occasionally connected Nabokov with James Joyce and D. H. Lawrence (on the grounds of censorship) and with Joseph Conrad (on the grounds of a transition into English), but they were not especially concerned to characterize his literary practice in relation to contemporary French or British fiction. Nor did they pay much attention to Nabokov's Russian literary heritage. The only Russian writer to feature prominently in these earliest reviews was Gogol, whose work had been brought to the attention of the American public by Nabokov's own biography, published in 1944. All of which suggests that, far from encompassing the world, the horizon of possibilities that shaped the novel's meaning and impact was rather more limited. *Lolita* was situated, and made sense of, principally within the American field.

Lolita's American homecoming was eventually consolidated in the unexpurgated edition published by Putnam in 1958. In 1942, the same firm had achieved notable success with Stefan Heym's *Hostages*, a novel set in German-occupied Prague that wove together tales of the Czech resistance with those of the Nazi practice of ransoming citizens for the compliance of their countrymen. When it appeared in October, film rights had already been purchased by Paramount, and, by the end of the year, *Hostages* had found its way onto bestseller lists.

This commercial success was not entirely surprising. Putnam had committed itself to the 'largest first printing of a first novel in the firm's history';[26] and thereafter pursued an intensive advertising campaign, producing an advanced notice which mentioned Heym alongside Hemingway and Steinbeck.[27] The approval of critics followed. Orville Prescott insisted *Hostages* would 'be ranked with the finest novels of 1942, if not of a much longer period';[28] and other reviewers compared Heym's novel favourably with Steinbeck's *The Moon is Down* (1942),[29] Maxim Gorky's *The Lower Depths* (1912 [1902]),[30] and Jaroslav Hašek's *The Good Soldier Švejk* (1930 [1923]).[31] When the Book-of-the-Month Club conducted its annual nationwide poll, *Hostages* was placed tenth on the list of outstanding novels of the year.

However, though *Hostages* was certainly acclaimed, its greatest champions were seldom prominent critics or novelists. Even then, some suspected *Hostages* of 'melodrama', deploying one of the period's 'standard terms [. . .]

used to designate a novel as entertainment'.[32] Reticence about Heym's literary standards was doubtless compounded by his formal conservatism. *Hostages* made little use of recent technical innovations in focalization, free indirect discourse, stylistic pastiche, surrealism, or reflexivity. Instead, its narrator was the familiar figure of the late nineteenth century: external, impersonal, and omniscient, sweeping freely back and forth across Prague, piercing prison walls and secret meeting places. As such, were we to characterize Heym's literary practice only in terms of Casanova's broad distinction between modernism and realism, we would necessarily incline to the latter, especially given that *Hostages* is set in the real and recognizable world at large.

Hostages thus comes into focus as a middlebrow fiction. It was by no means pulp – it came out in hardback from a prestigious firm at the time when the US paperback market was emerging – but nor was it purely literary.[33] A serious but commercially oriented work, it seems to belong at what Bourdieu describes as the 'heteronomous' end of the 'sub-field of restricted production', a siting further encouraged by Casanova's identification of heteronomy, not only with commerce, but also with realism, politics, and parochialism. This assessment is complicated, however, by a broader view of the American field. To begin with, *Hostages* was not alone in achieving both commercial and critical success. Steinbeck's *The Moon is Down*, Pearl Buck's *Dragon Seed*, and Anna Seghers's *The Seventh Cross* had done considerably better on both fronts. This might indicate that properly autonomous American fiction no longer existed in the 1940s, as American literary culture became increasingly mercenary; except that, crucially, these novels were also linked thematically, by a preoccupation with the war, or with events leading to the war. Rather than literary value being subordinated to market value, it seems that both were being subsumed by moral and political imperatives, in particular by the demands of the war effort. These demands were clear to Putnam's publicity director, who committed to ensuring 'the sale of every possible copy' of *Hostages*, 'not only because of the profit' but also because 'you might as well have the facts even if you must get them from a novel'.[34] As for Heym, far from guarding his artistic freedom, he threw himself into anti-fascist activities, and would soon enlist in the US army.

If the local fate of *Hostages* suggests that priorities were shifting within the American literary field, its international trajectory hints at far broader, even systemic, changes. Before the novel's US publication, rights had been sold for Czech, Swedish, Slovak, Portuguese, and Spanish translations; and soon after, *Hostages* was reviewed positively in the French press in Algeria, and in Britain. There too, war themes were increasingly prominent, and novels concerned with the conflict could achieve both commercial and critical success. Clearly, even the most autonomous literary regions were becoming increasingly politicized.

Hostages thus alerts us to structural changes across the literary world. A sense of this altered 'transnational space' helps, in turn, to explain the speed and breadth of the work's circulation. However, such a 'detour' hardly facilitates better understandings of the captivating, breathless intensity of Heym's novel – its 'thrilling suspense',[35] 'constant excitement',[36] and 'terrific swiftness'[37] – or the ambivalence of its reviewers. In short, Casanova's heteronomous realism brings us little closer to *Hostages* than her cosmopolitan modernism brought us to *Lolita*, not least because lumpy categories of this kind – ubiquitous in world literary studies – lack the precision required to identify features that may be more granular, but are no less properly distinctive. In the case of Heym's novel, these include its strategic deployment of the conventions of the crime novel.

Hostages opens with what seems to be a murder. Soon after, the Nazi policeman Reinhardt begins his investigation. On the pretext of identifying the culprit, he takes hostages, whilst scouring the city for members of the underground, mimicking in his search the hard-boiled detectives already associated with American pulp magazines of the 1920s and 1930s. A story of Czech resistance is thereby harnessed to a powerful generic motor of suspense, and, while reviewers resisted identifying *Hostages* with 'Continental espionage' and 'crime fiction' (for the same reasons they equivocated about 'melodrama'), Heym had no such qualms. Describing his earliest plans for *Hostages*, he recalls reflecting, first, on the American demand for detective novels, and, second, on the need to frustrate the genre's formulaic conclusion, which he did by inventing Reinhardt, a detective whose investigation fails.[38] In fact, it seems Heym was thinking along similar lines long before he had conceived of *Hostages*. In 1939, after completing 'The Courier from Strasbourg', a short story in which a resistance movement is infiltrated by a spy, he offered it to a literary agent as 'a mixture of detective fiction and underground', suggesting that it might be 'sold on the glossy or pulp market'.[39]

Heym's literary practice was thus shaped from early on by a desire to remake commercial fiction as democratic fiction, entwining two versions of the popular. For this, he cultivated sensitivity to local conditions, especially the tastes of American readers and publishers. But, in pursuing this project, Heym also aligned himself with a particular tradition of American novelists, who had used their works to expose social ills, and to evoke animosity towards the powerful as well as sympathy with the downtrodden. When asked to contribute an article to a series on memorable books, Heym chose a signal work of this tradition, Upton Sinclair's *The Jungle* (1906). Of it, he remarked: 'Mr Sinclair's style is not necessarily exquisite; [...] but I like a man who sees things as they are – writes them down – and points an accusing finger squarely'.[40] In Heym, then, we find a further example of an exiled author attuning his work to a local literary field. He shapes his practice so as to position himself both alongside a group of American writers identified with socially conscious novels, and also against the conventions of mass-market American crime fiction, even whilst drawing on the energies of those conventions.

We might anticipate Heym's literary localism more readily than Nabokov's, especially if we assume, like Casanova, an alignment between political art and parochialism. But, in important ways, Heym was a cosmopolitan writer too, which is signalled even by his engagement with American literature, since this predated his emigration. In the piece on Sinclair, Heym recalls reading *The Jungle* long before he arrived in Chicago: 'It was the first of the books I read on America by an American author. I read it, then, in its German translation.'[41] Moreover, the very first of Heym's works to appear on stage – in Vienna as well as Prague – was *Tom Sawyer und Huckleberry Finn*, an adaptation of *The Adventures of Tom Sawyer* (1876). Addressing a youth audience, but with the purpose of sounding a warning to German-speaking communities in the shadow of Nazism, Heym reworked Twain's novel to produce a play explicitly about racist conspiracies and violence.

Moving across media, as well as linguistic–cultural bounds, *Tom Sawyer und Huckleberry Finn* is evidence that neither technical innovation nor a worldly orientation is the preserve of autonomous art. The play also points towards another important context for Heym's practice, by connecting him with a German tradition of epic theatre that was associated then, as it is today, with the works of Bertolt Brecht and Erwin Piscator. Heym himself identified his one-act *Execution*, performed in Chicago in 1936, as an 'epic play'; and, once in the United States, corresponded several times with Piscator. The fact that Piscator himself produced an adaptation of Theodore Dreiser's *An American Tragedy*, which had premiered in Vienna in 1932 before crossing the Atlantic in 1935, hints at the possible existence of a more systemic relation between the American and Weimar literary fields, one having little to do with global flows of literary prestige.

From the outset, then, Heym's literary as well as his political interests were cosmopolitan in outlook. But the point really to be emphasized is that the capacity of *Hostages* to be gripping and suspenseful, as well as provocative and unsettling, was the result of an aesthetic disposition that was formed in Germany in the 1920s and early 1930s and that came to fruition as a position-taking within the American literary field in the early 1940s. As with Nabokov, however, this cosmopolitan inheritance would remain invisible to local readers, unless made explicit by the author or his reviewers. In this regard, it is interesting, first, that the advanced notice for *Hostages* mentioned *Tom Sawyer und Huckleberry Finn*; and, second, that the non-American work to which reviewers most frequently referred was not a German novel, but a Czech one: Hašek's *The Good Soldier Švejk*. If the former assured readers of Heym's long-standing familiarity with American authors, the latter framed the worldliness of the novel in terms of its themes, rather than its author's origins.

In closing, I offer a few observations about the kind of readings attempted in this chapter, as well as their consequences for an approach to the literary world that draws on Bourdieu's field-based model. I have tried not only to explain the circulation and successes of *Lolita* and *Hostages*, but also to understand how these novels were related to works of significant peers and predecessors. I have therefore considered aspects of publication and reception, and even, broadly speaking, of biography and history. I have remarked also on genre, style, and narration, attending especially to those features that seem both distinctive and pertinent to the effects of these novels on their readers. The chapter thus indicates some of the ways in which a field-based approach demands, but also facilitates, internal as well as external analysis.

As to claims for the necessity of a transnational perspective, it is certainly true that we gain richer understandings of their aesthetic dispositions if we consider Nabokov's Russian and Heym's German literary inheritances. It is also true that the relative prestige of different literary cultures, and the structure of their relations, are relevant to the ways in which *Lolita* and *Hostages* circulated and were consecrated. However, once we shift our focus from the value of a work to its meaning, there is little to suggest that we ought to keep in view the global totality of literary production. On the contrary, if we are trying to determine a work's 'context of intelligibility', it seems far more important to begin within a particular community of practice.[42] In the case of Heym and Nabokov, this was the American literary field, the existence of which both authors presumed in addressing or responding to the constraints and possibilities of American themes, tastes, and conventions.

This is not to say we should never lift our eyes to the wider world. In all kinds of ways, the American field was impinged upon by outside forces, literary as well as socio-political and economic. The outbreak of global conflict, for example, affected the movement and valuation of literary works, and perhaps also the relations between fields. What is more – and this is something not yet touched upon – it may also have provided the kind of common ground necessary for the emergence of relationality, in confronting writers from very different communities with the same themes and even challenges. This returns us to a question with which I began: what are the limits to cooperative and competitive activity, and to relationality? How, for that matter, does relationality arise, and of what does it consist? These questions have hardly been posed by sociologically minded scholars of world literature, yet they are clearly vital to understanding how we might expand the ambit of Bourdieu's insights beyond the boundaries of the nation.

Intuitively, it seems that relationality can extend only so far. While the existence of transnational or even non-national spaces of position-taking is inevitable (there are no practical or theoretical reasons for limiting relational dynamics to national borders), imagining such a space on anything like a global scale is more challenging. It is especially difficult to understand why or how writers would shape their works in response to one another's aesthetic decisions if they were faced by very different constraints and choices, and if they lacked a common repertoire of meaningful forms, genres, techniques, and themes. Yet without this – without, that is, an effort on the part of writers to craft their practices and measure themselves alongside and against one another – it is quite meaningless to speak of a literary field in Bourdieu's terms. Unless, of course, we abstract literary practices so far as to banalize them, for example, by relying entirely on categories such as realism and modernism; or unless we conflate value and meaning, and thus understand the global field as little more than a global market, unified by the common currency of symbolic capital.

Confronting actual works and practices, and attempting to understand whether and in what ways particular instances of relational position-taking operate over narrower or broader terrain than any nation's, would be one way of adapting Bourdieu's vision of the literary world. In the case of individual authors, relations across fields might prove to be singular, idiosyncratic, and also superficial, amounting to little more than what is often called 'influence'; but, if we look carefully, patterns may emerge, pointing to deeper structural or systemic relations across and also between fields, which cannot be accounted for by models of global prestige. To begin with, this may only prompt further questions – what is and is not portable across fields? What, if any, of a literary material can be shared? – but these would at least lead us closer to, rather than away from, understanding how much of the world is relevant to articulating those horizons of expectation and possibility that impel, constrain, and shape any work's emergence into meaning.

Notes

* Research for this chapter received funding from the European Union's Horizon 2020 research and innovation programme under Marie Skłodowska-Curie grant agreement No. 708030.

1. The now classic account of this understanding is found in H. S. Becker, *Art Worlds* (Berkeley: University of California Press, 1982). It continues to frame social-scientific research into cultural production. See, for example: H. van Maanen, *How to Study Art Worlds: On the Societal Function of Aesthetic Value* (Amsterdam: Amsterdam University Press, 2009).

2. Elaborated across his career, this model is given clearest expression in P. Bourdieu, *The Rules of Art*, S. Emanuel (trans.) (Cambridge: Polity Press, 1996).

3. A similar focus on the nation characterizes research by scholars influenced by Bourdieu, such as Michel Hockx, Peter D. McDonald, and Gisèle Sapiro, in their respective accounts of the Chinese, British, and French literary fields.

4. See, for example: A. Boschetti, 'How Field Theory Can Contribute to Knowledge of World Literary Space', *Paragraph*, 35.1 (2012), 10–19; G. Sapiro, 'How Do Literary Works Cross Borders (or Not)?: A Sociological Approach to World Literature', *Journal of World Literature*, 1 (2016), 81–96; P. Casanova, *The World Republic of Letters*, M. B. DeBevoise (trans.) (Cambridge: Harvard University Press, 2004).

5. Casanova, pp. 87–103.

6. For an early, incisive and influential critique, see: C. Prendergast, 'The World Republic of Letters', in C. Prendergast (ed.), *Debating World Literature* (London: Verso, 2004), pp. 1–25.

7. Analysis of literary production, circulation, and consecration from a global or transnational perspective can be found in a number of recent studies, including those of James English, Sarah Brouillette, Stefan Helgesson, Ruth Bush, and Peter D. McDonald. See Further Reading for details.

8. Casanova, p. xii.

9. Bourdieu, p. 205.

10. We are thus dealing here with actual authors moving 'from space to space', and not merely with the disembodied forms pursued in F. Moretti, *Graphs, Maps, Trees: Abstract Models for Literary History* (London: Verso, 2007), p. 90.

11. G. Culligan, '*Lolita*, Or As You Like It', *Washington Post*, 17 August 1958, p. E6.

12. This approach to reviews is explained in more detail in J. Zimbler, *J. M. Coetzee and the Politics of Style* (Cambridge: Cambridge University Press, 2014), pp. 4–7. For an account of the status, dispositions, and institutional contexts of American reviewers in the mid-twentieth century, see J. S. Rubin, *The Making of Middlebrow Culture* (Chapel Hill: University of North Carolina Press, 1992).

13. R. W. Flint, 'Nabokov's Love Affairs', *New Republic*, 17 June 1957, 18–19 (p. 19)

14. C. Brenner, 'Nabokov: The Art of the Perverse', *New Republic*, 23 June 1958, 18–21 (p. 20).

15. L. Trilling, 'The Last Lover: Vladimir Nabokov's *Lolita*', *Encounter*, 11 (1958), 9–19 (p. 19).

16. P. Lauter, '" ... elementary errors"', *New Republic*, 3 November 1958, 23–24 (p. 23).
17. Flint, p. 19.
18. V. Nabokov, 'On a Book Entitled *Lolita*', *Anchor Review*, 2 (1957), 105–112 (p. 110).
19. On the surge in popularity of the American road narrative in the 1960s, and the significance of *On the Road*, see: R. Primeau, *Romance of the Road: The Literature of the American Highway* (Bowling Green: BGSU Popular Press, 1996), pp. 8–9.
20. Brenner, p. 21.
21. Lauter, p. 24.
22. Flint, p. 19.
23. Nabokov, 'On a Book Entitled *Lolita*', p. 105.
24. V. Nabokov, *The Enchanter* (London: Penguin, 2009), p. 15.
25. V. Nabokov, *The Annotated Lolita* (London: Penguin, 2000), p. 37.
26. 'Notes on Books and Authors', *New York Times*, 5 September 1942, p. 11.
27. 'Hostages', *Four Star Final*, September 1942.
28. O. Prescott, 'Books of the Times', *New York Times*, 16 October 1942, p. 17.
29. D. Daiches, 'Grim Picture of Life Under "New Order"', *Chicago Sunday Tribune*, 18 October 1942, p. 6.26.
30. W. Soskin, 'Books and Things', *New York Herald Tribune*, 17 October 1942, p. 11.
31. F. Seyd, 'Without Fear of Failure, Torture or Death', *New York Herald Tribune Books*, 18 October 1942, p. 5.
32. B. G. Ekelund and M. Borjesson, 'The Shape of the Literary Career: An Analysis of Publishing Trajectories', *Poetics*, 30 (2012), 341–364 (p. 353). The term is used in this way, with varying degrees of circumspection, by Soskin, 'Books and Things'; H. Strauss, 'A Czech Patriot', *New York Times Book Review*, 25 October 1942, p. 28; and H. S. Canby, 'Hostages', *Book of the Month News*, November 1942, p. 10.
33. This sense of 'middlebrow' is discussed by Rubin in *Middlebrow Culture*, pp. xi–xvi.
34. C. B. Boutell, 'Analysis of Novel by Stefan Heym: The Source of the Power in *Hostages* Lies in Five Basic Factors', *Four Star Final*, October 1942.
35. Prescott, p. 17.
36. Canby, 'Hostages', p. 10.
37. A. D. Bond, 'Novel of Life in Conquered Czechoslovakia', *Boston Herald*, 23 October 1942, p. 3.
38. S. Heym, 'Wie ich anfing: "Stefan Heym"', Stefan Heym Archive, A107.
39. S. Heym, Letter to Henriette Herz, 7 July 1939, Stefan Heym Archive, C1/H7.
40. S. Heym, 'Upton Sinclair's *The Jungle*', Stefan Heym Archive, D2.
41. Ibid.
42. The notion of 'context of intelligibility' is explored in B. Etherington and J. Zimbler, 'Field, Material, Technique: On Renewing Postcolonial Literary Criticism', *Journal of Commonwealth Literature*, 49.3 (2014), 279–297.

5

STEFAN HELGESSON

Translation and the Circuits of World Literature

> There is nothing special about English. It is just one language among many.
>
> (J. M. Coetzee, *Summertime*, 161)

Humans may be defined as speaking animals, yet even if the most avid polyglot masters fifteen or twenty languages, 5,000 – approximately – will remain beyond his or her purview. Of course, if we limit ourselves to the domain of printed literature, numbers drop. UNESCO's translation database, the *Index Translationum*, has about 500 language options, many of them making distinctions that are not self-evident, such as those between 'German' and 'German, dialects of', or between 'Gujarati' and 'Gujarati, old'. Yet even here, within the restricted realm of print (with its dozen or more writing systems), linguistic diversity is overwhelming. As a corollary to the claim that language is a means of communication, one must therefore insist to an equal degree that human language after Babel *obstructs* communication. Any substantial discussion of world literature that wishes to challenge the distortions of what Emily Apter calls 'oneworldliness' needs to take this into account.[1] As I soon will explain, my aim in this chapter is to situate the question of world literature in the context of linguistic diversity, with a focus on translation as the medium of uneven literary exchange. I do this in opposition to inadequate monolingual subdivisions of world literature – 'world literature in English', '*littérature-monde*' in French – and will argue that what makes world literature matter as a critical paradigm has rather to do with how literature is (and is not) connected across languages and communities. This involves both the 'worldliness' of the individual text and systemic forms of networking, exchange, and recognition.

If we review current debates on world literature, we see that two distinct yet overlapping perspectives have been dominant. One is David Damrosch's view of world literary texts as those that circulate beyond their cultural and linguistic point of origin and manage to 'gain in translation'.[2] The other is the systemic understanding of world literature as an interconnected international hierarchy with a centre, a semi-periphery, and a periphery. In Pascale

Casanova's Bourdieusian model, world literary space is defined by rivalry and a struggle for international recognition. In Moretti's version of the world-system, the focus is less on canonization and authorships, more on the transnational spread of certain genres (notably the novel) and aspects of literary form.

Both perspectives, which have been extensively developed as well as criticized by other scholars, presuppose that translation is a key component of world literature.[3] However, only the systemic view insists that translation occurs under unequal conditions. Contrary to the nominal linguistic diversity presented by the *Index Translationum*, a tiny handful of languages completely dominate the sum total of book translations. With regard to *source languages* (languages *from* which books are translated), roughly half of the world's translations in recent decades have originated in English. This language is so dominant that it is regarded as 'hyper-central',[4] overshadowing the other languages that nonetheless enjoy a central position: French, German, and Russian. In the 1980s, each of these provided around 10 per cent of the source texts in published translations, while another group of 'semi-peripheral' languages each had a 1–3 per cent share. Here, we find languages such as Spanish, Italian, Swedish, Danish, Polish, and Czech. This is, however, a dynamic hierarchy. In recent decades, Russian has weakened and Japanese and Chinese have strengthened. Even so, the hypercentrality of English is more firmly entrenched than ever and European languages in general remain dominant.

If we switch perspectives and look at *target languages* (languages *into* which books are translated), the ranking changes, but not the inferences regarding centrality. It is striking that in the book markets of the United States and the United Kingdom, translations account for no more than 3–4 per cent of all published books. For the book markets in France and Germany, the corresponding figure is roughly 15 per cent; in Sweden, Spain, and Holland it is around 25 per cent; while in Greece and Portugal, up to 40 or even 45 per cent of all published books are translations.[5] Reframing this in terms of languages, one notes that Portuguese is semi-peripheral as a target language, but is peripheral as a source language; with Greek, the relations are exactly inverse.

These statistics are riddled with uncertainties, yet they enable a number of indicative observations. One is that the number of speakers of a language does not necessarily correspond with the position of the language in translation exchanges. Arabic and Hindi, for example, rank among the top five or six most spoken languages in the world, but in current translation statistics they fall behind. As source languages, Arabic is in place 17 and Hindi in place 45; as target languages, their positions are 29 and 44, respectively.[6] Another conclusion is that there seems to be an inverse relationship between source and target languages: English provides global publishing with half of its source texts, but admits proportionately few target texts; Portuguese, by contrast, supplies the international system with few source texts, but receives an overwhelming number of target texts. Even Portuguese is relatively privileged, however, by virtue of being a highly active partner in the exchange system for published translations. Most languages in the world stand outside of the system altogether. This presents a methodological and conceptual limit for world literature studies insofar as it focuses on the interconnectedness of *printed* literature.

It is, nonetheless, within these restrictions that the present chapter operates. It investigates the nexus of language, literary works, and their published translations, first by expanding on the claim that 'world literature' can be framed as the study of (translational) relations between literatures, and subsequently by exploring the two contrasting cases of José Craveirinha and J. M. Coetzee. Towards the end of this chapter, I will suggest that the circulation of works across languages can be understood in terms of expandable, multilingual 'textual zones'. Rather than viewing originals as bounded entities, the notion of textual zones accounts for the effective, unfolding life of a literary work in its many versions.

My focus on translation has affinities with Damrosch's emphasis on circulation, as well as with the systemic approach of Casanova especially, yet it develops a more differentiated understanding of these systemic relations. It is for this reason that I also make extensive use of Alexander Beecroft's notion of literary 'ecologies'. Understood as a typology of circulation, it complements the Bourdieusian field-concept by defining different modes of literary relations. An earlier attempt at such differentiation was made by Itamar Even-Zohar, whose abstract and agentless polysystem theory posited that particular literatures (mostly national ones) are shaped by a multiplicity of intersections, which is what the term 'polysystem' indicates. Translations are of crucial importance to the polysystem, not least because they enter discrete literatures differently, depending on the relative strength of a particular literary culture. For a 'young' or 'weak' literature, 'features (both principles and elements) are introduced into the home literature which did not exist there before', whereas translations can be (but don't have to be) relegated to a marginal position in a strong literary culture.[7]

In Beecroft's *An Ecology of World Literature*, a more empirically grounded attempt is made to categorize the variety of literary contacts and circulations. Three of Beecroft's six ecologies seem particularly relevant to my present discussion, namely the cosmopolitan, national, and global.[8]

Cosmopolitan literary circulation is premised on the transcultural currency of a particular language. Cosmopolitan languages typically project their values as universal.[9] Historical examples are Latin and Sanskrit; contemporary cases include English and Arabic. The number of cosmopolitan languages at any given moment is, however, strictly limited. Cosmopolitan languages are not necessarily amenable to translation, even though historical examples such as the Latin *Vulgata* or the rich translation culture of the Abbasid empire require us to nuance this claim. In the more characteristic scenario, writers for whom the cosmopolitan language is not their own, but who nevertheless need to operate within its ambit for political and cultural reasons, self-translate or 'pre-emptively' translate their work. The entire complex of contemporary postcolonial African and Asian writing in English, French, and Portuguese could, in other words, be described as a subset of the wider and older phenomenon of cosmopolitan literary circulation.

National circulation, by contrast, has often emerged in tandem with translation – a paradigmatic example being the importance of translation in German literary culture around 1800.[10] The national ecology is exclusive to the modern era, yet the extent of its formative impact on the very conception of literature has become all the clearer as this dominance has been challenged by postcolonial and world-literary paradigms of inquiry.

The *global* ecology, finally, in Beecroft's estimation is still emergent. The key point about the global ecology, as distinct from cosmopolitan circulation, is the degree of *systemic integration* of literatures, evident not least in the acceleration of translation and the global dominance of a handful of publishing houses.[11] A fully developed global ecology, whose condition of possibility is economic globalization and the rampant proliferation of media technologies, could therefore be resolutely multilingual, yet remarkably synchronized in terms of genre, form, and frames of reference. This represents something qualitatively different from cosmopolitan circulation, even if the 'critical difference [...] in terms of access to the global literary system' persists.[12] In fact, Casanova's model, as well the comparative translation statistics presented at the outset, could be seen as ways of theorizing global circulation. This makes it clear, however, that one and the same element can be coded differently depending on which 'ecology' one is investigating. If Portuguese, for example, is semi-peripheral and even peripheral in view of global translation exchanges, it can just as well be understood as a cosmopolitan language in view of its imperial history.

Both Even-Zohar and Beecroft emphasize change over time, and it is crucial to understand that their models are relational. Beecroft demonstrates, for example, how even national literatures can be understood as 'world-literary', either by having rejected a cosmopolitan other or, more positively, by establishing new connections with other literatures through translation. Such a differentiated understanding of world literature enabled by the ecologies approach is significantly different from conceiving world literature as only a global canon, as a singularly constituted 'Republic', as the teaching of literature in English, or simply as the globalization of genres.

My discussion thus far could be described as working within the remit of 'distant reading', taking only large-scale entities such as book markets, languages, literatures, and translation statistics into account. Looking qualitatively at individual literary works involves a shift in methodological scale. They can *illustrate* systemic hypotheses, but cannot falsify or verify them. They enable, however, a different type of knowledge about the same set of problems we have been discussing. Here, we can approach the linguistic fabric of the texts themselves, as well as their contextual circumstances, as sources of knowledge in their own right. This allows for a fine-grained understanding of the dynamics at play and brings the reader back into the picture.

The systemic distance between my chosen authors is considerable, and deliberately so. J. M. Coetzee (b. 1940), who received the highest international literary consecration (the Nobel Prize) in 2003, belongs to the select group of contemporary authors whose works are 'born translated', to use Rebecca Walkowitz's influential term.[13] It is a foregone conclusion that a new book by Coetzee will be translated into thirty or more languages; indeed, since the late 1990s, these translations have often appeared simultaneous with or even ahead of the English-language original. In the contemporary system of world-literary exchange, Coetzee scores highly on every chart: he writes in the hypercentral language of English, he is widely translated, and his works are recognized globally for their aesthetic qualities.

José Craveirinha (1922–2003), by contrast, belongs to a group of what we might dub 'scarcely translated' writers. This pre-eminent Mozambican poet published numerous collections during his lifetime and further work has appeared posthumously, yet the circulation of his work beyond the Portuguese language has been limited. Although the work of poets tends to be translated less often than that of novelists, this makes it all the more interesting to look at the translations that *have* been published, in view both of their editorial circumstances and the actual choices made by translators. There is, for instance, a striking anomaly in the translation history of Craveirinha: although only around thirty of his poems have been translated into English, two book-length selections by two different translators have appeared in Swedish. This challenges the structural axioms of translation sociology: the Swedish translations of Craveirinha are not attributable to prior translations into the hypercentral language of English. Instead, we find a direct link between two linguistic (semi-)peripheries – the Mozambican periphery of the semi-peripheral language of Portuguese, and Swedish.

Craveirinha was censored and persecuted during the late-colonial period and only four volumes appeared in his lifetime: *Chigubo, Karingana ua Karingana, Cela 1*, and *Maria*. Throughout his career, however, he published poems in the press, as well as in anthologies. He was above all a poet of *moçambicanidade*, 'Mozambicanness'.[14] By introducing a distinction between poetry *in* Moçambique and poetry *of* Moçambique, Craveirinha forced the hand of those Portuguese poets in Mozambique who remained aloof from the question of national liberation. However, from a world-literary perspective, it is worth emphasizing that this was an *internal* rupture within the Portuguese language, occurring in the midst of colonial conflict, the vehicle of which was the imperial cosmopolitan language. The flipside to this ambivalent attachment can be seen in Craveirinha's gradual consecration within the transcontinental circuit of lusophony, most spectacularly when he received the Camões Prize in 1991, the most prestigious international prize for Portuguese-language writing.

If Craveirinha's work resolutely affirmed the nationalist cause, the condition of possibility for his writerly endeavour remained linguistically cosmopolitan – but not global – by default. What needs to be asked, then, is to what extent Craveirinha's poetry moves beyond the circuit of Portuguese altogether by entering other languages and modes of circulation. This seemingly straightforward question is hard to answer definitively, but searches on the *Index Translationum, Karlsruher Virtueller Katalog*, and a wide range of national library catalogues, suggest that he has *not* been much translated. I have so far found a handful of *untranslated* poems in a 1966 issue of *Présence Africaine* and nothing in German; searches in Spanish, Czech, Serbian, Dutch, Danish, and Finnish yield no results at all.[15] Beyond the europhone sphere, the picture is just as bleak: Craveirinha has apparently not made it into Arabic, Chinese, Japanese, Farsi, Hindi, Indonesian, or Swahili. It may seem odd to present non-results in this way (and I must emphasize they are not conclusive), but I believe it dramatizes the 'negative space' of world literature effectively, highlighting just how restricted the linguistic range of translation in the circuits of world literature can be. The positive results are in fact limited to seven languages: some poems are in French; one is in Russian (a slim sixty-three-page volume published in 1984); one poem is in Polish; two poems are in Norwegian and appeared in 1974; thirty-four of his poems (plus a short essay) have been translated into English by various translators; eight undated poems, available on the Internet, are in Italian; and, finally, two full collections in Swedish have been produced independently by the translators Örjan Sjögren and Marianne Sandels in 2002 and

2006 respectively, comprising, with overlaps, roughly ninety different poems.[16]

For reasons of space, as well as linguistic competence, I will focus on the English and Swedish versions. The English translations are to be found in anthologies or journals of various kinds. They have been produced by five different translators and published over a period of twenty-five years. The places of publication themselves illustrate the wide dispersal of the English language: Margaret Dickinson's 1972 volume *When Bullets Begin to Flower* was published in Nairobi; Chris Searle's selection was published in London; Don Burness's anthologies were published in the United States; the London-based journal *Portuguese Studies* has published Michael Wolfers's translations as well as a few of Luís Rafael and Stephen Gray's collaborative translations; other translations by Rafael and Gray appeared mainly in South African journals in the 1990s. Several poems have been published repeatedly, and a handful have been retranslated by different translators.[17] Taken as a whole, these thirty-four poems provide a reasonably varied representation of Craveirinha's oeuvre. They are dispersed across ten rather obscure publications, however, and very few readers will ever encounter them together. These publication events represent three different principles of selection: Dickinson and Searle especially, but also Burness, insert Craveirinha into the general category of anti-colonial revolutionary writing; Wolfers's selection, which includes 'To My Beautiful Ex-Emigrant Father' and 'The Tasty "Tanjarines" of Inhambane', presents a more personal side of Craveirinha's development as a poet, as well as his sharp criticism of the revolutionary order in the 1980s; Rafael and Gray, finally, are particularly interested in Craveirinha as a *regional*, southern African poet, which is evident not least from the fact that several of their translations were produced in direct collaboration with the critic Fátima Mendonça in Maputo and the *Associação dos Escritores Moçambicanos* (AEMO), the Mozambican Writers' Association.[18]

We see then how the translational dissemination of Craveirinha's work in English is distributed across three transnational circuits: the political circuit of anti-colonial solidarity, an academic and literary circuit specializing in Portuguese studies, and finally a literary circuit invested in the cultivation of a regional southern African literature. This causes some strain in the neat distinctions between ecologies: the first supports nationalist liberation by exploiting the cosmopolitan resonance of English, the second is cosmopolitan in a restricted academic sense, whereas the third issues in a national space but is regionalist in spirit. Arguably, it is the anti-colonial circuit that has led to the strongest breakthrough beyond English. The Norwegian 1974 translation clearly emerged on the back of decolonization. The precise motives behind the Russian 1984 translation are hard to determine, but the massive translation industry of the Soviet period and its imbrication with official policies are well known.[19] Rafael and Gray's southern African translations, by contrast, can be read in more straightforward Bourdieusian terms as participating in the local accumulation of cultural capital, not least because they appeared after the Camões Prize, and in the wake of the 1992 peace agreement in Mozambique and the democratic breakthrough in South Africa in 1994. They orient themselves, in other words, towards a place-sensitive 'literary' pole (appearing, for example, in the small South African literary journals *New Coin* and *New Contrast*). Wolfers's four translations in *Portuguese Studies* are not as obviously rooted in the region, but serve to complicate the image of the poet of anti-colonial liberation.

If we accept the general polarity between anti-colonial and literary tendencies, the Swedish translations provide us with several surprises. The first Swedish collection, translated by Örjan Sjögren and called simply *Dikter* ('Poems'), was produced by the independent left-leaning press, Ordfront, in direct connection with the short-lived literary prize '*Afrikas röst*' ('The Voice of Africa'). This prize was awarded only twice, first to the Zimbabwean writer Yvonne Vera in 1998, second to Craveirinha in 2002. The initiator of the prize was the bestselling author Henning Mankell (1948–2015), who was famous across the world for his 'Nordic noir' crime novels, but also known in Sweden for his long-standing commitment to African independence and development. From the late 1980s, he lived for parts of the year in Maputo, Mozambique, working as the director of the theatre company *Teatro Avenida*. Mankell was well known among Mozambican writers, he knew Craveirinha personally, and wrote an afterword to *Dikter*. Behind the single most comprehensive translation of Craveirinha's work, with its 136 pages and seventy-one poems selected from four books, there is, in other words, an unusual combination of personal relationships, political commitments in the socialist anti-colonial tradition, and, yes, financial muscle. Mankell was at the time one of the world's bestselling authors, translated into all of the central and many of the peripheral languages in the world-system.[20] It was, of course, this success that made it possible for him to establish '*Afrikas röst*'. Translation spawned translation: Mankell's success in the global field of large-scale literary production enabled this intervention in the Swedish field of restricted production. What, from one angle, can be seen as a direct translational link between two (semi-)peripheries without mediation by way of a central language was nonetheless implicated structurally in the workings of the global ecology.

The second Swedish translation of Craveirinha springs another set of surprises. Entitled *Att stava till ett kosmos* ('To Spell a Cosmos'), it was issued by Almaviva, a tiny enterprise managed by the translator Marianne

Sandels. Sandels trained as a librarian and, as early as the 1970s, had started to translate poetry from the romance languages.[21] Almaviva has a limited and mostly dormant catalogue, but the handful of writers it has published since 2001 include the Angolan writer José Eduardo Agualusa and the Portuguese writers Almeida Faria and Nuno Júdice. It thus conforms with Bourdieu's claim that it is small publishers, deprived of resources, that adhere to strictly literary norms and whose existence depends on their capacity to differ from the mainstream by, for instance, translating from languages other than English. In Bourdieu's estimation, 'they make use of their talent and pioneer audacity to discover minor authors writing in minor languages (Catalan, Brazilian, Korean, Hungarian, etc.), authors who are less expensive to buy in but far more "interesting" from a literary point of view'.[22] Yet being deprived of resources is a relative condition: Almaviva's edition of Craveirinha announces that the translation was supported by the *Instituto Camões* and the *Instituto Português do Livro e das Bibliotecas*, both based in Portugal with a brief to support the international circulation of national Portuguese as well as lusophone literature more generally. On top of this, Sandels's edition (but not Sjögren's) received post-production support from the Swedish Arts Council, a government agency.[23] Sandels's personal interest and competence colluded here in somewhat ironic ways with several enabling structural factors: first, the post-imperial, cosmopolitan network of the Portuguese language; and second, a national agency whose primary purpose is to support the diversity of Swedish cultural production.

In Craveirinha's translation history we see a constant traffic between national, cosmopolitan, and global forms of circulation. Translations may be 'facts of target cultures', but these cultures are themselves complex entities.[24] If we move down the ladder of generality and abstraction, complexities will accumulate. What, for example, can we say of the translations themselves? What are the meaningful differences and characteristics that speak to the shaping of world literature? Briefly, I offer a few observations. First, we see that a few poems recur repeatedly in English and Swedish, and thereby accumulate representative authority. 'Grito negro' is one of them, translated as 'Black Cry' (Searle), 'Black Outcry' (Rafael and Gray), 'Black Protest' (Burness), '*Svart rop*' (Sjögren), and '*Svart skri*' (Sandels). This is a signal poem in Craveirinha's corpus and one of the most effective anticolonial protest poems ever written. Its first stanza reads:

> *Eu sou carvão!*
> *E tu arrancas-me brutalmente do chão*
> *E fazes me tua mina*
> *Patrão!* (11)

The thundering repetition of the ['ẽw̃] sound is immediately silenced in translation, and all translators tend therefore towards semantic rather than auditory and rhythmic fidelity in their reinscription of the poem (with the exception of the Italian translation, whose *'carbone'*/ *'padrone'* comes close).[25] But, as always, even on the semantic level, translators make different choices, giving the poem different orientations. Translation can be described, in Theo Hermans's intriguing phrase, as 'delegated speech', and hence as 'discourse that represents another discourse'.[26] With poetry translation, this can, however, become a problematic claim. Poems can be treated as discourse, but they may also be approached as events, or linguistic objects. The question then follows if a translated poem can *be* an event or an object in its own right, or if it merely *represents* that event or object. Already in the translations of the title we can register a push and pull between being and representing: modulating *'grito'* in the abstract and political direction of 'protest', Burness signals a discursive treatment of the poem, whereas Searle's 'cry' and Rafael and Gray's 'outcry' emphasize its visceral eventfulness. A similar, if less obvious, tension can be found between Sjögren's *'rop'* ('call') and Sandels's *'skri'* ('cry' or 'shriek'), the latter conveying pain and the former presenting a more balanced image of the speaker. As for the first stanza, here are the three English versions:

> I'm coal!
> And you pull me brutally from the ground
> And you make me your mine, boss.[27]

> I am coal!
> And you uproot me brutally from the earth
> And make me your mine
> Boss![28]

> I am coal!
> Brutally you wrench me from the ground
> And you make me your mine
> Boss![29]

The differences are slight but not insignificant. The eventness of the poem as a speech act is underscored by the interjective self-affirmation ('I am coal!') and the open address to the colonial exploiter ('Boss!'), but in Searle's version (the first quote) these elements are weakened. The various choices of 'pull', 'uproot', and 'wrench' also push the poem in different directions. Burness's 'uproot' is the most interpretive, tending towards what translation scholars call 'explicitation' in the same vein as 'protest' in his title. Searle's 'pull', by contrast, weakens the force of *'arrancas'*, while Rafael and Gray's 'wrench' instead shifts the semantic field towards the inorganic domain of tools, which is more in line with the image of mining and colonial exploitation. Together with their decision to change the syntax and foreground 'Brutally', this produces a starker, less intellectualizing text-event. What we see happening here is something quite paradoxical. On the one hand, this single poem by Craveirinha accumulates canonical authority by being repeatedly published and translated. But on the other, this very process blurs the identity of the poem, transforming it into an agglomeration of versions and publication events. The paradox touches on the very definitions of 'authorship', 'work', and 'text' – questions too large to address here, but which will motivate my closing remarks on 'textual zones'.

If even an infrequently translated poet such as Craveirinha opens a wide range of world-literary issues, the stakes rise dramatically in the case of Coetzee, a prose writer whose English works have gradually been translated into more and more languages, including Arabic, Hebrew, Farsi, Chinese, Japanese, and Malayalam. The translational resonance of his work has been remarked by Coetzee himself in essays such as 'Speaking in Tongues' and, more importantly, through his fictions.[30] Here we enter the domain of the 'born-translated' novel, which makes it necessary to enumerate some of the crucial differences between my two cases. If Craveirinha's poetry can be located almost entirely within an anti-colonial nationalist context, Coetzee not only works in the far more translation-friendly medium of prose, but has been at pains not to be pigeonholed as a 'South African writer'. As Sarah Brouillette and Rebecca Walkowitz show in very different ways, this has entailed an increasing imbrication with a global publishing industry in a manner that was not conceivable for Craveirinha. Intriguingly, Coetzee has come to thematize these very conditions of translational circulation. In *Diary of a Bad Year*, we follow the writer J. C., who is preparing a book of essays destined for publication in German and French. In *Summertime*, the third and seemingly final of his 'autrebiographical' fictions, we encounter a range of different voices, supposedly speaking from different linguistic vantage points. The exchanges between John and his cousin Margot are understood to take place in Afrikaans; his former colleague Sophie Denoël speaks English but is French; and in the chapter where we encounter the Brazilian Adriana Nascimento, the interview is supposedly conducted by means of an interpreter, shuttling between English and Portuguese.

The latter case is particularly interesting, given that the English version of the narrative presents itself as being already translated, and therefore not in the 'immediate' voice of Adriana. This self-reflexive mediation of a mediation has been perceptively discussed by Walkowitz.[31] If we follow it across several languages, it becomes even more intriguing. Comparing the French, German, Swedish, Brazilian Portuguese, and European Portuguese versions, we find differences in how they reveal or conceal the fact of translation. Adriana uses certain French words such as '*célibataire*' and '*comme il faut*'; in the French edition, translated by Catherine Lauga du Plessis, these are highlighted with an asterisk to indicate that they were in French in the original.[32] The European Portuguese translator J. Teixeira Aguilar does the same, whereas the German, Brazilian, and Swedish retain the French words without explicitly indicating their status in the original.[33]

When it comes to the two Portuguese translations, they could – if we accept the fiction – be read as back translations, restoring Adriana's translated anglophone voice to her own Portuguese. But here, of course, the instability not just of translation but of the literary text itself becomes apparent. Adriana is explicitly portrayed as a Brazilian, although she has lived several years in Angola and South Africa. Yet, Aguilar's version makes her sound more Portuguese than Brazilian. When the Brazilian translator José Rubens Siqueira has Adriana say, in colloquial Brazilian fashion, '*é*' for 'yes' or '*está vendo*' for 'look', Aguilar renders this as '*sim*' or '*pois*' and '*olhe*', which reads as more 'correct', European Portuguese.[34] These comparisons could be developed further, but the main point I wish to make concerns the relationship between Coetzee's deliberate thematization of the born-translated nature of *Summertime* and the relative instability of its versions. To begin with, Coetzee ironizes English hypercentrality by letting the character John, portrayed as an English teacher, disingenuously claim that English 'is just one language among many'.[35] But by producing a translational charade – the fiction that Adriana is 'actually' speaking Portuguese – Coetzee introduces an element of instability in the source text that functions as a mode of 'linguistic hospitality' towards translations-to-come.[36] As Hermans observes, there is in any given translation a 'latent gesturing towards additional possibilities and alternative renderings'.[37] Uncharacteristically for a source text, *Summertime* itself inscribes the possibility of such alternative renderings into its fictional world. Hence,

> [w]hile the production of a new translation shows the underlying original to be translatable, the provisionality of the rendering intimates the dimension of the untranslatable, understood here as the impossibility of arriving at a definitive version [...] The potential for retranslation thus undermines any claim an individual translation may have to be the original's sole representative.[38]

On such an understanding, therefore, by presenting the Adriana chapter as a translation into English, *Summertime* is in fact unsettling the claim of the *source text* to be the sole representative of 'the original'. Understanding *Summertime* as a world-literary text requires, therefore, that one expands into the multilingual effective life of *Summertime, Sommer des Lebens,*

Sommartid, Verão, L'été de la vie, and so on. The world-literary text – understood here as the text that travels through translation – is therefore never stable, yet always shaped and constrained by its systemic circumstances. Each translation is relational, being produced in response to, and together with, one or several source texts. Taken together, then, each new translation contributes to establishing not 'a' text, but an expandable, multilingual *textual zone*, issuing from multiple subjectivities, produced in discrete systems of publication, and constituting thereby the effective world-literary existence of a poem or a novel. These textual zones are not reducible to the poem that Craveirinha himself once wrote, or to the book authored by the individual known as J. M. Coetzee, but nor could they exist without them.

Notes

1. E. Apter, *Against World Literature: On the Politics of Untranslatability* (London: Verso, 2013), pp. 31–114.
2. D. Damrosch, *What Is World Literature?* (Princeton: Princeton University Press, 2003), p. 4.
3. See, for example, C. Prendergast (ed.), *Debating World Literature* (London: Verso, 2004); G. Lindberg-Wada (ed.), *Studying Transcultural Literary History* (Berlin: De Gruyter, 2006); M. R. Thomsen, *Mapping World Literature: International Canonization and Transnational Literature* (London: Continuum, 2008); WreC (Warwick Research Collective), *Combined and Uneven Development: Towards a New Theory of World-Literature* (Liverpool: Liverpool University Press, 2015); A. Mufti, *Forget English! Orientalisms and World Literatures* (Cambridge: Harvard University Press, 2016).
4. J. Heilbron, 'Toward a Sociology of Translation: Book Translations as a Cultural World-System', *European Journal of Social Theory*, 2 (1999), 429–444 (p. 434).
5. J. Heilbron and G. Sapiro, 'Outline for a Sociology of Translation. Current Issues and Future Prospects', in M. Wolf and A. Fukari (eds.), *Constructing a Sociology of Translation* (Amsterdam: John Benjamins, 2007), pp. 96–97. For the sake of comparison, I would also refer the reader to Beecroft's table on page 255 of *An Ecology of World Literature*, which looks at the number of published books rather than percentages. Small differences notwithstanding, it supports the broad conclusions above. A. Beecroft, *An Ecology of World Literature* (London: Verso, 2015).
6. *Index Translationum*, http://portal.unesco.org/culture/en/ev.php-URL_ID=7810&URL_DO=DO_TOPIC&URL_SECTION=201.html.
7. I. Even-Zohar, 'Polysystem Studies', *Poetics Today*, 11.1 (1990), 1–268 (p. 47).
8. Beecroft, *Ecology*, pp. 33–36.
9. Beecroft, *Ecology*, p. 103.
10. A. Berman, *L'Épreuve de l'étranger: culture et traduction dans l'Allemagne romantique* (Paris: Gallimard, 1995).

11. S. Brouillette, *Postcolonial Writers in the Global Literary Marketplace* (New York: Palgrave, 2007); R. Walkowitz, *Born Translated: The Contemporary Novel in an Age of World Literature* (New York: Columbia University Press, 2015).

12. Beecroft, *Ecology*, p. 246.

13. Walkowitz, *Born Translated*.

14. G. Matusse, *A construção de imagem de Moçambicanidade em José Craveirinha, Mia Couto e Ungulani Ba Ka Khosa* (Maputo: Universidade Eduardo Mondlane, 1998).

15. *Présence Africaine*, 57 (1966), 472–480.

16. D. Burness (ed.), *A Horse of White Clouds: Poems from Lusophone Africa* (Athens: Ohio University Center for International Studies, 1989); D. Burness (ed.), *Echoes of the Sunbird: An Anthology of Contemporary African Poetry* (Athens: Ohio University Center for International Studies, 1993); J. Craveirinha, *Karingana ua karingana* (Lourenço Marques: Academica, 1974); J. Craveirinha, *Xigubo* (Lisbon: Edições 70, 1980 [1964]); J. Craveirinha, *Cela 1* (Lisbon: Edições 70, 1980); J. Craveirinha, *Izbrannoe*, Vjačeslav Kuprijanov et al. (trans.) (Moscow: Mol. Gvardija, 1984); José Craveirinha, 'A Translation of Four Poems by José Craveirinha', Michael Wolfers (trans.), *Portuguese Studies*, 3 (1987), 193–204; J. Craveirinha, 'Szigubo', Eugeniusz Rzewuski (trans.), *Okolice*, 11.10 (1990), 54–55; J. Craveirinha, 'Seven Poems by José Craveirinha', L. Rafael and S. Gray (trans.), *New Coin*, 31.1 (1995), 1–5; J. Craveirinha 'Seven Poems', Luís Rafael and S. Gray (trans.), *Portuguese Studies*, 12 (1996), 201–209; J. Craveirinha 'Five Poems', L. Rafael and Stephen Gray (trans.), *The Journal of African Travel-Writing*, 2 (1997), 66–69; J. Craveirinha, *Dikter*, Ö. Sjögren (trans.), (Stockholm: Ordfront, 2003); J. Craveirinha, *Att stava till ett kosmos*, M. Sandels (trans. and intr.) (Uppsala: Almaviva, 2006); K. Falkeid (ed. and trans.), *Mitt Afrika, mitt Afrika: gjendiktninger* (Oslo: Cappelen, 1974); M. Dickinson (ed. and trans.), *When Bullets Begin to Flower* (Nairobi: East African Publishing House, 1972); C. Searle (ed. and trans.), *The Sunflower of Hope: Poems from the Mozambican Revolution* (London: Allison & Busby, 1982).

17. To this could be added a few impromptu translations of quoted verses by P. Chabal in his discussion of Craveirinha in *The Postcolonial Literature of Lusophone Africa* (Johannesburg: Witwatersrand University Press, 1996). There is also a small selection by Julio Finn that I have been unable to track down.

18. S. Gray, 'Seven Poems by José Craveirinha', *Portuguese Studies*, 12 (1996), 201–209 (p. 201).

19. S. Witt, 'Between the Lines: Totalitarianism and Translation in the USSR', in B. J. Baer (ed.), *Contexts, Subtexts and Pretexts: Literary Translation in Eastern Europe and Russia* (Amsterdam: John Benjamins, 2011), pp. 149–170.

20. According to his publisher his books have sold forty million copies in forty languages. See Leopard Förlag's website, www.leopardforlag.se.

21. M. Sandels, *Att tänka på henne: provensalsk trubadurlyrik från medeltiden* (Stockholm: FIBs lyrikklubb, 1980); M. Sandels (ed. and trans.), *Smaken av oceanerna: tjugosju portugisiska 1900-talspoeter* (Stockholm: FIBs lyrikklubb, 1982).

22. P. Bourdieu, 'A Conservative Revolution in Publishing', Ryan Fraser (trans.), *Translation Studies*, 1.2 (2008), 123–153 (p. 135).

23. See www.kulturradet.se/upload/kr/distributionsstod/06_nov.pdf.

24. G. Toury, *Descriptive Translation Studies and Beyond* (Amsterdam: John Benjamins, 1995), p. 29.
25. www.ponto.altervista.org/Livros/Doc/craveirinha.html
26. T. Hermans, 'Translation, Irritation and Resonance' in M. Wolf and A. Fukari (eds.), *Constructing a Sociology of Translation* (Amsterdam: John Benjamins, 2007), pp. 57–75 (p. 67). See also T. Hermans, *The Conference of the Tongues* (Manchester: St Jerome, 2007).
27. Searle, *Sunflower*, p. 1.
28. Burness, *A Horse of White Clouds*, p. 159.
29. Craveirinha, 'Seven Poems by José Craveirinha', p. 5.
30. J. M. Coetzee, 'Speaking in Tongues', *The Australian, Weekend Review*, 28 January 2006, 4–6.
31. Walkowitz, pp. 72–76.
32. J. M. Coetzee, *L'Été de la vie*, C. L. du Plessis (trans.) (Paris: Seuil, 2010), pp. 191, 196, 201.
33. J. M. Coetzee, *Verão*, J. T. Aguilar (trans.) (Lisbon: Dom Quixote, 2010), pp. 179, 185; J. M. Coetzee, *Sommartid*, U. Danielsson (trans.) (Stockholm: Brombergs, 2009), pp. 187, 190; J. M. Coetzee, *Verão*, J. R. Siqueira (trans.) (São Paulo, 2009), pp. 168, 175; J. M. Coetzee, *Sommer des Lebens*, R. Böhnke (trans.) (Frankfurt: Fischer Verlag, 2010), pp. 184, 190, 197.
34. Coetzee, *Verão*, Siqueira (trans.), pp. 164, 180, 182; Coetzee, *Verão*, Aguilar (trans.), pp. 168, 184, 186.
35. Coetzee, *Summertime*, p. 161.
36. P. Ricoeur, *On Translation*, E. Brennan (trans.) (London: Routledge, 2006), p. 23.
37. Hermans, p. 61.
38. Hermans, p. 61.

6

SOWON S. PARK[*]

Scriptworlds

Script and World

Thinking about literature in relation to 'world' tends to invite the broad sweep. But the widened scope needn't take in only the majestic, as conjured up in lofty concepts such as planetarity or world-historical totality. Sometimes the scale of world can produce a multifocal optic that helps us pay renewed attention to the literary commonplace. Taking script, the most basic component of literature, as one of the lenses through which to view the world literary landscape, this chapter will examine if, and how, ideas about writing can influence both our close and distant reading.

Script is something that usually escapes notice under traditional classifications of literature, which organize subjects along linguistic borders, whether as English, French, or Spanish; or as Anglophone, Francophone, or Hispanophone studies. The construction of literatures by discrete language categories supports the widespread view that differences between languages are not just a matter of different phonemes, lexemes, and grammars but of distinct ways of conceiving, apprehending, and relating to the world. This was a view that was developed into a political stance in Europe in the nineteenth century.[1] It posited a language as an embodiment of cultural or national distinctiveness, and a literature written in a national language as the sovereign expression of a particular worldview. One of the facets this stance obscured was the script in which the texts were written. Writing was defined as a medium for transcribing 'language' with no particular significance in itself.

The conflation of spoken language and written text is steeped in the tradition of European philology that bases the concept of language on speech. The primacy of speech, which persists in Western linguistics today, renders writing an ancillary form of spoken language. The underlying consensus remains that text cannot be transformed into meaning without being calibrated by spoken language, as individual words cannot acquire meaning in the absence of an overall system, which is speech.[2] This merging of writing and spoken language does not pose an immediate problem when one is working within the confines of European languages, because the Roman alphabet has been the unified standard.

However, when we take a wider view and bring diverse literatures of the world onto a single platform in a relation of putative equivalence, it immediately becomes apparent that the view of writing as a neutral and value-free tool for encoding spoken language is insufficient. Seeing texts in Arabic, the Roman alphabet, *Hanzi,* and Cyrillic, side by side requires the reader to make distinctions between spoken language and written language. For the thousands of spoken languages, there are hundreds of scripts, and script and speech do not correlate to each other along the recognized linguistic borders. The relation between writing and speech is much more complex than that which emerges from within the European frame.

One need only look to the literary history of pre-colonial India to see manifold relations between orality and textuality, which, in their rich multi-scriptal and polyglot manifestations, defy the standard ways of classifying languages and literatures.[3] Elsewhere, it is not hard to note that many spoken languages are digraphic, which is to say that they use more than one script for writing. Digraphia can be synchronic, as in the examples of Serbian, which is written in both Cyrillic and the Roman alphabet, and contemporary Konkani, which is written in Devanagari, Kannada, Perso-Arabic, the Roman alphabet and Malayalam. Digraphia can also be sequential. Azerbaijani was written in the Runic alphabet (fourth to eighth century), Arabic (seventh to twentieth century), the Roman alphabet (1929–1939), and then Cyrillic (1939–1991), before returning to a modified version of the Roman alphabet after 1992. Conversely, many different languages are written in a common script even if they are unrelated to one another. *Hanzi,* for example, was once the 'universal script' used for writing the many dialects and languages of China, Korea, Japan, and Vietnam. Today, the Roman alphabet is the *scripta franca,* transcribing over 130 languages as various as Swedish, Cherokee, and Zulu.

Scrutinizing literature through the lens of script allows us to see that there has always been a gap between speech and the written sign. The gap calls upon us to notice the various organizing conventions by which written knowledge is produced. One might begin to investigate these conventions by considering the ways in which the graphic shapes of script place constraints on meaning, which, in turn, condition the form, structure, and even the mode or genre of particular literary works – a point to which this chapter will return. And it should be remembered that learning a script is not just a matter of acquiring an understanding of the coding system by which spoken language is rendered into a visual form of communication; it is also a process of absorbing the ideas and traditions that are inscribed in the canonical texts through which literacy was traditionally acquired. 'Scriptworlds', such as those of the Roman, Chinese, Arabic, and Pali scripts, overlap with Christian, Confucian, Islamic, and Buddhist cultures respectively. The dominant script in a given culture establishes the relations between what is present and what will be preserved, in the technological sense, as well as in the character of knowledge that culture seeks to transmit and perpetuate.

It also determines who will have access to written information and for what purpose. This point is illustrated by the famous case of the Rosetta stone, on which is inscribed Egyptian hieroglyphics (which were used for writing religious documents at the time of its inscription), Egyptian demotic (the common script of Egypt), and the Greek alphabet (used by the rulers of Egypt at that time). As can be inferred, the choice of script discloses the text's immediate audience, whom it intends to exclude, as well as whom it aims to address. The choice of script is also an indication of the generic and literary tradition in which the text situates itself, and further gestures towards the particular social and cultural sphere it is meant to reach. For example, that *The Tale of Genji* was written in phonetic *Hiragana* and not classical *Kanji* served to remove it from the male elite class in eleventh-century Kyoto and firmly situated it in the intimate female circle of concubines and consorts of the imperial court.[4] Script is not as neutral as it may seem.

But in our alphabetic age, where the Roman alphabet has become the global script, it can be difficult for some, especially for monolingual speakers of English, to imagine how script can shape meaning. To discuss the ways in which scripts differ and to consider their implications for literary studies, the next section will look to an historical example.

When a Slovenian Jesuit met a Korean Philosopher in Eighteenth-Century Beijing[5]

On the 2nd of November 1765, the Korean astronomer and Confucian philosopher *Damheon* Hong DaeYong (담 헌 홍 대용, 湛軒 洪大容, 1731–1783) set off from Seoul (then called *GyeongSeong*, 경성, 京城) on a six-month tour to Beijing as part of the *Joseon* mission (조선 연행사, 朝鮮 燕行使) to imperial China.[6] Hong was not an official delegate of the *Joseon* court, but was able to secure his place as the nephew of Hong Eok (홍억, 洪檍), who was heading the delegation. What spurred him on was not political, but intellectual ambition. Hong was an early advocate of the Korean enlightenment and, independently of other intellectual traditions, had developed a theory of heliocentrism, an idea that was widely dismissed and resisted by the Confucian intellectual orthodoxy of *Joseon*. Mathematics and astronomy in particular drew him to Beijing, then the intellectual centre of the Chinese 'scriptworld'.[7]

The mission reached Beijing in the bitter winter of 1765–1766.[8] Upon arrival, Hong requested, with some persistence, a meeting with the Head of the Imperial Board of Astronomy and Mathematics of the Qing dynasty. This was Ferdinand Augustin Haller von Hallerstein (1703–1774), a Jesuit missionary born in Carniola, an area with a largely Slovenian population, which was then part of the Hapsburg Empire.[9] From 1746 until his death in 1774, Hallerstein, known in China as Liu SongLing, worked closely with the Qianlong Emperor and led research into astronomy and mathematics at the Qing court. Hallerstein eventually agreed to meet with Hong in the South Catholic Church of Beijing, then called Yenjing, where Hallerstein was resident. After the first encounter, they met again on two occasions to continue their discussion on mathematics, astronomy, and music. Hong gives an account of the journey and the meetings in his *Damheon Yenjing Records* (담헌연기, 湛軒燕記), a chronicle in six books, written in classical Chinese, which is now generally regarded as one of the three finest travelogues of premodern Korea.[10]

Hong and Hallerstein could not communicate through spoken language, but they were able to converse through a form of written exchange that was common across East Asia, called 'brush conversation', that is, written communication in classical Chinese. At one point in their discussion, Hong asked Hallerstein: 'Do Europeans use Chinese characters to write?' The question, at first, seems so absurd that it might have set an historical benchmark for parochialism. No doubt it reflected something of the cultural conditions of the time and place. In this region, China was then perceived as the only civilization, the source of all learning and knowledge, and the centre of the universe – as suggested by the characters for China (中國), meaning literally, centre (中) kingdom (國). This perspective had dominated East Asia for over 2,500 years. By the eighteenth century, Beijing had become a multi-ethnic, polyglot city. Hundreds of different Chinese dialects and scores of languages were spoken there – Burmese, Mongolian, Manchu, Tibetan, Uyghur, Thai, Korean, Japanese, Vietnamese, Nepalese, as well as Arabic, Uzbek, Turkish, Russian, and all the major European languages. By contrast, official written communication was uniformly in Chinese script or Han characters (漢子), known across East Asia as the universal script. Given this, Hong's question, taken out of context, could be put down to the sinocentrism of the time. But Hong was no innocent abroad, blundering headlong into solipsistic confirmation of the provincial; *Records* is a systematic reconstruction of Chinese civilization, in which he notes, with anthropological perceptivity, what people say and what they think, so as to reproduce for the reader at home accurate information about a more advanced civilization. Hallerstein's answer opens up an alternative reading: 'No' is his reply; in Europe, 'we only use speech-writing (諺字).'

Alphabetic Writing and Ideographic Writing

Hong and Hallerstein's dialogue discriminates between 'speech-writing' and 'idea-writing', or between phonetic writing and 'ideographic' writing.[11] This is a distinction that has all but disappeared from view in Western literary scholarship. Especially within standardized Roman alphabetic cultures, the general tendency is to think that writing *is* the encoding of the sound of speech by way of a phonetic system. The idea that writing is 'visible speech' can be traced at least as far back as the seventeenth-century French poet and translator Georges de Brebeuf's assertion that writing is 'speech for the eyes'.

But as the exchange between Hong and Hallerstein indicates, transcribing speech in a sound-based script is but one kind of written communication from a range of historic examples. Of course, writing is often a transcription of the sound of speech, but at the other end of the spectrum there are sign systems that communicate visually, independently of orality. To regard all writing as speech-writing is, as Jacques Derrida famously argued, to assume a phonocentric conception of language, which subordinates writing to 'an essential relationship to the presence of a speaking subject'.[12]

Examining language and literature through the lens of script affords us a view of text where writing is more autonomous because it is not reduced to voice. In other words, script reveals in concrete terms what phonocentric assumptions conceal. One script that brings clearly to the fore the visual dimension of writing, as separate from the aural, is Chinese. In China, Korea, Japan, and Vietnam, various and distinct indigenous languages were spoken, but the writing of these various East Asian languages was in 'ideographic' Chinese. (Ideographs or ideograms are script symbols that represent ideas, objects, and events; logographs or logograms are script symbols that represent words; and pictographs or pictograms are picture symbols that represent ideas, objects, and events.)[13] Even today, after successive major script reforms, there are still 808 Chinese characters commonly used in everyday writing across China, South Korea, Japan, and Taiwan.[14] This is possible because Chinese characters, or *Hanzi,* are visual units, which can transmit meaning independently of sound – hence the claim to 'idea writing'. This is not to suggest that Chinese is detached from sound and communicates by image alone. A sound component is attached to each visual sign, and the sound and idea work in parallel and in combination. Characters at times signal visually while at others what they transmit is mainly an approximation of sound. The distinction between ideographic script and phonetic script is not absolute.

For example, the Chinese characters 文學 are used in China, Korea, and Japan to mean literature, but are spoken as *wenxue* in Mandarin, *munhak* in Korean, and *bungaku* in Japanese. To reduce this example to a single character, 文 means letters or writing, and is pronounced as *wen* by Mandarin speakers, *mun* by Korean speakers, and *bun* in Japanese. The sounds attached to the character 文 are spoken differently according to the language or dialect of the speaker. The local phonologies vary too widely for oral communication to be possible but the image signifier 文 retains its meaning across the borders of spoken languages.

The example of Chinese adds to the discussion of world literature not because it is a script unlike any other but because it emphasizes the degree to which signification through image is achieved. The visual aspect of Chinese makes available a perspective that enables us to see that, at times, alphabetic script also communicates by image. Indeed, one could go so far as to say that all scripts, from Hieroglyphics to Hebrew to Tibetan, communicate visually as well as phonologically, and in the context of a larger social semiotic system.[15] But so naturalized is the view that alphabetic writing is exclusively a phonetic transcription of the sound of speech that it often obscures the wider context of semiotic communication – visual and contextual – within which it functions.

This is a view of writing that is corrected by reflecting on everyday experience. We can see that even the most phonologically ambitious alphabetic writing, for example, the International Phonetic Alphabet, has elements of 'idea writing', which are separate from speech. In English, the most obvious components of 'idea writing' can be seen in non-phonetic signs such as =, $, %, +, @, !, " ", ..., ;, :, CAPITALIZATION, line breaks, line direction, visual puns, *enjamb/ment*, font types and size, and the ever-increasing range of emoticons available on our keyboards. The polyphonic sounds of north-west London consummately captured in Zadie Smith's *NW* (2012) are not created by phonetic transcription, but through an abundant range of visual effects stimulated by the variation of form that works alongside, and in collaboration with, our auditory imagination. One of the most powerful passages of Toni Morrison's *Beloved* (1987) is the eponymous character's monologue in chapter twenty-two, where the lack of punctuation and irregular spacing are central to its choric, haunting effect. The blank single page on which Gertrude Colmore's *Suffragette Sally* (1911) ends gives us a sense of the resolve, hope, and uncertainty experienced by first-wave feminists at the height of the suffragette movement. The history of the English novel is rich with examples where authors, if not directly experimenting with typography, have nevertheless drawn on and made use of visual textuality, from Laurence Sterne's *Tristram Shandy* (1759–1767) to Donald Barthelme's *Snow White* (1965) to Mark Z. Danielewski's *House of Leaves* (2000). Currently, we are witnessing the flourishing of a diverse range of 'ergodic' literature, which is finding new relevance by means of media technology.

More ordinarily, readers of the Roman script might think of instances where meaning registers straight from the written word without there being a need to convert the letters into sound and then sound to meaning. The instances where we engage in reading that by-passes sound and operates directly from visual image to meaning are more frequent than a narrow conception of writing leads us to suppose. In the context of our present digital age, where technology allows for increasingly diverse means of visual communication and cybertexts are part of the mainstream, and where visual units of meaning such as GIFs and emoticons are rapidly becoming part of our everyday semiotic system, the view of writing as visible speech is becoming increasingly inadequate.

The dissociation of the visual from writing reflects a wider progression in post-reformation Europe, when there was a gradual transference of the model of poetry from one rooted in written Latin to one based on voice and the natural rhythm of the 'vernacular'. In the English tradition, poetry was recast as 'man speaking to man' in the eighteenth century and from there developed the idea that it should aspire to the level of music. By the middle of the twentieth century, T. S. Eliot declared that the music of poetry is not something which exists apart from the meaning.[16] Notwithstanding the counter-tradition, as most ebulliently represented by the Imagists, the ascendency of a vocal type of literature in modern Europe unquestioningly privileges speech. And hidden in plain sight are the ways in which scripts influence form, structure, and genre to produce our experience of literature.

To return to the question of script and literary form raised previously, an example of how one influences the other is found in Chinese poetics. The foundational unit of Chinese poetry is the character. Each character provides the image of a condensed, compact, free-standing unit. The composition scheme prescribes the *number* of characters per line, whether the poem be found in *The Book of Songs* (诗经, 11–7 BC), the earliest poetry collection in Chinese, in a set by Du Fu (a poet of the Tang dynasty), or in a modern volume of *haiku*. As we read, each character takes centre stage in the cognitive theatre, each suspended in time for a millisecond. The sound of the poem will be different according to the spoken language of the speaker. Nevertheless, the grapheme, the morpheme and the word are combined in every unit, each offering multiple levels of meaning. There is stillness in the sign because each character is solid, dense and specific. Each sign is separated by space and the space is charged with implication. Some of the joys of Chinese poetry have to do with the allusiveness, the sharp contrast, the swift and ferocious reversals made possible by the conceptual density that concentrated visual communication affords.

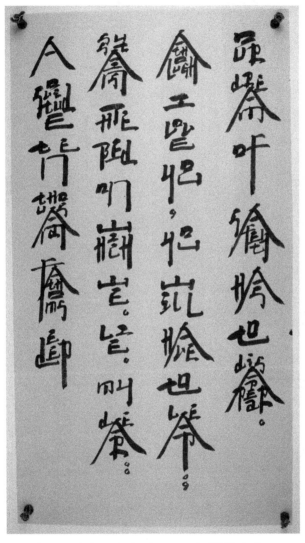

Figure 6.1 Xu Bing, 'Leap Before You Look' – poem by W. H. Auden, 1940, 2007, last paragraph. Ink on paper; 8 panels; 69 x 124 cm (6P), 23.5 x 124 cm (2P).
©Xu Bing Studio. Text reads (downwards, starting from the left): 'A solitude ten thousand fathoms deep/ Sustains the bed on which we lie, my dear: / Although I love you, you will have to leap; / Our dream of safety has to disappear.'

Figure 6.2 Xu Bing, 'Art for the People', 1999. Silk banner; 36 x 9 ft. Installation view at
Museum of Modern Art, 1999.
© Xu Bing Studio.

This distinctly graphic example might serve as a springboard for considering the more general, but nevertheless *visual* ways we experience literariness in alphabetic writing. The elaborate pictorial structures of George Herbert's 'The Altar' and 'Easter Wings' are obviously written for the eye. Edwin Morgan's concrete poetry draws attention to how space sets the pace for our visual experience. More commonly, we might think of the basic method of recognizing an English sonnet by its thirteen line breaks. An abiding definition of poetry, as opposed to prose, is that it is a form of writing where the author determines the lineation. Lineation creates discrete graphic units of meaning that provide the structure upon which the poet's deployment of end-stopping and *enjambment* create effects of sense and syntax. As T. S. Eliot noted: 'Verse, whatever else it may or may not be, is itself a system of *punctuation*'.[17]

A striking example of the influence of image on our reading experience is provided by Xu Bing's English square word calligraphy. The characters appear to be Chinese at first sight yet when the eye settles on the individual unit, it is able to decipher alphabetic letters that have been compacted into free-standing signs. Figure 6.1 shows the last stanza of W. H. Auden's 'Leap Before You Look' in square word calligraphy.

The compactness of each word produces differences in pace and rhythm. Reading Xu Bing's version illustrates that space, shape, and visual flow are not things that exist apart from the meaning. Another more immediately legible example of square word calligraphy is the 'Art For The People' banner at the entrance of Museum of Modern Art, New York (Figure 6.2).

The Politics of Script

Awareness of the differences between script systems opens up new vistas and allows us to reimagine the cartography of the literary world. Frames through which we commonly view literature, such as language and nation, appear to take on new forms, showing unfamiliar connections and disconnections. New categories are generated, such as the Chinese scriptworld, the Arabic scriptworld, the Sanscrit scriptworld, and so on, the comparative study of which provides the basis for charting a new world-literary landscape.

But structuring the world in terms of script also raises a number of quite difficult issues which need rather careful examination before rushing towards a new model. If a script is selected to represent a scriptworld, what are the ways in which that single representation adds to knowledge of a greater literary abundance and what are the ways in which it blinds us to the differences within it? If the analytical unit of a scriptworld is to provide a foundation for gauging and productively addressing the relations between national literatures of different linguistic traditions, how are the commonly held ideas about the relations between language and nation affected? This chapter has put forward the idea that 'writing as visible speech' curtails knowledge in our criticism and interpretation. Exactly how does the awareness of phonocentric thinking open up ways of approaching world literature?

Beginning with the last point, one of the most powerful consequences of defining written language in relation to speech is that text is tethered to the speaking subject. The presence of the subject then lends itself readily to the notion that a literature – say Norwegian or Zulu or Mongolian – is organically tied to a people or a demotic worldview. From the nineteenth century onwards, this conception of language hardened into the idea of a national language, which best embodies a people, their way of life, and their mode of thought. Modern literatures and literary histories have encouraged this view by mostly being written along national lines. The novel, in particular, has been defined as a genre closely linked to ideas of nationhood, so we can speak of the great English, Russian, or American novel. While transnationalism and cosmopolitanism are no less important registers in the twentieth-century novel, they necessarily presuppose the frame of nation in the attempt to transcend it, thereby reconsolidating the category of nation.

One form of world literary studies actively lends support to the alliance between language, nation, and people by conceptualizing world literature as the total sum of various literatures as classified by distinct language categories – Turkish literature, Vietnamese literature, Nepali literature, and so on. But if the basis for this 'world' is the congregation of various literatures drawn up along standardized national and linguistic borders, an entirely predictable outcome of this conception is a reproduction of nineteenth-century imperialist cartography. For the borders of modern languages emerged as part of the development of the modern nation state and the majority of what are now accepted as non-European standardized modern national languages were defined by traditional European philology during the period of colonialism. Postcolonial literary histories have shown how 'dialects' were marshalled into supposedly distinct wholes, classified according to the model of European languages, and then constructed as discrete languages to represent the part of the world the colonial administrators sought to govern.[18] As Robert Young has argued: 'It was not simply that particular languages were engineered, largely for political reasons, but that in order to represent the nation, the concept of language had to be dreamt up as well.'[19] If we call into question the very concept of a discrete language and recast it as an entity rooted in configurations of political hegemony, the artificiality of supposedly organic links between literature, nation, and culture that have become normalized and naturalized are suddenly brought into view. What further destabilizes the alliance of nation, language, and literature is the complex history of script. Or, to see this from a reverse perspective, the ideology of a national language represses perhaps the most obvious feature of literature – its writing system.

Foregrounding script in interpretation helps to uncover the critical situatedness of texts. Digraphia, outside of Europe, is the norm not the exception: multiple scripts co-exist and have co-existed in virtually all literary cultures. The wealth of scripts may be more noticeable in the southern hemisphere but even in Europe, the standardized use of the Roman alphabet did not completely eliminate the use of Runes, Cyrillic, Glagolitic, and the Hebrew alphabet. The *choice* of script embeds the text in its socio-political and intertextual setting.

So we might consider what the circumstances are in which a script is selected officially to represent a language or a nation. Is it the case that writing systems gradually evolve until the fittest survives? And is the predominance of one script over another purely based on the efficacy of the system, as the champions of the Roman alphabet would have it? The case of Korea provides an example that allows us to proceed to a more general observation. Korea has been simultaneously digraphic – in Chinese and 'Korean' – since around 1443, when the phonological *Hangul,* an alphabetic system of writing tailored to capture spoken Korean, was devised.[20] *Hangul* is today celebrated as the national script of South Korea, while in North Korea it is the only script permitted.[21] Translated, it means the writing of the Han race. Yet before the twentieth century, there was virtually no discussion of abjuring Chinese in favour of the 'national', scientific, alphabetic writing. The phonological alphabetic or 'speech writing' that is *Hangul* was universally considered an inferior script, suitable only for women and children who had not had the benefit of a classical education. For example, Hong wrote his *Damheon Yenjing Records* in a *Hangul* version, as well as in Chinese, ostensibly for his mother, and this version was read widely by women.[22] It would not have occurred to any reader of the time that the *Hangul* version was somehow more intrinsically tied to Korean culture. During the *Joseon* dynasty, Chinese was not considered alien or foreign as it came to be seen over the course of the twentieth century. It was only during the Japanese colonial occupation of Korea, when Korean culture was subject to near total suppression, that *Hangul* came to be embraced as typifying the spirit of a nation.[23] The chequered history of writing does not bear out the idea that writing systems evolve organically and systematically to become as efficacious as possible in mediating between speech and thought.

Official, standardized writing systems are political institutions. They are instituted by social and political forces in order to regulate often disparate communities of polyglot, multi-scriptal peoples. This creates a cultural sphere, or at least key parts of a cultural sphere, which transcend boundaries of spoken language and integrate people into an administrative whole. The reason why Chinese, or *Hanzi,* the Roman alphabet, Arabic, and Cyrillic formed 'scriptworlds' is because they were imperial scripts. The borders of 'scriptworlds' are often the borders of empires. In all these scriptworlds, multiple writing systems existed, as did multiple languages, but the system that had currency was the one whose foundations were laid upon the edifice of political and economic ascendency. An official script is an expression of economic dominance, political power, and cultural prestige, rather than a rational reflection of how people can best communicate.

The view of writing as institutionally driven is corroborated by the observations and comparisons of script systems made by those who take a longer view. In evolutionary terms, the unique ability of humans to encode and decode language through vision is a recent development: writing emerged approximately 5,400 years ago and the alphabet is only 3,800 years old. Early writing was not devised to record stories or poems, or to express feelings and articulate internal states, or even to represent speech, but to keep track of accounting and to administer clerical and governmental processes. Early manuscript cultures are rich in legal, military, medical, philosophical, religious, and even mathematical texts. What this points to is that all writing, including imaginative fiction and poetry, is the outcome of institutional forces, which continue to govern and regulate writing systems, even if they appear naturalized and transparent. This aspect of writing should help us to question any simplistic idea of a script being a mere technological device, and to discern the ways in which it disguises the hegemonic nature of writing.

Script and Cognitive Worlds

The previous section addressed the issue of writing as a political institution; now arises the different question of how various writing systems reflect in their structure the relations between speech and cognition. One of the most influential works to deal with this problem was Derrida's *Of Grammatology* (1967). Derrida proposed that the history of Western metaphysics is a by-product of phonetic writing. The 'metaphysics of presence', of a speaking subject that pervades logocentric thinking, divests writing of an essential relationship to what it means. Controversially, he asserted that Chinese culture is distinct by the absence of logocentrism on account of its ideographic writing system. Other Western thinkers, for example Ernest Fenollosa, A. C. Graham, Chad Hansen, Roland Barthes, and John Gray, have also reflected that the differences between ideographic Chinese and phonetic alphabets engenders a different kind of thinking. Summarized, their arguments go something like this: when one acquires a phonetic alphabet to encode what exists in the world, the world of written language becomes an autonomous system independent of the world it represents. This is because instead of words being names for things, words are produced within their own separate and arbitrary system of difference and deferral. There is no trace of the *thing* in the alphabet, as there is in the pictographic or ideographic systems, and thus phonetic encoding affords the kind of abstract, transcendental thinking that we find in the history of Western thought. John Gray is the latest in a long line of philosophers who have pondered the effect of script on thought. In his much-discussed book, *Straw Dogs* (2002), he writes:

> It is scarcely possible to imagine a philosophy such as Platonism emerging from an oral culture. It is equally difficult to imagine it in Sumeria. How could a world of bodiless Forms be represented in pictograms? How could abstract entities be represented as the ultimate realities in a mode of writing that still recalled the realm of the senses? It is significant that nothing resembling Platonism arose in China. Classical Chinese [...] did not encourage the kind of abstract thinking that produced Plato's philosophy. Plato is what historians of philosophy call a realist – he believed that abstract terms designated spiritual or intellectual entities. In contrast, throughout its long history, Chinese thought has been nominalist – it has understood that even the more abstract terms are only labels, names for the diversity of things in the world.[24]

To what degree distinct cognitive worlds are produced through different scripts is an extremely difficult problem that demands further research. Answers to the questions posed by literary theorists and philosophers are now more likely to come from a wide variety of investigative approaches within the humanities, as well as the neurobiological sciences with important technological input from the physical sciences. What has already been established, however, is the answer to the narrower cognitive question that has divided literary theorists and linguists for thirty years: whether visual linguistic communication is possible independently of sound. Recent developments in cognitive neuroscience concerning how we read have verified that the brain network which interprets word meaning is quite distinct from that which decodes characters/letters into sound.[25] The empirical discovery of two kinds of mental organization for reading language, the lexical and the phonological, helps free ideas about writing from the primacy of speech.

In focusing on script as a relevant issue in world literary studies, this chapter has sought to delve into a deep history of world languages and literatures. If at certain moments literature could be said to represent a history, a language, or a world, it is imperative that the framework of analysis takes into account the hegemonic force of standardized discrete languages and official writing systems, against and within which particular literary expressions were crafted. The more precision with which we explore what these texts have situated themselves against, the more we can expect to be rewarded by general insights into normative and ideal world literary categories that reflect the actual practice of reading and writing across the world.

Notes

* This essay was written with the support of the Arts and Humanities Research Council as part of the Open World Research Initiative, Prismatic Translation after 'Initiative'.

1. See B. Anderson, *Imagined Communities: Reflections on the Origins and Spread of Nationalism* (London: Verso, 1983); E. J. Hobsbawm, *Nations and Nationalism since 1870: Programme, Myth, Reality* (Cambridge: Cambridge University Press, 1990); J. E. Joseph, *Language and Identity: Nation, Ethnic, Religious* (London: Palgrave Macmillan, 2004).

2. See J. Defrancis, *Visible Speech* (Hawaii: University of Hawaii Press, 1989).

3. See F. Orsini (ed.), *Before the Divide: Hindi and Urdu Literary Culture* (New Delhi: Orient Blackswan, 2010).

4. See M. Chozick, 'Eating Murasaki Shikibu: Scriptworlds, Reverse-importation, and the *Tale of Genji*', *Journal of World Literature*, 1.2 (2016), 259–274.

5. I am indebted to Marko Juvan and Mitja Saje for the material on Augustin Hallerstein, and to the Hong DaeYong Science Museum in Cheonan, Korea, for access to the *Damheon Yenjing Records* archive.

6. The *Joseon* dynasty ruled what is now Korea between 1392 and 1910. *Damheon* (담헌, 湛軒) is Hong DaeYong's (홍대용, 洪大容) 'brush name' (호), a literary title conferred on a writer traditionally by a teacher or his peers. His given Korean name, DaeYong, is transcribed in *Pinyin* as 'Darong'.

7. See S. S. Park, 'Introduction: Transnational Scriptworlds', *Journal of World Literature*, 1.2 (2016), 129–141.

8. The mission left Beijing on the March 11, 1766, and arrived back in Seoul on April 27, 1766.

9. For further details see M. Saje (ed.), *A. Hallerstein – Liu Songling: The Multicultural Legacy of Jesuit Wisdom and Piety at the Qing Dynasty Court* (Slovenia: KIBLA, 2009), pp. 76–115.

10. The other two are Kim ChangEop's (김창업, 金昌業) *Yeon Haengilgi* (연행일기, 燕行日記, 1712), and Park JiWon's (박지원, 朴趾源) *Yeolhailgi* (열하일기, 熱河日記, 1780).

11. This chapter does not engage with or address the specialized connotations accrued to the English word 'ideographic' in the field of Sinology. 'Ideographic'

in this chapter is used in a simpler sense of idea-writing. See Z. Handel, *Sinography: The borrowing and adaptation of the Chinese script* (Leiden: Brill, 2018).

12. J. Derrida, *Of Grammatology*, G. C. Spivak (trans.), (Baltimore: Johns Hopkins University Press, 1976), p. 303.

13. Pictographs form the basis of writing systems such as cuneiform and hieroglyphs, though all writing systems contain a combination of ideographic and phonetic elements.

14. See K. Tyson, '808 ways to Write Chinese, Korean and Japanese: Update', *The World of Chinese*. www.theworldofchinese.com/2014/04/808-ways-to-write-chinese-korean-and-japanese/.

15. See D. Sperber and D. Wilson, *Relevance: Communication and Cognition* (Oxford: Blackwell, 1986).

16. T. S. Eliot, 'The Music of Poetry' (1942), in *T. S. Eliot on Poetry and Poets* (London: Faber and Faber, 1957), p. 29.

17. T. S. Eliot, 'Questions of Prose', in *The Letters of T. S. Eliot, Vol. 3 1926–1927*, V. Eliot and J. Haffenden (eds.) (New Haven: Yale University Press, 2013), p. 260.

18. See O. Dann, 'The Invention of National Languages', in *Unity and Diversity in European Culture c. 1800*, T. Blanning and H. Schulz (eds.) (Oxford: Oxford University Press, 2006), pp. 121–134; R. J. C. Young, *Colonial Desire: Hybridity in Theory, Culture and Race* (London: Routledge, 1995).

19. R. J. C. Young, 'That Which Is Casually Called a Language', *PMLA*, 131.5 (2016), 1207–1221 (p. 1209).

20. The *Hunminjeongeum* ('Correct Sounds for the Instruction of the People'), which sets out the *Hangul* writing system, was proclaimed by King Sejong in 1446.

21. See the special issue, 'Hangul and Korean Culture', *Korea Journal*, 36.3 (1996).

22. The Chinese version was first published in 1939 and the *Hangul* version appeared in 1974. They are on permanent exhibition in the Hong DaeYong Science Museum in Cheonan, Korea.

23. See H. Lim, 'From the Universal to the National: The Question of Language and Writing in Twentieth Century Korea', *Journal of World Literature*, 1.2 (2016), 245–258.

24. J. Gray, *Straw Dogs: Thoughts on Humans and Other Animals* (London: Granta Books, 2003), p. 57.

25. S. Dehaene, *The Reading in the Brain: The New Science of How We Read* (London: Penguin, 2009), p. 26.

7

LIZ GUNNER

Ecologies of Orality

Orality is often seen as existing outside the confines of world literature, excluded largely because the heavy weight of print pushes it aside: words spoken, sung, or performed as aesthetic events are considered to be external to the domain of print, and thus to the modes of circulation conventionally associated with the term 'world literature'. Even if we keep to the term 'oral literature' we confine orality to a zone so peripheral that its points of connectivity, its potential links to 'world literature', are virtually erased.[1] How then do we begin to rethink orality, in order to bring about a model of world literature which is truer to the broad spectrum of verbal arts?

At one level, to provide a model of world literature that does not include orality is comparable to an act of self-amputation; it entails the excision of a huge field of human cultural endeavour. A great many techniques of aesthetic patterning and formal qualities, linked to the use of voice and body, mark this variety of verbal art and for this reason alone orality has a place within world literature. I argue that, for many reasons, an erasure of such a storehouse of creativity is unfeasible. We need to find a way of arriving at a possible model where orality remains, or becomes, a site of the literary within world literature. With this search in mind, what needs to be clear is that oral and written/printed forms of verbal art have intersected and overlapped in many cultures and at different points in human history. Orality may 'work' differently in its vast range of expressive forms; it may be complicated, shifting, and have fluid boundaries, but at base, as verbal art, it belongs to a universal practice of making or creating in language. This position is set out most clearly by Roman Jakobson and the Prague School of Linguists, and still stands today.[2]

My brief in what follows is to lay out a terrain of orality that makes it possible to ponder what *might* be, or even should or could be included within a domain of world literature, a site which recognizes a number of literary ecologies, to take on Alexander Beecroft's helpful, even liberating conceptualization.[3] Here, we may be able to escape from any fixed idea of a normative centre and thus undo the correlative notion of power emanating from such a fixed point – a Western centre of literary influence and one dominated by the genre of the novel.

Rendering or realizing oral works involves a body, a voice, a moment in time, and an audience. Attending to the poetics of orality must take into account the *somatic*, that is, physical and material elements. The possibilities and actualities these variables give rise to are vast, but the fact of a somatic rendering, where body, voice, and movement are part of the textual performance, has to be considered when theorizing orality. This is so particularly if the question of *how* orality, and the vast and extensive practice of orature, is to sit within the models of world literature that currently dominate.

I here discuss orality as a phenomenon of human culture that is particularly rich on the African continent. To understand this fully, some long-standing Western images of Africa need setting aside; in particular, the notion of Africa as a continent apart, home of the strange and the exotic. What does not bear forgetting are its agonistic ties to European colonialism and, linked to this, its history as a region of slavery which for centuries fed the economies of powerful states of the Western and Arab world.

Orality in Africa, manifested as types of formal speech, song, and dance, has produced a range of genres tied into social, political, and spiritual existence.[4] In order to suggest how a decentred world literature might look, I will address the sphere of orality as it pertains to Africa, although it exists as practices of verbal art across all of human cultures, including those as distant from each other as Inuit and indigenous Australian.[5] I will then analyse an example of African epic, before I focus on praise poetry, which can be seen as one of the great African forms of orality. First, though, I further discuss the sphere of orality in relation to the current debates and dominant models of world literature. Why, I ask, has orality been so absent from the debates in this field?

Notions of temporality are important. Pascale Casanova's model of a world 'republic of letters' has immense appeal in some ways, but deals a *coup de grâce* to any serious consideration of world genres other than the novel – a relatively recent one in terms of world culture – and to the regions of the literary world covered by the term postcolonial.[6] Orality as verbal and performed art is very much part of the present. It is not simply a fascinating relic of earlier epochs, nor can it be viewed as an outmoded repository for folk art that belongs to the literary past of the national-romantic moment. Casanova's insistence on a progression of modes in the West thus ensures no contemporary place for orality, and indeed no acceptance of its place as living literary art.

Also important is the question of 'pastness' and 'presentness' in relation to Africa, as its deep timeline may be left out of an easily accessible global knowledge of the past. While David Damrosch's model of world literature, with its canon of global circulating texts, may seem exclusionary, Damrosch makes the important point that a model of world literature which focuses only on the last 500 years of human culture is intensely presentist.[7] He opens up texts from deep history, such as the Mesopotamian Epic of Gilgamesh, for inclusion into a body of transculturally circulating literary items, each of which comes with its own history, speaks across time, and is engaged with from a new perspective by its readers in their moment. It also sets up for contemplation a text with a shadow history of performance, where there is a hint of particular moments of theatricality, listeners, performers, and perhaps also a particular philosophy of life and death. Unlike Franco Moretti's dynamic, contrastive model of 'trees and waves', Damrosch takes us out of the trap of a narrow focus on the novel genre and gestures to a point which suggests a connection with orality and world literature, namely the active, performative life of a text being made and remade in a visceral sense. Could this be a point of connectivity from which to contemplate orality?[8]

For all its appeal, the Damrosch model makes it impossible to understand as literary art the kinds of orality whose base is not script, but the craft of words as an activity characteristic of human communities. Orality is not a practice that was *before* writing and which therefore is now obsolete, part of a past to be treasured or discarded. To think like this is to think in a developmental and teleological way. Rather, orality in many instances flows into and out of print/writing, and changes itself; the borders are not fixed. As Mikhail Bakhtin notes: 'The shift of boundaries between various strata (including literature) in a culture is an extremely slow and complex process [...] which occurs at a great depth'.[9] Bakhtin thus signals the tenacity of literary forms even in cultures which are changing swiftly. Stability and innovation, he stresses, are not incompatible, but can co-exist.

Travelling Genres: Epic and Praise Poetry

How do oral forms of verbal art travel over time and distance? And how do they maintain a place in one or multiple cultures, even as they shift and change? How do they relate to the complicated process of slowly shifting strata in a culture? My main focus will be praise poetry as an African performance mode – primarily an oral one – which operates across a number of cultures and eras. I will begin, though, with epic, a form of verbal art which shares some of the characteristics of praise poetry. Both epic and praise poetry carry as part of their discursive conventions the practice of *naming*. This, at least, is their great shared bond in African expression. I focus here on the epic of *Sunjata*.

In a conventional or, perhaps, Western world, the taxonomy of genres prescribes a pecking order that sets epic above praise poetry: praise poetry is *not quite* epic; it *lacks* the broad sweep and wide narrative landscape; epic is *longer*; it has *more* substance, and so on.[10] Epic is without doubt a very ancient and powerful genre if we consider the sweep of world cultures, and one that predates print and script. The oral base of the *Iliad*, for instance, argued for first by Milman Parry and after him by Albert Lord, now has broad acceptance.[11] Often, the purchase of epic is that it retains, in artistic form, the deep history of a region, a people, or group of peoples. For this reason, examples of the epic genre have tended to make the transition from orality to written form, and such records are frequently used to validate, even shape a particular history and identity.

The epic of *Sunjata* from the Mande region of West Africa, one of the great epics of the world, still exists as a performed resource; it is sung and chanted/spoken by specialist artists to particular communities from Senegambia across to the modern Republic of Mali. It has also migrated across media and maintains a presence in digital and electronic media, and on the airwaves of radio and television. The roots of the epic lie in the era of Sunjata Keita (the spelling in French is Sundiata), founder of the kingdom of Mali in the thirteenth century CE, who returned from exile to defeat his enemy, the powerful Susu magician king, Sumanguru.[12] Mali, the empire founded by Sunjata, which lasted for over two centuries, was the second of three great West African empires: Ghana, Mali, and Songhai. These existed contemporaneously with the Song Dynasty in China and the Kamakura era in Japan. At its height in the early fourteenth century CE, the Malian Empire stretched from Senegal as far as Timbuktu and Gao in modern Mali.

Present as an epic in the oral tradition, *Sunjata* incorporates earlier hunters' songs, praise songs, praise names (in particular those of Sunjata Keita himself), and historical narrative; it is performed by skilled artists known as *jali* (in French, often called griots), and has circulated in the Mande region over many centuries. It thus provides a site of shared cultural memory and artistic practice and binds together millions of West African peoples, all of whom speak closely related languages and can trace their ancestry to the empire of Sunjata. It forms part of a living tradition, constantly finding new life as performers give it their own particular renditions. The epic, with roots in an era which had absorbed Islamic influence but which predated any substantial contact with the Christian West, has also come to represent a vindication of Africa's deep history and culture.

The *Sunjata* epic's character as a living example of the oral epic tradition became far clearer after Gordon Innes published three Mandinka versions recorded by him in the Gambia in 1970. Here, we can see how the details of the Sunjata story vary according to the *jalis* who perform it, and this is part of the nature of the live performance tradition. The outline of the narrative is as follows: it covers the difficult early years of the hero Sunjata and his mother Sogolon, the Buffalo Woman, including his exile – in some versions with his mother, in some, alone. In the rendition of some *jalis*, his sister, Nene Faamaga, plays an important role during his years in exile. Then there are Sunjata's battles, in particular against his main adversary, the Susu magician king, Sumanguru, followed by his triumphant final return along with his key generals from the region, and the founding of a new kingdom, Mali.

Before 1970, a prose version of the epic by the historian Djibril Niane had already been published in French in 1960, and then in English in 1965. Aimed largely at a Western audience, the published epic met with great success and was hailed as a mark of African deep history and a vindication of African artistic presence at a time of continent-wide African nationalism. Niane's text, which was compiled from several performances by a renowned Guinean *jali*, Mamadou Kouyate, gave a powerful account of the drama and historical flavour of the epic and its key songs, but it did not highlight the fluid, oral quality of the epic, its *living* presence. Nor did it allow readers an opportunity to grasp the changing nature of each performance, and the differences between the *jalis* as *artists*, who learnt the mastery of the epic but performed it in different styles and shaped it according to their own talents, also modifying it for each particular audience.

With the publication of Innes's three Mandinka versions, what became evident was the central role of each performer in shaping the epic according to his own set of skills, and the importance of the audience in each performance. The line-by-line transcription showed the very different techniques and ways of rendering the epic of the *jalis* whom he recorded. Bamba Suso and Banna Kanute were regarded as masters of the eastern Mandinka tradition, steeped in the classical and historical repertoires of the *jalis*, going back to the era of the empire of Mali.[13] Bamba Suso was considered an authority on Sunjata and other heroes of Mande history. He was above all a storyteller with speech, rather than song, as his preferred performance mode; in Mande terms he was an historian and 'master of the word'. Banna Kanute, on the other hand, preferred a more flamboyant style of delivery, consisting of more song, the dazzling use of the balafon (xylophone), and less spoken narrative. Suso's voice, in contrast, boomed out with perfect diction and authority, as he gave his history of Sunjata, and was accompanied by a musician playing the kora, a harp-lute instrument with twenty-one strings, an alternative to the xylophone. Suso was most interested in the relations between the central characters, especially the relations between Sunjata and his mother and sister, and in the shift in Sunjata's character, from headstrong youth to mature leader and warrior. Banna Kanute, more of a charismatic showman, dwelt on the battles, the magical elements of the narrative, and the praise songs of the generals of famous lineages who had supported Sunjata.

The role of women as singers within the Mande music tradition is also linked to the *Sunjata* epic. Praise songs, associated with particular points of the Sunjata story and holding their own dynamic powers of affect, are most often the preserve of women *jalis*. They sing the melodies that are part of the great Mande epics, such as *Sunjata*, and the songs themselves create a sense of history which is not always tied to a particular lineage but can have a far broader, more inclusive reach. They are associated, too, with the circulation of the epic across media. Fanta Damba, famed for her looks as well as her clear and beautiful voice, toured Europe in the 1970s and was one of the stars of the Mali National Ensemble at the Second World Black and African Festival of Arts and Culture (FESTAC), in Lagos, in 1977. A decade later, Amy Koita, a star of Malian music, made the *Sunjata* praise songs central to her repertoire. Glamorous, and dressed in the flowing and majestic robes of damask or tie-dye that are famous in the region, such singing celebrities attract adoration and lavish gifts such as houses, gold, and cars from wealthy admirers.[14]

Artists of both genders have contributed to the expansion of the epic tradition across a range of media. Nowadays, full-length recitations of the epic are rare but songs from the epic may be heard on public holidays over the airwaves, and at public rallies; and one tune from *Sunjata*, 'Death is Better than Disgrace', is the Republic of Mali's national anthem. Alongside the proliferation of songs from *Sunjata* in recordings and on the airwaves, performances by *jalis* and accompanying musicians for their patrons continue. Here, the skill of the *jali* is to fit parts from the Sunjata story – and other stories of the region – to suit the particular occasion. Choice and a knowledge of the lineage of one's patron will shape each performance.

Since the early 1980s, the art of the *jalis* has been on display also on the international concert circuits, where it has even extended into new kinds of popular musical performance. Tunes and songs from the *Sunjata* epic find their way into a range of recordings by artists such as Salif Keita, who originate from the countries where the *Sunjata* epic circulates – Guinea, Mali, Senegambia, and Burkina Faso. For example, a CD published in 2004 with recordings by the most eminent of contemporary male and female performers is labelled *Mandekalou: The Art and Soul of the Mande Griots*.[15] Such recordings, which circulate in the West African diaspora and worldwide, show the *jalis* as modern artists working across media. They may modify the thick epic tradition of the whole region, and perform it in non-traditional styles, but such changes are a mark of the resilience of the oral epic tradition in the Mande region.

How can we place the *Sunjata* epic within a frame of world literature? One way, taking up Beecroft's model, would be to view it as circulating simultaneously within different spheres or ecologies of literary practice. As a printed publication, in particular the version authored by D. T. Niane, the epic circulates as a literary text much like the modern *Iliad*. It may be far closer to its origins in orality, but the *Sunjata* text, like the *Iliad,* speaks from a narrative in the deep past to a particular modern consciousness of history and region, nation, and historical tradition. Yet the rich multimedia presence of the *Sunjata* epic points to its dissemination by other technologies, electronic or digital, on CDs, and on the airwaves of radio and television. In these instances, it may be only fragments of the full epic that circulate, but they remain part of the performed footprint of the epic. In these cases, *Sunjata* reaches a home audience in the Mande region, but it also reaches a global audience, as well as those parts of the Mande diaspora scattered elsewhere in Africa and further afield. This digital mode of circulation constitutes a different ecology. In addition to these there are the continuing performances by *jalis* for patrons in a social setting reminiscent of older performances to wealthy nobles and rulers, which need not be seen as the most authentic kind of performance of the epic or songs and fragments from it. Each kind of circulation still conveys the conventions through which the epic is generated, but differently. The oral epic tradition of *Sunjata* thus exists through multiple practices, each of which sustains its presence in the modern world.

Praise Poetry

Praise poetry is important in both past and present eras of literary practice in Africa. In what follows I do not make a case for the canonical status of a single tradition of praise poetry within the wider ambit of orality. Instead, I focus on particular practices of praising which differ according to the history and context to which they relate, and yet are connected, most significantly by the value placed on *naming*, by means of particular aesthetic conventions, the individual who is being praised.

Praise poetry is a mode of poetic communication which profiles, defines, and in this broad sense praises through turning the spotlight on an individual, his/her personality, and social or historical being, with great clarity and force. The craft of praising is usually the work of gifted individuals, but in some traditions it is a skill shared by those who know the basic style and rules of composing. The dense and compact praise epithets, which may be piled on one after the other, often creating a strong rhythm through repetition and the device of parallelism, aim to capture the essence of an individual's life, her/his history, and personality. Sometimes the truth of the praise captures startling but not necessarily flattering aspects of a personality. The definition, though, is the essence. In a number of praising traditions, the person praised, either man or woman, is set within a larger social frame. There is a connection to a genealogy, a clan, a wider regional group, even in some instances a kingdom or nation.

The aesthetic of praising and naming can be found in the praise poetry of different regions and peoples in Africa, and has a range of defining features which vary according to each locale's specific language and cultural practices. Praise poetry can also shift its technologies of production, and find a place in different literary ecologies, as Beecroft would put it. In the southern African tradition of praise poetry, for example, in its Zulu form known as *izibongo*, praise poetry has been the preserve of royalty. But it has also been widely used by less powerful groups and to praise individuals who are not at all famous. Sometimes composers familiar with praising conventions will praise, and thus define and name, *themselves*.[16] Praise poetry in the South African instance has shown a capacity to migrate, to follow power, to challenge existing power and seek the new. In that way, it differs from the Rwandan praise tradition which I discuss below. Linked to royalty and cultivated by the nineteenth-century king Shaka and his praise poets, the Zulu practice of praising, marked by its formal speech, its store of poetic skills, and its set of dramatic gestures, maintained a place in cultural and political repertoires well into the modern period of South African race segregation known as apartheid. As late as the 1980s, and shortly before the start of the new post-apartheid era, it was still present. Its coupling of poetic rhetoric with the use of poetry to envision the public space, and to comment on history and powerful individuals, meant it continued to inspire its audiences. Some poets worked in the frame of the older praise tradition, others shifted to English and used praise poetry's sanctioned public role, rather than its precise features of style.[17]

Zulu praise poetry also migrated more directly – in terms of form and technique – into the arena of worker poetry and political insurgence. In the 1980s, a new trade union, FOSATU (the Federation of South African Trade Unions), was praised by a worker imbongi (praise poet) as:

> You moving forest of Africa
> When I arrived the children
> Were all crying [...]

You are the hen with wide wings
That protects its chickens.[18]

Here, we see how profiling and definition through praise naming and invocation is directed at an organization, not an individual. Also striking is the impulse to situate the thing/person praised in a particular historical narrative and to associate it with power. At the same time that the praise poetry tradition was being captured for this new role, to support the workers' struggle, praising continued in its more established role. The Zulu king at the time had no political power but was still widely revered as the descendant of Shaka, founder of the Zulu kingdom. His young imbongi, Thulilwenkosi Dlamini, hailed him as:

> Horned Viper with the Feathered Head, descendant of Menzi! [...]
> Persistent young man
> Because he persisted with the men of Zululand when his strength was gone.[19]

Linked to the words themselves, in the first case pointing to a new political formation, and in the second to the weight of a kingdom with its own history and value, was the *act of performing* the praise poetry. The trade union praise poets, such as Alfred Qabula, Mi Hlatshwayo, and Nise Malange, performed at worker rallies, often in Durban. The king's imbongi chanted his patron's praises at meetings and ceremonial occasions, mainly in rural KwaZulu-Natal but also sometimes at stadiums, open grounds, and other public spaces of the cities of Johannesburg and Durban in particular. Each imbongi had his/her own recognizable delivery style, but worked within the performance frame of the dramatically raised voice, which also entails following the rhythm of the praise names, drawing out the final word and at the same time dropping tonally to a break, before beginning the next raised entry. Action and costume could vary. Dlamini, the royal imbongi, relied mainly on his powerful voice for dramatic effects. Qabula devised his own striking rags and tatters costume to signify the plight of the workers. Body and voice combined with skilled phrasing of the clusters of praise names, as each poet strode across the stage with a microphone or simply projected their voices for their often huge audiences. Those present knew the aesthetic and practice of praise poetry and could respond with equal intensity and *knowledge* to both the trade union poets and the royal praise poet. The ideas conveyed in the praise poems, however, carried different messages in terms of loyalty and a vision of the state.

In the contemporary era, more than two decades since the release of Nelson Mandela from jail, and the fall of apartheid in 1990, these poetic skills of praise poetry have found a place on radio, and electronic and digital media. In a popular weekly Zulu-language radio programme, '*Sigiya ngengoma*' (We show off with the dance), men fit their own *izibongo* into a popular genre, *maskanda*. Sometimes the aesthetic is diluted or redirected. New generations of poets, women and men, who draw on the dynamic of praise poetry, mixing it with other performance modes drawn from the British and African-American voice traditions, command attention. Still, praise poets may keep to the older form at national and regional events. Zolani Mkiva, imbongi of the late President Nelson Mandela, would travel widely with him in Africa and praise Mandela in the distinctively gruff and more staccato Xhosa praising style. The popular base of the art of praising may be reduced, but it still sits within social knowledge as a repertoire to be drawn on, and as a mark of a person's social and interpersonal skills, and their access to cultural capital. The Zulu king's praises and those of the kings before him, can still be heard on the radio, on special days and in recordings. Alongside it, the newer offshoots flourish.[20]

If we turn to poetry and praise in Northern Nigerian Hausa society, we see a long tradition of praise song, *waka*, one which is 'intimately tied up with relations of power'.[21] Patronage plays a part in this and thus a particular centre of power may have the services of a certain praise singer. Yet it is not always so clear-cut. The famous poet, Jankidi, travelled through parts of Nigeria and sang the praises of many individuals and rulers before he was finally given a formal position in the court of Sokoto.[22] Relations between praiser and praisee are further complicated because being praised can put demands on patron as well as praise singer. The praise singer will scrutinize and assess both the individual he is praising, and the office he holds. How well the praisee performs the duties expected of his office is a question likely to be addressed, and answered, in the praise songs of a competent praise poet. As one writer has put it, 'Vilification is the "co-wife" to praise'.[23] This links with other traditions of rhetoric such as that which nourishes European Renaissance poetry, where praise and blame could sit together in terms of the rules of rhetoric laid down by Aristotle.

As expected from a praise tradition such as that of the Hausa, where the praise singer has some freedom to travel in search of the best client, contemporary praise singers have moved into high-profile roles in the media and, in some cases, adapted the focus of their praise. Here too, like the earlier example of the sudden irruption of South African trade union poetry into adversarial state politics, the art of praising can migrate – in this case to a different medium, that of television. The praise singer Dan Marya Jos, for instance, moved away from the binaries of praise and vilification aimed at people of status. Instead, he began to sing in praise of himself, but then turned his praise songs to focus on the problems faced by ordinary people, such as truck drivers, labourers, and peasants.[24] In other cases, praise singers have been sought after by politicians and political parties.[25] The didactic and moralizing element, so important in Hausa praise poetry, is worked into the poetic structure: certain ideas and values are foregrounded, often through the device of parallelism. The poetry works aesthetically but *teaches* at the same time. What is clear from the continuing role of praise poetry/song in Hausa society is that the power to cause the praisee to shine lies – in part – with the praise singer, the artist who assesses the object of his praise, and makes the song. Hausa praise singing, as it operates now, circulates both electronically through the media and in the live performances of court artists. Here too, as in the case of the epic of *Sunjata*, we see *co-existing* rather than *successive* modes of production and circulation.

Other praise poetry has not travelled, nor has it found a place in co-existing technologies of production and circulation. The genres of court poetry in the East African kingdom of Rwanda flourished for several centuries but faded with the kingdom's demise in 1959. The exacting craft of the poets, practised over centuries, was passed from one cohort of poets to the next by intensive training, but now exists only in published accounts as an archive of a past era. This was elaborate praise poetry, marked by particular rhythmic and metrical structures, with elevated praise names and dense historical references tied to the royal dynasties. Some genres were secret, others circulated more widely. Animals were praised as well. Alongside the dynastic praise poems full of forgotten skirmishes and conquests, war poems, and ritual poetry, were the pastoral praises of the royal cattle – the long-horned *inyambo* cows. These treasured animals were praised as bovine heroines of courage and beauty. Their praises were in a particular metre made up of short and long vowels, with an assortment of narratives and invocatory praise names. At special ceremonies, including the national harvest celebrations, the *umuganura*, they were trained to parade and dance, draped with beads, in honour of the king.[26] The demise of the moral and political economy with which this poetic tradition was intertwined meant the value of the poetry itself, and its ability to produce meaning, faded away. Nevertheless, as one of Africa's significant sites of praise poetry, prestige, and power Rwandan court poetry still holds great interest for comparative literary work.

Other traditions of praise poetry cut through historical eras and remain resilient. Yorùbá praise poetry, *oriki,* found in the west of Nigeria, is one such practice of praising. Dynamic and dialogic, the process of naming and praising an individual folds the past into the present, deliberately blurring temporal distinctions. Here too, as in one aspect of Hausa praises, the astute gaze of the poet can call up critique as well as eulogy. While focusing intensely on a particular figure, often a 'big man', the praise keeps a certain openness and a multiplicity of voices in play. This is part of its particular aesthetic, its conventions to which audiences remain attuned. Karin Barber remarks that such a performance:

> Does not exclude other voices which sound a note of difference, if not of outright dissent [...] The kick in *oriki* seems to come from the never-resolved textual confrontations that are continually arising and as continually falling behind as the performer moves on [...] No final view is proposed just as no closure is sought.[27]

Orality and New Possibilities for World Literature

The desire to fit orality in all its breadth and complexity within the study of world literature presents us with choices and challenges. It offers new understandings of how the practice of literary art makes meaning within vastly different societies over time and regions. This essay has suggested how ecologies of orality, in Beecroft's sense, could operate in a wider system. We can see the possibilities of a single genre, epic for instance, sustaining and transforming itself through historical and aesthetic changes. Convergences across languages, epochs, and regions are there to be explored and worked into longer comparisons. How might we read the *Iliad* and *Sunjata* concurrently as epics with origins in orality, which work across time and within the present? How do we begin to think of co-existing and competing literatures within a single ecology? In the case of praise poetry, do we see its transference into different media – radio, television, or the internet, for instance – as a continuity? A new beginning? A loss? Lastly, precisely *how* do we bring orality and its bodies of meaning, and its systems of value, into the frame of world literature? Where are the texts? The voices? The theories? And how do we assemble them?

Notes

1. This term was coined by Ruth Finnegan in her monumental *Oral Literature in Africa* (Oxford: Clarendon Press, 1970).
2. R. Jakobson, 'The Poetry of Grammar and the Grammar of Poetry', *Lingua*, 21 (1968), 597–609; R. Jakobson, 'Subliminal Verbal Patterning in Poetry', in R. Jakobson (ed.), *Studies in General and Oriental Linguistics Presented to Shiro Hattori* (Tokyo: T. E. C. Company, 1970), pp. 302–308.
3. A. Beecroft, *An Ecology of World Literature: From Antiquity to the Present Day* (London: Verso, 2015).
4. L. Gunner, 'Africa and Orality', in F.A. Irele and S. Gikandi (eds.), *The Cambridge History of African and Caribbean Literature*, vol 1 (Cambridge: University of Cambridge Press, 2004), pp. 1–18.

5. L. Gunner, 'Names and the Land: Poetry of Belonging and Unbelonging, a Comparative Approach', in K. Darian-Smith, L. Gunner, and S. Nuttall (eds.), *Text, Theory, Space: Land, Literature and History in South Africa and Australia* (London: Routledge, 1996), pp. 115–130.

6. P. Casanova, *The World Republic of Letters*, M. B. DeBevoise (trans.) (Cambridge: Harvard University Press, 2004).

7. D. Damrosch, *What Is World Literature?* (Princeton: Princeton University Press, 2003), p. 17.

8. F. Morretti, 'Conjectures on World Literature', *New Left Review*, 1 (2000), 54–68.

9. M. Bakhtin, *The Dialogic Imagination: Four Essays*, M. Holquist (ed.), C. Emmerson and M. Holquist (trans.) (Austin: University of Texas Press, 1990), p. 33.

10. See the 'placing' of praise poetry in such a taxonomy in T. Cope, *Izibongo: Zulu Praise Poems* (Oxford: Oxford University Press, 1968).

11. A. B. Lord, *The Singer of Tales* (Cambridge, MA: Harvard University Press, 1960).

12. See: L. Duran, '*Jelimusow*: the Superwomen of Malian Music', in G. Furniss and L. Gunner (eds.), *Power, Marginality and African Oral Literature* (Cambridge: Cambridge University Press, 2008 [1995]) pp. 197–207; T. A. Hale, *Griots and Griottes: Masters of Words and Music* (Bloomington: Indiana University Press, 1998); G. Innes, *Sunjata: Three Mandinka Versions* (London: School of Oriental and African Studies, 1974); B. Suso and S. Kanute, *Sunjata: Gambian Versions of the Mande Epic by Bamba Suso and Banna Kanute*, L. Duran and G. Furniss (ed. and intro.), G. Innes and B. Sidibe (trans.), (London: Penguin, 1999).

13. For more information about both, see Duran and Furniss, 'Introduction', in Suso and Kanute, *Sunjata*, pp. vii–xxix.

14. See Duran, '*Jelimusow*'.

15. Various Artists, *Mandekalou: Art and Soul of Mande Griots* (Syllart/Melodie, 2004). See K. Kouyaté, M. Damba, S. Sidibé, and O. Sangaré, *Mali: The Divas from Mali* (WDR World Network, 1997). See also: R. C. Newton, 'Out of Print: The Epic Cassette as Intervention, Reinvention, and Commodity', in R. A. Austen (ed.), *In Search of Sunjata: The Mande Oral Epic as History, Literature and Performance* (Bloomington: Indiana University Press, 1999), pp. 313–326.

16. See the *izibongo* in L. Gunner and M. Gwala (eds.), *Zulu Popular Praises* (East Lansing: Michigan State University Press, 1991).

17. See Ingoapeli Madingoane's 'Black Trial', in I. Madingoane, *Africa My Beginning* (Johannesburg: Ravan Press, 1979), pp. 24–31.

18. A. Sitas (ed.), *Black Mamba Rising: South African Worker Poets in Struggle* (Durban: Worker Resistance and Culture Publications, 1986).

19. Gunner and Gwala, *Musho!*, p. 55.

20. See Koleka Putuma's 'Timelines', in K. Putuma, *Collective Amnesia* (Cape Town: uHlanga Press, 2017).

21. G. Furniss, 'The Power of Words and the Relation between Hausa Genres', in Furniss and Gunner, *Power*, p. 131.

22. B. W. Andrzejewski, S. Piłaszewicz, and W. Tyloch (eds.), *Literatures in African Languages: Theoretical Issues and Sample Surveys* (Cambridge: Cambridge University Press, 1984), pp. 273–274.

23. G. Bello 'Yabo, zuga da zambo a wakokin sarauta' (Praise, exhortation and ridicule in songs of the aristocracy), *Harsunnan Nijeriya*, 6 (1976) 21–34.
24. Furniss, 'The Power of Words', p. 135.
25. Furniss, 'The Power of Words', p. 135.
26. A. Coupez and T. Kamanzi, *Littérature de Cour au Rwanda* (Oxford: Oxford University Press, 1970), pp. 115–157; J.-P. Bucyensenge, 'Inyambo, the Royal Cattle Trained to "Parade and Dance"', *The New Times*. www.newtimes.co.rw/section/Printer/2014-10-08/181717/
27. K. Barber, 'Interpreting Oriki as History and as Literature', in K. Barber and P. F. de Moraes Farias (eds.), *Discourse and Its Disguises: The Interpretation of African Oral Texts* (Birmingham: Birmingham University African Studies Series 1, 1989), pp. 13–23.

PART II

Practices

8

BORIS MASLOV

Lyric Universality

Lyric and (World) Literature

'World literature' is a concept that, historically, has depended on a particular notion of literature, understood as a body of socially significant as well as artistically refined texts. This notion is, in turn, intrinsically related to the ideas of society and the public sphere as they came to be defined during the European Enlightenment. Increasingly since that period, Western readers have come to place at the centre of their literary canons works that have a critical, polemical, or questioning stance. We still live in a literary-historical epoch dominated by the novel as it was moulded in the nineteenth century. Yet if we turn to earlier periods of European history or survey varieties of verbal art practised outside of the 'Western' world, we have to adopt a very different outlook. Globally, the most widespread kinds of verbal art known to ethnographers are (folk) tales, often founded on collectively shared myths, and lyrics, that is, sung texts which are often performed communally, sometimes to the accompaniment of musical instruments. Leaving aside the popular art of storytelling, a crucial antecedent to all narrative forms, there are many cultures that have no epic or drama (not to speak of the novel!), and yet lyric seems ubiquitous, particularly those of its genres that are most obviously embedded in social life, such as ritual invocations, songs tied to the agrarian cycle, lullabies, and laments. The purpose of these forms of verbal art was not to question or critique, but to explain the world, influence it for the good of the performer(s), as well as to maintain shared values and ways of thinking; functions that, in the West, have tended to be relegated to other spheres, admittedly not always easily separable from literature, but more recently increasingly opposed to it, such as religion, science, varieties of non-fiction, and mass communication.

In the premodern 'West', what we now call literature used to be described first and foremost by terms cognate with the English *poetry* or *poesy*, derived from Ancient Greek words for creating objects and texts (*poiêtikê* 'the art of creation', *poiêtês* 'the poet'). The single most important characteristic of poetic works has long been their crafted quality or masterly design, which is most perceptible in their material form, first and foremost in diverse prosodic properties that historically are tied to a marked performance mode (song or expressive recitation). These range from the patterning of syllables (rhythm) to the use of consonance (including rhyme or alliteration) and pauses (in written texts, visible in the breaking of text into 'lines'). In discussing poetry, a broader notion of metered discourse (in the sense of being specially organized and measured) may therefore be more opportune than a simple reference to metre or rhythm. A variety of genres populates the domain of poetry understood as metered discourse, yet the distinction that is most patent is that between epic and lyric. By the former, we refer to longer narrative works in verse that tend to be *stichic* (works in which all lines use the same metre); by the latter, to shorter pieces that prefer *stanzaic* structures, ranging from quartets to sonnets and to the most intricate odic forms.

Universal characteristics of lyric, which are anchored in globally observed patterns of verbal art, can only be uncovered if we pay attention to basic structural features of metered discourse. That, in part, has been recognized as the task of linguistics, and it is not incidental that much important work on metre has been done by phonologists.[1] It is on this foundation that we can attempt to construct a historical poetics of lyric. While aware of both the historicity of each and every literary form and their participation in the 'great time' of literary and cultural history (to use Mikhail Bakhtin's term), we must be attentive to typologically prevalent structures that are variously inflected, experienced, and put to work in poetic cultures worldwide. In lyric, we may indeed be able to access humanity at its most elemental, yet we should not forget that this access can only be gained via philological exploration of language-specific qualities of particular poems. At least three levels of analysis are thus at play: the universal aspects of metered discourse deriving from patterns of human cognition; literary forms that cross-cut yet are energized by historical time; and the specific manifestation of both in the concrete materiality of verse. The perspective of world literature demands that we provisionally bracket language-specific aspects of lyric, so this chapter focuses on the former two levels of analysis.

It is in the context of our exploration of historically inflected universals of literature that the Ancient Greek etymology of the term *lyric* – 'poetry accompanied by a string instrument' – becomes relevant. For the Greeks, lyric was a synonym for melic (sung) poetry, which used complex stanzas, in contradistinction both to (1) recited verse composed stichically in epic hexameter and (2) recited (possibly, originally sung) verse in elegiac couplets, a very simple two-line stanzaic form. Stanzaic forms – which the term 'lyric' invites us to privilege – proved more resilient in some traditions of lyric composition than in others, yet even in poetic cultures that have largely abandoned not only the idea of musical accompaniment, but also the notion that poetry calls for a special type of performance (recitation from memory, expressive voicing, pausing at line divisions), quatrains are readily recognized as a form associated with lyric.

The approach taken in this chapter continues a particular strand in the tradition of Historical Poetics that reaches back to Alexander Veselovsky's disagreement with German Romantic narratives of the evolution of literary 'kinds' such as epic, lyric, and drama. Veselovsky noted that elemental forms of narrative, song, and dialogue 'had no reason to await history in order to manifest themselves', as they have been available at least since the time of the Vedas.[2] Historical Poetics, as it was understood by Veselovsky and later by Bakhtin, is opposed to teleological historiography of literary forms (with a distinct Western European bias), whose Hegelian inspiration is quite overt in scholars like Erich Auerbach and Bruno Snell. Instead, it advocates for an inclusive, empirically grounded account of verbal creativity whose broad comparative scope permits us to discern and experience, in any particular literary text, non-synchronous elements that may appear to us as 'primitive', 'archaic', 'folk-communal', belonging to the 'great time' of world culture, the deep 'memory' of a genre, or deriving from shared facts of human cognition and perception. These elements may be termed *panchronic* in the sense that they cannot be arranged in a chronological, intention-laden series (often referred to as 'tradition'). While not timeless, they tend to recur in different historical circumstances, with an insistence that makes any attempt to trace their complete genealogy highly tentative. These panchronic elements represent the most effective and most elusive aspect of literature; they, in particular, account for the often mystified view of 'lyric powers', the compelling force of a great lyric poem, unmistakable yet difficult to elucidate analytically.[3]

In the following two sections I will endeavour to elucidate some of the basic panchronic elements of lyric with reference to Roman Jakobson's notion of the poetic function, Veselovsky's theory of psychological parallelism, as well as empirical work in comparative prosody. On this basis, I present a brief account of lyric literary forms (genres) within the Western tradition (the ode, elegy, and the epigram), as a token of the kind of comparative work that Historical Poetics enables. As I argue, valid generalizations across different time periods – and, *a fortiori*, across the whole spectrum of world literature – are feasible only if comparative literary history is conceived as a history of literary forms that variously elaborate universally shared poetic principles rather than, say, as a history of the reception of individual texts, of great authors and their influence, or of literary movements and practices spreading through trade, colonial aggression, or cultural imperialism.

The current understandings of world literature, most of which are rooted in the idea of dissemination through translation, are less amenable to a truly inclusive account of lyric.[4] Jettisoning the universality of the object of study (only a fraction of world lyric will ever be translated!), they are necessarily swayed by current patterns of global domination and concomitant culturally overdetermined preferences. It is surely not an accident that the current vogue for world literature, understood as the study of translation and circulation of texts in a globalizing world, has become widespread in the post-Cold War United States, which has seen both a steep decline of interest in 'folklore', that is, in pre-literary forms of verbal art that are too unlike modern (questioning, unsettling, anti-dogmatic) ones, and the deterioration of the study of foreign languages, now perceptible even at most well-endowed universities. Countering these trends, the perspective of world literature ought to challenge us not to privilege our own notions of literature. Focusing on lyric's objectively given formal characteristics offers one way of opening our minds to its truly universal aspects. It is imperative that we acknowledge the risks of imposing an alien hermeneutic paradigm on other cultures. Nevertheless, in this case, as in many others, techniques of 'Western' rationality can be wielded as tools for dislodging our pre-set intellectual dispositions (be they aestheticism, exoticism, or a penchant for the political).

The Poetic Function

Possibly the most promising methodological starting point for empirically minded comparative work on lyric is the study of metrics. For example, a classic study of English folk songs reveals tantalizing general patterns in the composition of stanzas.[5] The most fundamental of such patterns is parallelism, which can obtain at the level of the line (as in quatrains with four stresses per line: 4444), the couplet (in which the second and fourth lines tend to be shorter: 4343), or the stanza (4443, 4443 ...).[6] Intuitively, the consistency of parallelism implies that the song is divided into segments that can be recognized as identical either aurally or graphically, or both. The phenomenon of rhythm – alternation of strong and weak positions – is also an example of parallelism. Such patterning is fundamentally alien to non-crafted forms of language, yet obviously akin to structural features of music. In short, verse is marked by a *double articulation*: it is composed of linguistic elements that are arranged according to rules of morphology and syntax, and this same linguistic material is subjected to patterning of a different order (at the very minimum, in free verse, of parallel segments called 'lines').

This insight is at the heart of Roman Jakobson's famous definition of the poetic function as the projection of the principle of selection (the paradigmatic principle) onto the plane of combination (the syntagm).[7] For example, sentence (1) is grammatically correct, arranged according to the rules of English syntax.[8]

(1) Following the death of the king his widow soon also died.

Each element in that sentence was selected from a series (a paradigm) of elements which all perform the same function: thus, we can pick 'after' instead of 'following' (within the paradigm of temporal prepositions), 'ruler of the land' instead of 'king' (within the paradigm of synonyms referring to solitary ruler), and so forth, in order to produce sentence (2).

(2) After the ruler of the land had perished it did not take long for his former consort to follow him.

In contrast to both (1) and (2), a different rephrasing of the same simple idea in sentence (3) might strike us as 'poetic':

(3) The king is dead. The queen has perished.

The reason for the different effect of (3) is that individual elements *within* the syntagm (sequence of elements) begin to echo one another, entering into small would-be paradigms. For example, 'the king' and 'the queen' are semantically aligned (both are lexemes, or headwords, belonging to the group 'members of the royal household'). The same is true of 'is dead' and 'has perished', verb phrases which obviously belong to the same semantic group. Moreover, the text is now broken into two clauses that are syntactically identical (noun followed by verb). Zooming in on more subtle manifestations of the poetic function, the phrases 'Following the king's death' and 'The king is dead' differ in that the latter consists of four syllables, whereas the former has six. In both cases, syllables form sequences (syntagms) that make perfect sense to us, yet in the case of 'The king is dead', they have an added quality of being arranged, assuming non-emphatic enunciation of 'the', into two groups of 'w S' (where 'w' stands for unstressed syllable and 'S' for stressed):

(4) The king is dead
    w   S   w   S

In sentence (4) each element 'S' is no longer just part of a sequence of syllables, but refers back to other 'S's in a regular fashion: each time a stressed syllable occurs, it makes us think back to previous stressed syllables. (In other words, all 'S's enter into a paradigmatic relationship.) Parallelism in the arrangement of strong positions creates *rhythm*. Once we recognize the rhythmic pattern, we extrapolate it beyond the beginning of the text, construing the sequence of nine syllables as an instance of iambic tetrameter (four groups of 'w S'), which, in the tradition of English verse, allows for an extra unstressed syllable at the end.

(6) The king is dead. The queen has perished
   w   S   w S   w   S   w   S w

Aside from rhythm and syntactic arrangement, parallelism in poetry is perhaps most obviously manifested in rhyme. Jakobson's poetic function, however, is not restricted to identifying parallelism. It encompasses such phenomena as alliteration, repetition of the same rhetorical device or the same image. Moreover, through stanzaic arrangement, larger chunks of metered discourse can be recognized as paradigm-setting within the text. The principle of the emergent paradigm, familiar to any attentive reader of lyric, whereby new meanings are born in the process of discovering elements within the text that appear to echo one another, brings Jakobson's structuralist insight to bear on the problem of unstable, inherently boundless semantics of any literary text, explored by reception aesthetics and deconstruction.

Lyric and its Deep Past

In Jakobson, poeticity thus receives a clear structural definition, applicable to widely divergent and historically unrelated poetic cultures. We may add that, of all kinds of literary production, it is lyric that claims the greatest share of the poetic function; it is, in this sense, the verbal art par excellence. While the particular manifestations of the double articulation of metered discourse – such as rhythm, rhyme, and stanzaic architecture – are highly complex and tradition-specific, the general underlying principle is a cross-cultural universal.

Jakobson's concept of poeticity rests on the earlier work of his fellow Russian Formalists, who detected in literary texts a tendency to endow language with a new kind of functionality by drawing attention to its own verbal material. The Formalists, moreover, stressed that poetic devices are historical variables, not aesthetic universals; thus, to recognize a type of patterning as a 'literary fact', we need to be trained to do so by our literary culture.[9] Particular types of parallelism detected by Jakobson, while employing the raw data of human language and an apparently universal principle of the poetic function, are cultural constructs.

One way of understanding the global importance of parallelism is offered in Alexander Veselovsky's article 'Psychological Parallelism and its Forms as Reflected in Poetic Style' (1898), an unacknowledged earlier source of Jakobson's thinking.[10] Veselovsky strives to derive 'formal parallelism' from 'psychological parallelism,' a juxtaposition of a living human being with an inanimate object or force. Veselovsky charts a development whereby an initial moment of comparative insight, which we would construe as animation, is absorbed into the melodic and syntactic parallelism of the poetic structure. As an illustration of this process, he cites a quatrain from a German folk song:

> Dass im Tannwald finster ist,
> Das macht das Holz,
> Dass mein Schatz finster schaut,
> Das macht der Stolz.

> The gloominess of fir forest is due to wood,
> The gloominess of my darling is due to pride.[11]

The psychological analogy between '*Holz*' ('wood') and '*Stolz*' ('pride') is somewhat opaque, yet this semantic vagueness is compensated for by the prosodic identity of the line's endings (rhyme) as well as by the parallel syntax of the couplets' second lines.

Veselovsky's study still stands as one of the most adventurous investigations of the formal features of poetry on a global scale.[12] Its fundamental finding was that formal parallelism is often mirrored by parallelism of meaning, and that such mirroring is more apparent in oral poetic cultures. The original parallel structure was generated in the encounter between the human and the outside world, which marked not a meeting between a subject and an object, as no such distinction was yet made, but an effort to make sense of the self in the categories of the other. In song, human beings conceived of themselves as part of nature. That imperative of self-cognizance may be thought of as the first in the series of 'popular-poetic demands' that, in Veselovskian Historical Poetics, motivates artistic production.[13] As it converted parallelism into a formal principle, lyric became the fundamental means of aligning humanity with the world.

Read side by side, Veselovsky's and Jakobson's works reveal that lyric's association with music is not merely incidental to some of its culturally conditioned uses; rather, lyric's essential structural property – its reliance on various kinds of parallel structure – should be seen as a result of sedimentation, pointing back to its origin in song. Building on the notion of lyric as the verbal art that is most consistently doubly articulated, we can take the next step towards a historical poetics of different forms of lyric, ranging from those closest to song, to those that minimize the poetic function. Although my focus is on lyric traditions that share a basis in Greek and Roman literatures, the principal aim of the following section is to illustrate an approach that can be extended to other poetic traditions. This approach combines the genealogical study of tradition-specific forms of literature with an awareness that their vitality derives from impulses not limited to that of continuing the tradition in question. In fact, as Veselovsky, Bakhtin, and Yuri Tynianov all recognized, a distinctive historical urgency in literary production often results in the rejection of a living tradition in favour of elements that had long been deemed obsolete. Perfect continuity is inimical to art's mode of historicity.

The persistence of the deep past in lyric is a testimony both to the transhistorical quality of basic human responses to the outside world conveyed by lyric and to its dependence on universally available resources of sung discourse. The poetic function enables human subjects to use language to impose a new order on the world, extending the particularity of their here-and-now into the past, as well as into the future. This stance of creative agency is always concretely motivated and thus 'expressive' of a self, yet the fundamental rules (such as varieties of parallelism) and devices (such as techniques of animation and comparison) that make this agency possible are so deeply ingrained in poetic praxis as to be shared by all humanity and, in their historically specific forms, ceaselessly iterated by both anonymous and self-consciously individual authors whose lives have come to energize these forms. In literature, as T. S. Eliot notes, the divide between creative freedom and inherited forms of expression is an illusion.[14] Verbal art not only rearranges the world in its own categories, conjuring new paradigms of being and meaning-making, but introduces the individual into the 'great time' inhabited by humanity as a universal collective.

When studying lyric as world literature, we should thus aim for an approach that calibrates three factors: (1) formal properties of the text or body of texts in question, considered in relation to the history of forms that arose, either as a result of evolution or borrowing, within a given literary culture; (2) ways in which these forms reveal principles of poetic language that obtain across different cultures, such as that of parallelism and of the emergent paradigm; and (3) the social demand that accounts for the vitality of particular formal elements within a given literary culture and that may arise independently due to similar social conditions. For example, the similarities between hymns or laments across world cultures are not simply typological, but profoundly historical: the similarity of 'popular-poetic demands' that obtain in different societies is due to analogous challenges and dilemmas that these societies confronted.[15] In other cases, however, similarities must be explained by reference either to an aspect of the poetic function or to the interaction between literary cultures.

Kinds of Lyric

In the second part of this chapter, I present a tentative taxonomy of three kinds of lyric, based on formal (prosodic) properties that can be correlated with historically evolving genres. These three kinds of lyric are the odic, the elegiac, and the epigrammatic. It will be useful to begin with a look at the Ancient Greek literary system as a whole, seeing that it has crucially influenced the shaping of lyric in the Euro-Atlantic cultural realm.

Sung lyric proper (melic verse) and prose, rather than constituting a binary opposition, stand at two ends of a continuum of forms. In Greek literature, those interim forms ranged from elegy to verse composed in iambic trimeters,

TABLE 8.1: The spectrum of prosodic rigor in Ancient Greek literary genres

Genre	Form and Performance Mode	Major Representatives	Dates
Melic poetry (<*melos* 'song')	Complex stanzas to be sung with musical accompaniment	Alcman, Sappho, Alcaeus, Anacreon, Simonides, Ibycus, Stesichorus, Pindar, Bacchylides	into mid. 5th *c.* BCE; cola reconstructed to Proto-Indo-European
Elegy (*cf. elegos* 'lament')	Two-line stanzas (hexameter + pentameter); initially meant to be accompanied on an *aulos* by another musician	Archilochus, Theognis, Solon, Mimnernus, Xenophanes	from the 7th *c.* BCE
Hexameter	Identical long lines; recited, originally to minimal accompaniment on a string instrument	Homer, Hesiod, cult hymns, later epic	from the 8th *c.* BCE
Iambic trimeter	Identical lines, recited without musical accompaniment	Attic drama	5th c. BCE
Prose	No double articulation	historiography, philosophy	From the 5th *c.* BCE

the metre used for dialogue in Attic tragedy and deemed by Aristotle to be most akin to spoken discourse.[16] The chart also has an important diachronic dimension: the late emergence of prose coincides with the eclipse of *melos* in the second half of the fifth century. Long before the ascendancy of the novel, the rise of prose is already linked to the decline of song culture.

The dominance of prose and the concomitant demise of song were part of a shift that affected the whole literary system. Within the domain of metered discourse, recited forms – hexameters and elegiac couplets – that had been used for a variety of purposes later associated with prose (including historiography and early philosophy) were restricted to literary genres. A spectacular fate was allotted to the Greek epigram, a short descriptive or gnomic type of verse, which remained in active use through the end of the Middle Ages. The epigram's success had much to do with its disavowal of oral performance, which is reflected in the term's etymology (*epi-gramma*: 'inscription, what is written upon something').

In the spectrum of prosodic rigor charted above, the ode is linked to sung poetry, the elegy occupies the niche of recited or spoken verse, and the epigram is closely tied to the medium of writing. The conventional narrative of literary history holds that distinctions of lyric deriving from Graeco-Roman antiquity became irrelevant in the post-Romantic period.[17] In the history of literary forms, however, transmutation, not oblivion, is the reigning principle. In the twentieth century a new, looser system of forms of lyric came into existence, in which earlier distinctions were in part maintained and in part reconfigured. In particular, the anthological (epigrammatic) form and the tradition of the lesser (Horatian and Anacreontic) ode, along with the Renaissance forms of amatory and confessional verse, were generalized into a notion of short 'lyric' poem (represented by Dickinson, Frost, and Pasternak); the Whitman–Mayakovsky line continued the paradigm of the greater (Pindaric) ode; and the meditative verse of poets such as Yeats, Valéry, Brodsky, and Ashbery was most dependent on the matrix of elegy. Most major poets felt comfortable moving between these varieties of lyric, and some cannot easily be fitted into any one of them. The focus of the following discussion, however, is on formal distinctions that not only cross-cut boundaries of national traditions (predictably so, inasmuch as they share the Graeco-Roman patrimony) but also enable us to discern aspects of lyric that have a global dimension.

The Odic

Folk song, in many varieties, is notable for its *potential chorality*: a song may be performed solo, yet others may join in. Bakhtin's important discussion of rhythm and lyric dwells on the phenomenon of *choral support* behind seemingly individualized poetic utterance.[18] The experience conveyed by this type of verbal art is essentially communal: it generates shared affect, be it of jubilation, lament, praise, or adoration. This pertains also to emotions that imply particularity and privacy, such as love or separation. For example, in Russian folk wedding songs, performed by a group of girls on behalf of the bride, singers vicariously experience what the text conveys, occasionally even switching into the first person.[19] Similar effects are observed in Pindar's victory odes.[20] This quality of lyric performance is remarked upon in the earliest text in the European literary tradition, the *Iliad*. Briseis leads the lamentation over the dead body of Patroclus, recalling the deaths in her own family, and the captive women respond, each 'grieving over her own sorrows, yet on the pretext of Patroclus' (19.300–301).

When reading a poem aloud we invite such forms of participation – ideally, not feigned or enacted but genuinely intersubjective. This dimension of lyric is fully in evidence in the Book of Psalms, perhaps the single most important resource of European lyric outside of the classical tradition. The poetics of Walt Whitman, one of the poets who moulded modern free verse, borrowed more from the Psalms than from the ancients, yet a sense of basic compatibility between the Whitmanesque style and the Pindaric ode is unmistakable.[21] In Vladimir Mayakovsky, for whom Whitman's precedent was important, we encounter perhaps the greatest twentieth-century practitioner of the odic mode. In the opening of an early poem, 'Listen!' (Послушайте (1914)), the poet reflects on the absolute imperatives issuing from the outside world, a compulsion that implies the presence of a human subject:

> Послушайте!
> Ведь, если звезды зажигают –
> значит – это кому-нибудь нужно?
> Значит – кто-то хочет, чтобы они были?
> Значит – кто-то называет эти плевочки жемчужиной?
>
> Listen!
> If stars are lighted up – does this not mean that
> it is needed by someone?
> That someone wishes that they exist?
> That someone actually calls these tiny gobs of spit gems?[22]

The opening invocation conjures the audience of this poem as fellow humans with whom the speaker shares his sense of the inter-subjective nature of the world, and from whom he is eliciting a response. The poem is first and foremost a collective act: the speaker does not have wisdom to dispense to others; he is no more than a focal point for posing questions to which each and all (should) seek an answer.

A similar underlying structure of participation is at work in Pindar's epinician odes, which enforce a sense of shared belonging, initially endangered but potentially enhanced by the individual aristocrat who distinguished himself in one of the Panhellenic games.[23] The odic must balance the unique and the communal. If the text tends toward the latter, it risks triviality; if toward the former, it can lose 'the choral support' (Bakhtin) that an ode must marshal to succeed.

The Elegiac

By contrast with *melos* proper, elegy tends to stress the individual's separation from the community. Formally, elegy stands very close to epic, a narrative form that presupposes an individuated speaker claiming special knowledge about the idealized past (as in heroic epic) or about the world (as in didactic epic or in theogonies). Epic generally does not lend itself to choral sharing, and nor does elegy. The performance of Ancient Greek elegy demanded musical accompaniment (on the *aulos*) that could not be provided by the singer/reciter himself. Greek elegists assert their particularity (Archilochus), tell stories (Simonides), give advice (Theognis) or encouragement (Tyrtaeus); they can even present a political agenda (Solon). Roman elegy retains this polemical, self-assertive quality: in Tibullus, Catullus, Ovid, and Propertius we encounter individuals who are not happy with the world, for different reasons, most commonly unrequited love or the loss of a loved one. Perhaps the most typical elegiac speaker in Roman elegy is the *exclusus amator* – a lover who, due to the lack of reciprocity, is reduced to spending time outside his beloved's door, in perfect solitude. One of the more famous *paraclausithyra* (poems sung beside closed doors) is Tibullus 1.2, an address to the door, in which the pain of being excluded from the world, which can only be overcome by sleep and oblivion, is foregrounded in a way that anticipates the lone wanderers of the Romantic lyric.

Rejection and dejection, a state of being evicted, becomes a mark of the elegy in the later tradition. Whereas the ode generates spontaneous shared emotion or actively mediates generic experiences, elegiac texts put forward a solitary reflective speaker who is neither at one nor at ease with the world. Lamentation over a loss, in elegy, is simply one form that individuation can take. Arguably, the importance of elegy for modern European poetry, along with the relative neglect of the ode, is first and foremost a result of the condition of the modern Western subject.[24]

The Epigrammatic

The third lyric mode is perhaps the most readily recognizable. The epigrammatic refers to poems that describe an aspect of the world, often pithily, and in a way that is not strongly inflected by an individuated authorial voice. Classical epigrams, as Hegel notes, tend toward maxims or 'apophthegms' that express timeless truths.[25]

The Greek (Palatine) Anthology presents an abundant selection of epigrammatic verse written over the course of Greek literary history, beginning in the Hellenistic and ending in the Byzantine period.[26] Many pieces are provided with a fictitious author, as in the case of an epigram curiously attributed to Plato:

> Μῆλον ἐγώ· βάλλει με φιλῶν σέ τις. ἀλλ' ἐπίνευσον,
> Ξανθίππη· κἀγὼ καὶ σὺ μαραινόμεθα.

> I am an apple. Someone who is in love with you has
>   thrown me. Come, nod your approval,
> Xanthippe: both I and you gradually expire.[27]

Once again, we seem to witness a dialogue, yet this time it is pure fiction. There is no subject beseeching the beloved, and no beloved spurning the lover. Instead, we are given a memorable picture of an object endowed with life (and speech), if only for a brief moment. The compelling paradox of life's brilliance and transience – the latter conveyed in the 'falling' part of the pentameter, most of it occupied by the verb μαραινόμεθα, 'we gradually expire' – is contained within the miniature artefact of a two-line poem. In an epigram the craftedness of the text, its status as an object in the world, is allied to the ontological status of objects as such. This quality of the epigram derives from its early association with inscription.

An epigrammatic poem makes an object or an aspect of the world present, either through *ekphrasis* or *prosopopeia*, while at the same time exposing its awareness of this presence as being dependent on the poem's endurance as object. A mere poetic description of an object can render its presence overwhelming, as in the following poem by Wallace Stevens:

> I placed a jar in Tennessee,
> And round it was, upon a hill.
> It made the slovenly wilderness
> Surround that hill.

> The wilderness rose up to it,
> And sprawled around, no longer wild.
> The jar was round upon the ground
> And tall and of a port in air.

It took dominion everywhere.
The jar was gray and bare.
It did not give of bird or bush,
Like nothing else in Tennessee.

The poem begins with a distant evocation of a dedicatory gesture; yet in lieu of a sacred vessel being deposited at a shrine, Stevens describes the simplest of containers placed in the most seemingly trivial surroundings. The poem thus tests the limits of the epigrammatic: simply by focusing attention on an object of human culture, it endows it with the power of a civilizing hero. The jar subdues the wilderness, taking dominion over the landscape. No longer 'slovenly', the outside world is rendered responsive and alive by the aesthetic quality of the object, made manifest by the epigrammatic convoy of the poetic text.

To read lyric as world literature is to make legible (and audible) its deepest sediments. Rather than serving as an object of contemplation and enjoyment by the few, poetic forms – and forms of lyric in particular – need to be recognized as carrying forward the experience of multitudes. Rather than created *ex nihilo* by the poet, form must be seen as humanity's collective response to the 'urgent call of the times'.[28] Interpreted in this way, European lyric is but one fascinating case study, an ethnographical datum among many others, notably complicated by a long and multilingual history reaching more than two millennia back to poetry written in two dead languages. The study of lyric as world literature faces the challenge of developing a methodology that would be adequate to these two tasks at once: (1) structural analysis of lyric as a globally attested epiphenomenon of the poetic function and (2) historically nuanced account of lyric's place within any given literary tradition. This chapter has provided only some initial suggestions for such a method. The typology of the three kinds of lyric, in part aligned with different positions on the oral/literary and collectivity/subjectivity spectra, aims not at exhaustive classification of the data, but at elucidating some objective criteria which would permit us to trace meaningful connections between poetic texts produced in different cultural environs and epochs. Needless to say, this typology would not hold for non-Western literary cultures, even though the criteria identified might be useful. Moreover, many texts central to the European lyric canon, even those demonstrably aware of their formal genealogy, do not lend themselves easily to taxonomic treatment in these categories. Keats's 'Ode on a Grecian Urn', for instance, is an epigrammatic piece that presents itself as an ode.[29] Goethe's 'Roman Elegies', while in many ways directly imitative of the Roman models, lack the tension of individuation we expect from elegy, tending instead toward the descriptive (epigrammatic) or outright celebratory form of amatory verse.[30] Akhmatova's *Requiem* aims at communal voicing even as it more directly continues the elegiac tradition. It is with reference to such borderline cases that the tentative formal-historical distinctions adumbrated in this chapter can be further nuanced and put to work.[*]

Acknowledgment

A draft of the chapter was discussed at the faculty seminar at the Department of Comparative Literature and Linguistics at the NRU HSE, St. Petersburg, and I thank all those who contributed their comments.

Notes

[*] My work on this chapter was aided by a research grant from the international project on 'Reconstructive Poetics', supported by Russian Science Foundation (RSF), project 16–18–10250.

1. See L. Blumenfeld, 'Generative Metrics: An Overview,' *Language and Linguistic Compass*, 10 (2016), 413–430; and C. Rice, 'Generative Metrics', *Glot International*, 2.7 (1996), 3–8.

2. A. Veselovsky, 'On the Methods and Aims of Literary History as a Science' (1870), H. Weber (trans.), *Yearbook of Comparative and General Literature*, 16 (1967), 33–42 (p. 39).

3. The phrase is borrowed from Robert von Hallberg's *Lyric Powers* (Chicago: University of Chicago Press, 2008).

4. Jahan Ramazani's *A Transnational Poetics* (Chicago: University of Chicago Press, 2009), which presents a case for a 'transnational poetics' based solely on Anglophone poetry, is one example of this general trend.

5. See B. Hayes and M. MacEachern, 'Quatrain Form in English Folk Verse', *Language*, 74.3 (1998), 473–507.

6. Ibid., pp. 487–488.

7. R. Jakobson, 'Closing Statement: Linguistics and Poetics' (1958) in T. A. Sebeok (ed.), *Style in Language* (Cambridge, MA: Technology Press of Massachusetts Institute of Technology, 1960), pp. 350–377.

8. The example rephrases the sentence used by E. M. Forster to illustrate the difference between story and plot. See *Aspects of the Novel* (New York: Harcourt, 1954), p. 86.

9. See Y. Tynianov, 'The Literary Fact' (1924), A. Shukman (trans.), in D. Duff (ed.), *Modern Genre Theory* (Harlow: Longman, 2000)., pp. 29–49.

10. A. Veselovskii, 'Psikhologicheskii parallelism i ego formy v otrazhenii poeticheskogo stilia' (1898) in *Izbrannoe: Istoricheskaia poetika* (Moscow: ROSSPEN, 2006), pp. 417–508.

11. Veselovskii, '*Psikhologicheskii parallelism*', p. 434 (my translation).

12. In addition to empirical data in languages of which he had intimate knowledge, Veselovsky drew on translations from languages such as Hausa, Chuvash, and Tatar.
13. A. Veselovsky, 'From the Introduction to Historical Poetics: Questions and Answers' (1898) in I. Kliger and B. Maslov (eds.), *Persistent Forms: Explorations in Historical Poetics* (New York: Fordham University Press, 2016), p. 60.
14. T. S. Eliot, 'Tradition and the Individual Talent' (1917) in *Selected Essays* (London: Faber and Faber, 1961), pp. 13–22.
15. On the importance of polygenesis for the study of world (comparative) literature see V. M. Zhirmunsky, 'On the Study of Comparative Literature', *Oxford Slavonic Papers*, 13 (1967), pp. 1–13.
16. Aristotle, *Poetics*, 1449a.25.
17. Perhaps the most symptomatic expression of this view is Theodor Adorno's 'On Lyric Poetry and Society' (1951) in *Notes to Literature*, Vol. 1, S. W. Nicholsen (trans.) (New York: Columbia University Press, 1991), pp. 37–54.
18. M. Bakhtin, *Art and Answerability: Early Philosophical Essays*, V. Liapunov (trans.) (Austin: University of Texas Press, 1990), pp. 120–121.
19. G. A. Levinton, 'Russkoe svadebnoe velichanie', *International Journal of Slavic Linguistics and Poetics*, 38 (1995), pp. 94–118.
20. See B. Maslov, *Pindar and the Emergence of Literature* (Cambridge: Cambridge University Press, 2015), pp. 21–22.
21. See L. Spitzer, '*Explication de Texte* Applied to Walt Whitman's Poem "Out of the Cradle Endlessly Rocking"', *ELH*, 16.3 (1949), pp. 247–249.
22. Translation is mine. A full text of this poem in English can be found in V. Mayakovsky, *Selected Poems*, J. H. McGavran III (trans.) (Evanston: Northwestern University Press, 2013), p. 50.
23. See L. Kurke, *The Traffic in Praise: Pindar and the Poetics of Social Economy* (Ithaca: Cornell University Press, 1991).
24. Note Adorno's formulation that generalizes the elegiac (as I have defined it) to all of (modern) lyric: 'the lyric work is always a subjective expression of a social antagonism', 'On Lyric', p. 45.
25. See G. W. F. Hegel, *Aesthetics: Lectures on Fine Art*, T. M. Knox (trans.) (Oxford: Clarendon Press, 1975), p. 1040.
26. The condensed version of the Palatine Anthology, the so-called Planudes Anthology, was published in 1494 and, along with Pindar's *epinicia* (published in 1513) and the Anacreontea (published in 1554), had a major impact on later European lyric.
27. Book 5, p. 80 (my translation).
28. Veselovsky, 'From the Introduction to Historical Poetics', p. 60.
29. Cf. L. Spitzer, 'The "Ode on a Grecian Urn", or Content vs. Metagrammar', *Comparative Literature*, 7.3 (1955), pp. 203–225.
30. See T. Ziolkowski, *The Classical German Elegy, 1795–1950* (Princeton: Princeton University Press, 1980), pp. 66–75.

9

ATO QUAYSON

On Worlding Tragedy

By its very nature and scope, the study of world literature involves comparison. This applies most obviously at the levels of themes, genres, and literary history. But what does comparison look like when we set out to compare texts that seem on first encounter to have very little in common? This question is especially pertinent for tragedy because it deals with suffering; something that seems to be common to all cultures. However, the way in which suffering is construed and represented varies so widely that it poses a fundamental challenge to any comparative framework. Studying tragedy therefore inevitably raises 'world literary' questions regarding critical genealogies, the dynamics of translation and adaptation, and the role of circuits of cultural transmission. But whereas the study of world literature in general is oriented towards the ever-expanding body of the world's writing, tragedy relates primarily to the ways in which suffering has been represented on stage and elsewhere since classical times.

To 'world' literary tragedy in a comparative framework means studying it simultaneously at the level of its formal elements, its various thematic inflections, and also at the level of the larger cultural and conceptual arenas that shape our understanding of it. If tragedy furnishes a productive way for thinking about world literature, it does so not by precluding other modes of literary historicization, but rather by providing us with an array of possibilities for understanding the changing relations between a set of core elements: suffering, identity, fate, contingency, society, representation, history, and ethics. The range of these elements also means that tragedy has intersected with the canon of 'World Literature' at a variety of points, something that requires us to take it seriously not just for its impact but also for the ways in which it illuminates questions that lie within other literary forms.

An Anatomy of Tragedy

As a dramatic genre, tragedy was formalized and consolidated in the Athenian theatre of the fifth century BCE, though scholars have long speculated on its more ancient roots in choric ritual and performance. From these origins, it has spread and been refashioned to such an extent that speaking of tragic literature today means acknowledging these Greek antecedents, while also invoking many other traditions, and, indeed, many other forms and media, from all parts of the world.

The unfolding of tragedy has hardly been linear, progressive or unidirectional. The plays of Aeschylus, Sophocles and Euripides are more familiar to present-day audiences than they were to those of sixteenth-century Europe, or, for that matter, to Arabic commentators of previous centuries, such as Ibn Rushd, whose role in preserving the Greek theories of tragedy was essential. Indeed, whilst Shakespeare and his contemporaries certainly knew of and about the great Attic tragedians, and likely encountered fragments, summary accounts, and translations of their works, for them 'Greek tragedy remained mostly on a distant horizon'.[1] In contrast, the Roman plays of Seneca, which are of considerably less interest to dramatists today, were powerful influences in Elizabethan and Jacobean England, especially on the revenge tragedies of Christopher Marlowe, Thomas Kyd, John Marston, John Webster, and Thomas Middleton.

Even for playwrights who could read Classical Greek and consult the relevant texts, much depended on how they understood ideas and practices of millennia past, and these understandings were inevitably shaped by local political, cultural, and intellectual currents. For this reason, elements vitally important in one tradition could be peripheral in another. For example, although unhappy and often bloody endings were the *sine qua non* of tragic theatre for the Elizabethans (and remain so for their inheritors, including most Anglophone readers and viewers today), in French neoclassical tragedy of the seventeenth century, which is associated above all with the plays of Pierre Corneille and Jean Racine, it was 'the serious danger for one of the main characters' that was 'the ultimate and indispensable requirement'.[2] It was the threat of death, rather than death itself, that provoked fear, and it was above all fear (and the pity it occasioned) that was the necessary condition of tragedy. A tragic play could therefore end quite happily, as happens in Corneille's *Le Cid* (1637) and Racine's *Athalie* (1691).

Corneille's *Trois Discours sur le poème dramatique* (*Three Discourses on Dramatic Poetry*, 1660), in which he reflected on the genre's basic characteristics, was, like many such texts, a theory written in defence of a practice. However, from the late eighteenth century, in philosophical works produced by German thinkers who were deeply immersed in Classical Greek culture, the theorization of the tragic (rather than merely of tragedy) became somewhat divorced from the practical demands of dramaturgy, and was used instead to explore 'central questions of human freedom, political autonomy, self-consciousness, and ethical action' and 'as a means to comprehend the self as a political, psychological and religious subject'.[3] For example, at the start of the nineteenth century, German philosophers drew on insights from the French Revolution to interpret the Kantian sublime so as to highlight various human responses to its representational incommensurability. This incommensurability was interpreted not in terms of defeat but rather as enlivening the human capacity for rebellion and thus the possibility for transcendence. F. W. J. von Schelling, G. W. F. Hegel, Friedrich Hölderlin, Arthur Schopenhauer, and others would inspire Friedrich Nietzsche, Sigmund Freud, Karl Marx, Walter Benjamin, Carl Schmitt, and Hannah Arendt well into the twentieth century as they attempted to set out new idioms by which to think about suffering and its representation.[4]

If scholars of tragedy have tended to identify its great achievements with two places and periods – Athens in the fifth century BCE, and Western Europe in the sixteenth and seventeenth centuries – we should not lose sight of the fact that, since the late nineteenth century, there has been an extraordinary proliferation of works imbued with a tragic sensibility of one variety or another. These include the plays of Anton Chekov, Henrik Ibsen, August Strindberg, T. S. Eliot, and W. B. Yeats; as well as the more recent works of dramatists such as Arthur Miller, Tennessee Williams, Samuel Beckett, Bertolt Brecht, Athol Fugard, Lorraine Hansberry, José Triana, Ariel Dorfman, Federico García Lorca, Wole Soyinka, Caryl Churchill, and Harold Pinter.

Individually and collectively, these authors have incorporated in the tragic repertoire new materials, new cultural mythologies and dispositions, and new philosophies of existence; and they have expanded the range of characters represented on stage, giving ever greater prominence to questions of class, gender, race, and identity. As a consequence, any attempt today to engage with tragedy as a world literary form has to pay attention to critical definitions of the term, to its appearance in different cultures and climes, and to the ways in which other literary and philosophical enterprises have drawn on it to reflect upon the individual's relationship to suffering, ethics, religion, history, culture, and society.

Tragic Adaptations and World Literature

My focus until now has been on tragedy in its theatrical varieties, and subsequent sections of this chapter will likewise address significant dramatists. It would be a mistake, however, to ignore the ways in which tragedy has migrated across forms and media, for adaptation has played a major role in shaping a common repertoire of tragic representations in world literature. Of course, these adaptations include dramatic works which reconfigure significant antecedents. To take the example only of Sophocles's *Antigone*, we find plays from Ireland (Tom Paulin's *The Riot Act*; Seamus Heaney's *The Burial at Thebes*), Nigeria (Femi Osofisan's *Tegonni*), Syria (Jihad Saad's *Antigone's Emigration*), and South Africa (Athol Fugard's *The Island*); and in a range of languages, including modern Greek (Aris Alexandrou's *Antigone*), Turkish (Sahika Tekand's *Eurydice's Cry*), Yup'ik (Dave Hunsaker's *Yup'ik Antigone*), and Haitian creole (Felix Morisseau-Leroy's *Antigòn an Kreyòl*).[5] But, over and beyond theatrical works of this kind, it is important to recognize the impact of operatic, cinematic and novelistic adaptations.

Here, Shakespeare's *Macbeth* is a useful example. In addition to the innumerable and varied dramatic re-workings of performance, staging, and text, there have also been at least five operas, more than a dozen films, and several novels based in some way on Shakespeare's play. Of the operas, the best known is Giuseppe Verdi's. First performed in Florence in 1847, and with a libretto written mostly by Francesco Maria Piave, *Macbeth* kept close to the plot of the original and was a considerable success. Fidelity to the source material has not, however, always been a principal concern. Norwegian crime novelist Jo Nesbø's recent *Macbeth* (2018) is, according to its publicity material, '[s]et in the 1970s in a run-down, rainy industrial town' in which Duncan is the chief of a police force 'struggling to shed an incessant drug problem'.[6] Others have taken similar license, so that only echoes of the original remain, as is the case in *Lady Macbeth of the Mtsensk District* (1867), a novella by Nikolai Leskov which was itself the basis for an opera by Dmitri Shostakovich, first performed in 1934.

Among film-makers, Orson Welles made relatively minor modifications to Shakespeare's play in his film of 1948, whereas Akira Kurosawa's hugely important *Throne of Blood* (1957) transferred the action to feudal Japan, and blended the 'realistic cinematic conventions popular in Western film' with the 'ritualized gesture of traditional Japanese Noh theater and the static frame'.[7] But, whether or not they have followed the source closely, the adaptations produced by various composers, directors, and novelists have necessarily confronted and exploited the limits and possibilities of the particular forms and media in which they have worked. This has ensured that tragedy has been constantly revivified as it has been transposed into new contexts, making it an exemplary world-literary form.

On Suffering and the Problem of Ethical Choice

If suffering is the central concern of tragedy, how do we, as spectators from different cultures, come to identify with the characters on stage? What constitutes suffering? And what is it about suffering that brings us to empathize with the plight of the tragic hero or heroine and entices us to return again and again to the tragic?[8] Answers to these questions vary widely, but most people would agree that suffering entails some form of pain, whether physical or emotional. While this is not controversial, for the purposes of thinking about literary tragedy, the central problem turns on the exercise of ethical choice, and the fact that unpredictable consequences may rebound upon the tragic protagonist when making such choices.

In the *Poetics*, Aristotle suggests that the spectator experiences pity and fear on seeing the tragic hero suffer a reversal of fortunes because of an error of judgement – *hamartia* in his formulation – an error that derives not from any intrinsic evil, but in the encounter between human nature and the conditions that complicate the exercise of ethical choice in the first place. 'Pity' in the *Poetics* does not connote the contemporary sense of condescending concern. The Greek ἔλεος (eleos) bears a meaning closer to the English word 'compassion'. To capture and retain the interest of the spectator, and thus to guarantee his or her compassion for the suffering depicted, Aristotle claims that the events in a tragedy must be plotted in such a way as to engender a sense of inevitability.

All these Aristotelian propositions have been subjects of intense debate and qualification, especially because they do not appear directly applicable to the vast number of tragic plays from different cultures and traditions that have found a place in the corpus of World Literature.[9] And yet, at the same time, Aristotle provides important critical touchstones for debating questions of tragedy because he focuses on ethico-cognitive matters, rather than exclusively on dramaturgical or aesthetic ones. When tragedy is conceived of in ethico-cognitive terms and focused on the question of suffering, it becomes possible to compare tragedies across different traditions and cultures. If the *Poetics* focuses specifically on tragedy in trying to outline its main elements and emotional effects, it is in the *Nichomachean Ethics* that Aristotle elaborates more fully the grounds for identification with the plight of a sufferer. Apart from the fact that the person that is afflicted by suffering must not be held directly or exclusively culpable for what befalls her, Aristotle notes in the *Ethics* that identification ultimately depends on the recognition of the role that certain conditions play in frustrating a person's expression of their true character (as a function of their choices) and in ultimately accessing worldly goods.[10] A negative or intractable destiny may be triggered by character error (*hamartia*), or may derive from the circumstances that circumscribe the character's capacity to exercise ethically significant choices in the first place.

The term 'ethics' in 'ethical choice' must not be confused with the act of weighing up the relative values of good and evil. Rather, for Aristotle, ethical choice is an expression of *eudaimonia*, which is glossed variously as 'settled orientation', 'virtue', and 'good living'. An ethical choice derives partly from a particular character's orientation (the just person acts justly and the soldier is courageous), and partly from the desire to gain access to worldly goods. But the category of worldly goods in Aristotle's usage does not include the material accoutrements that people might consider as constituting the basis of a good life. Rather, as Martha Nussbaum points out, the category of worldly goods implies the 'interactions of *philia*, either familial or friendly', and good health, as well as the benefits of citizenship and communal belonging.[11] For Aristotle, the frustration of access to worldly goods serves to atrophy the self-perceptions of characters, making it difficult or even impossible for them to draw upon the internal and external resources that would enable them to exercise ethically significant choices.

If the plight of the tragic protagonist has the power to evoke our sympathies, it is not just because he or she experiences physical and emotional pain, important though these are. Rather, it is because tragedy demonstrates that the conditions for the exercise of meaningful choices that have consequences for how a life is crafted and lived do not remain entirely within the grasp of the individual. It is the iconic condensation of this central fact about human suffering, and its immediate presentation to us in dramatic form, that encourages us to return to tragedy despite all the discomfort that may come with it.

We find, then, that there are at least three central elements to suffering that are pertinent to tragic representation: the question of choice, the conditions of possibility that underpin choice-making, and the unpredictable consequences that derive from such choices once they are made. At the same time, suffering is not given to us unmediated, but must be grasped as the product of tragic dramaturgy. And tragic dramaturgy fulfils certain formal demands that are generated by traditions of performance that are themselves historically and culturally specific. But the differences between historical traditions do not preclude comparison, especially when the focus is on suffering and ethical choice. It is possible, then, to illustrate the various dimensions of suffering by looking at Sophocles's *Oedipus Rex* and *Philoctetes*, Shakespeare's *Hamlet* and *Othello*, and Wole Soyinka's *Death and the King's Horseman*. Even though these works will hardly allow us to exhaust the complex questions pertaining to the representation of tragic suffering, they present a range of historical and dramatic traditions, enabling us to focus on certain of these questions from a world-literary perspective.

Sophocles

Famously, Oedipus's main decisions take place before the stage action of *Oedipus Rex* begins. When, in the opening scene, the priest and a crowd of Theban children come to Oedipus and beseech him to do something about the plague that has afflicted their town and well-being, he has already fulfilled the oracle's prediction, by unknowingly killing his own father, Laius, the preceding king of Thebes, and marrying the Queen Jocasta, who is his own mother. It is these acts, which have gone unpunished, that bring down the plague. Thus, Sophocles's play is about Oedipus's discovery of his deeds of parricide and incest, and his terrible reaction to them. If our own sense of pity and fear grow with the inexorable progress of Oedipus's self-discovery, this is directly modulated, first, by the final sight of Oedipus emerging from Jocasta's chamber with eyes streaming blood, and second, by the response to this 'terrible sight' provided by the Chorus:

> **Chorus:** This is a terrible sight for men to see!
> I never found a worse!
> Poor wretch, what madness came upon you!
> What evil spirit leaped upon your life
> to your ill-luck – a leap beyond man's strength!
> Indeed I pity you, but I cannot
> look at you, though there's much I want to ask
> and much to learn and much to see.
> I shudder at the sight of you. (1298–1306)[12]

The spectacle that Oedipus presents at the end is a vivid tableau of physical pain and deep emotional suffering. By this point, several enigmatic transpositions have taken place within the play that all come together to define the tragic reversal. Oedipus has moved from self-assured speech and grandeur to being a spectacle of shock and horror; from being a law-giver, whose every edict must be obeyed, to being a pitiable supplicant; and from having almost divine status to being the expression of sacred pollution. That he arrives at this particular impasse as a result of his own decisions, ignorant though he might have been of what he was doing, makes his suffering all the more poignant.

The modulation of the spectators' pity and fear by the responses of the chorus is also to be found in Sophocles's *Philoctetes,* where pity for the eponymous hero's condition of disability and abandonment on the island of Lemnos is first expressed by the Chorus early in the play. Much later, it becomes a central feature of the process by which Neoptolemus gains a form of conscience. The son of Achilles, Neoptolemus had originally agreed to trick Philoctetes out of the bow of Herakles with which he had hunted for food and fended for himself while alone on Lemnos. The turn to conscience is effectively prompted when Neoptolemus is forced to bear witness to Philoctetes's anguished cries, which are triggered by the unbearable pain from his diseased foot. Neoptolemus himself becomes distraught and anguished as the older man's pain brings into question everything that he had hitherto taken for granted. This bifurcation of suffering – for Philoctetes, extreme physical pain and for Neoptolemus, emotional anguish – means that the play makes the question of pity central to the unfolding of its own internal moral dilemma, while also projecting it as a question pertinent to the spectator's sense of judgement.

Similarly, in Sophocles's *Antigone* and Euripides's *Bacchae*, and in Aeschylus's *Prometheus Bound,* different characters are invited to bear witness to physical and emotional suffering, while in Euripides's *Medea*, the eponymous principal character debates with the chorus directly in laying out her rationale for killing her two sons in her attempt to punish Jason, thus taking the question of pity in a completely different ethical direction. In all these instances, there are no comforting answers. As Jean-Pierre Vernant adroitly notes, one of the key elements of Greek tragedy was the ambiguity with which the hero was presented: 'In a tragic perspective man and human action are seen, not as things that can be defined or described, but as problems. They are presented as riddles whose double meanings can never be pinned down or exhausted.'[13]

Shakespeare

Even though there are tragedies in which we can identify the precise moment when an ethically decisive choice is made, in most cases pivotal choices are not confined to a particular moment, but are, rather, a matter of process. A particular choice may be informed by a series of earlier choices that either appeared inconsequential at the time, or whose potential consequences were not apparent to the protagonist and spectators. Thus, in Shakespeare we find that the question of ethical choice does not derive exclusively from self-volitional identity (what is popularly designated by the word 'agency') but rather from the interactions that a tragic agent has with principles that reside outside of his or her own consciousness. These principles are encapsulated by other agents through whom such principles gain expression within the dramatic action.[14]

At the same time, the tragic character may also be seen as embodying contradictory principles that complicate the exercise of ethical choice. This is amply illustrated in *Hamlet*. In one sense, the play is about the gradual purging of extraneous principles so that Hamlet can be the cleanser of the corrupt court of Denmark and the true avenger enjoined by the ghost of his father. But Hamlet has contradictory orientations within the play. He is at once philosopher, son, friend, poet, and playwright, as well as potential avenger, and he takes each of these roles extremely seriously when deliberating on the decisions that confront him. In this context, the encounter with his father's ghost in Act 1, Scene v can be read as a form of invitation for him to focus his identity exclusively through the singular orientation of avenger. But Hamlet is incapable of obliterating entirely the other orientations that define his being. The play may then be read as a series of manoeuvres to find not only a justification for killing Claudius, his father's murderer, but also a means or process by which to purge himself of the several orientations that inhere in his being and frustrate him.

This is, of course, an overly teleological reading of *Hamlet*, something that Shakespeare counters by deliberately revising the Senecan revenge plot of one of his sources of inspiration, Thomas Kyd's *The Spanish Tragedy* (or *Hieronimo is Mad Again*), a tragedy which involves various violent murders and which even personifies Revenge as a character. It is also to ignore *Hamlet*'s many twists and turns and the tragic hero's mood swings; factors that make Shakespeare's play such a masterpiece of world literature. For the process of Hamlet's purgation is neither smooth nor straightforward, but incorporates an aesthetic dimension whose ultimate objective is delayed action. The deferment of action could be said to lie at the heart of aesthetic judgement, a mode of reflection to which Hamlet gravitates throughout the play, such as during the First Player's mournful rendition of Hecuba in Act 2, Scene ii.

A similar observation can be made for the character Othello, whose problem is a fixation with an ideal of epistemological certainty. Othello's demand for 'ocular proof' from Iago in Act 3, Scene iii is correctly interpreted by the latter as a request for certainty of knowledge. In delivering ocular proof in the form of the staged conversation that he has with the unsuspecting Cassio about the handkerchief, Iago raises a problem with the quest for epistemological certainty that is not made visible to Othello until the very end of the play. For Othello bases his decision to kill his wife on his interaction with an ideal of epistemological knowledge, that is to say, with what is visible and thus has forensic verifiability. But, as we know from that scene, Othello has visual proof, without any auditory access to the conversation between Iago and Cassio. What he sees is essentially a mimetic representation of how

Cassio procures the handkerchief, one that is utterly shorn of any truth. It is Othello's interaction with this idealization of the value of absolute certainty that confirms his jealousy and certifies the course of action he decides to undertake (see his soliloquy as he makes his way to his wife's chamber at Act 5, Scene ii). He is manipulated and not self-volitional, but the manipulations go beyond the deceptions of Iago. They go to the heart of the quest for certainty itself, which is the ultimate source of suffering for Othello.

Soyinka

Set among the Yorùbá in colonial Nigeria, Wole Soyinka's *Death and the King's Horseman* illustrates another set of conditions that circumscribe ethical choice and thus engender suffering.[15] The emotional crux of the play centres on the failed ritual suicide of Elesin Oba, the king's horseman of the title, who, by tradition, is supposed to extinguish himself some forty days after the death of the King. The play stages a confrontation between the colonial administration, represented by the fumbling yet dangerously interventionist Simon Pilkings, and, on the other side, a colourful cast of Yorùbá characters that includes Elesin Oba, Iyaloja (head of market women), and Praise-Singer.

The first scene of the play opens on the closing stages of a market, with bolts of cloth being taken down by market women at dusk. The setting signals that, from the outset, the action is to be embedded within Yorùbá cultural processes, for as a Yorùbá proverb has it '*Ayé lojà; òrun nilé*' (the earth is a marketplace; heaven is home). This points to the conjunctural nature of the market in Yorùbá culture as a place for the meeting of the living, the dead, and the yet-to-be-born.[16] Into this cultural setting enters the energetic Elesin Oba, pursued by Praise-Singer and his drummers. We are told in the stage directions that Elesin 'is a man of enormous vitality, speaks, dances and sings with that infectious enjoyment of life which accompanies all his actions' (9). It is only much later that we realize that the contrast between a tableau of temporal transition and Elesin Oba's 'enormous vitality' in the opening scene is the visual codification of the central contradiction in the play. This is the conflict between the cultural demands of ritual suicide enjoined upon the central character and the insistent attachment to life that is expressed in his every conscious *and* unconscious gesture.

As soon as Elesin enters, the market becomes an interactive dramatic arena. In a structure not dissimilar to what we see in Greek tragedy, the market women, along with the Praise-Singer, adopt the role of the chorus and Elesin is cast as the tragic hero. In the scene that unfolds, however, these roles are reconfigured to align with the expectations attaching to this particular

Yorùbá ritual. As Praise-Singer proceeds to lay out the process that lies before Elesin in a densely poetic language replete with epithets and praise names, it is soon clear that the latter's destiny is bound up in the renewal of his community and so can follow only one pathway. With this, the generic conventions also are reconfigured. The dialogue between Praise-Singer and Elesin proceeds as a call and response in an idiom thick with Yorùbá proverb:

PRAISE-SINGER: In their time the great wars came and went, the little wars came and went; the white slavers came and went, they took away the heart of our race, they bore away the mind and muscle of our race. The city fell and was rebuilt; the city fell and our people trudged through mountain and forest to found a new home but – Elesin Oba do you hear me?

ELESIN: I hear your voice Olohun-iyo.(10)[17]

As the scene further unfolds, Elesin interrupts the ritual elicitation three times. The ritual call-and-response with Praise-Singer resumes after the first two interruptions, but the third will turn out to be decisive. Elesin's head is turned by a beautiful young woman who enters the market, and he becomes determined to possess her ahead of his crossing. Here lies the seed for the tragic scenario, for she is already committed to the son of Iyaloja, the 'Mother' of the market. After hesitating, Iyaloja accedes to Elesin's request. She agrees to transgress against the ethics of affiance in order to preserve the continuity and autonomy of Yorùbá cultural processes. She concedes to something that fundamentally contradicts the idea of the ritual preparation for death that has governed the action up to this point. It turns out to be a terrible mistake.

When Elesin fails to make the ritual crossing and is confronted by Iyaloja while in detention, we see that social relationships have been inverted. For, at that moment of confrontation, Elesin is no longer an object of admiration for Iyaloja, but only one of revulsion. Her condemnation is both ruthless and vociferous:

IYALOJA: You have betrayed us. We fed you sweetmeats such as we hoped awaited you on the other side. But you said No, I must eat the world's left-overs. We said you were the hunter who brought the quarry down; to you were the vital portions of the game. No, you said, I am the hunter's dog and I shall eat the entrails of the game and the faeces of the hunter. We said you were the hunter returning home in triumph, a slain buffalo pressing down on his neck; you said wait, I first must turn up this cricket hole with my toes . . . We said, the dew on earth's surface was for you to wash your feet along the slopes of honour. You said No, I shall step in the vomit of cats and the droppings of mice; I shall fight them for the left-overs of the world.(68)

Here, Iyaloja launches into what is the opposite of Praise-Singer's *oríkì,* for each of her insults is designed to take Elesin down from the cultural pedestal on which he had originally been placed. But it is Elesin's response to these insults that elicits our pity, for here he reveals why he has become an enigma to his culture:

ELESIN: What were warnings beside the moist contact of living earth between my fingers? What were warnings beside the renewal of famished embers lodged eternally in the heart of man? But even that, even if it overwhelmed one with a thousand fold temptations to linger a little while, a man could overcome it. It is when the alien hand pollutes the source of will, when a stranger force of violence shatters the mind's calm resolution, this is when a man is made to commit the awful treachery of relief, *commit in his thought the unspeakable blasphemy of seeing the hand of the gods in this alien rupture of his world.* I know it was this thought that killed me, sapped my powers and turned me into an infant in the hands of unnameable strangers. I made to utter my spells anew but my tongue merely rattled in my mouth. I fingered hidden charms and the contact was damp; there was no spark left to sever the life-strings that should stretch from every finger-tip. My will was squelched in the spittle of an alien race, and all because I had committed this blasphemy of thought – that there might be the hand of the gods in a stranger's intervention. (69; my italics)

Elesin's *hamartia* is founded in misrecognition. He believed that the intervention of the white colonizer might accord with the will of his own gods, that this 'alien rupture' could enable him to prolong his enjoyment of life. He did not foresee that his indulgence would fundamentally compromise the categories and procedures that had given his world order.

Elesin's reasoning takes us back to the contradictory tableau that we were presented with at the start of the play. It is a painful form of self-recognition that produces no reciprocal recognition or pity in the eyes of his interlocutor and is much like Othello's futile appeal at the end of Shakespeare's play: 'I pray you, in your letters, / [...] Speak of me as I am. Nothing extenuate' (*Othello* Act 5, Scene ii). For Elesin's decision is not mere individual error but plays into the hands of the broader cultural fragmentation set in train by colonization. He now stands entirely outside the cultural framework within which his transgressions could be understood and by which he could be reintegrated into the community. Iyaloja is only disdainful of his appeals for pity. At the end of the play Elesin, whose hands are bound, throws his shackles around his neck and strangles himself. He dies not as a hero of his community, but as a sad and dejected man. He is moved to this final act by the sight of the dead body of his son Olunde, who, having only recently returned from his medical studies in England, had offered himself as the sacrificial carrier in his father's place. It is too much for Elesin.

In *Death and the King's Horseman*, the exercise of ethical choice is expressed according to two mutually negating principles. On the one hand, there is the principle of cultural obligation, which enjoins that the master of the king's stables (and thus traditionally the commander of the king's army) commit ritual suicide. Every aspect of Elesin Oba's life has been a preparation for this moment, and it is clear that he embraces the role with great pride. And yet at the same time he is a hedonist, and completely attached to the pleasures of the living. His request for the hand of the young betrothed on the very night on which he is supposed to make the crossing shows the contradictory impulses that reside within him. When he pleads to Iyaloja for understanding, he speaks not as a cultural representative but as an individual. Thus, the reversal of fortunes is two-fold: he is individualized as a tragic figure at the same time as he is severed from the role of cultural representative. The shock and devastation of this severance is what elicits pity.

Conclusion

If the idea of world literature calls for us to engage vicariously with worlds beyond our own, then it is tragedy that schools us in the proper distribution of our attention. Tragedy invites us to reflect seriously on the question of suffering: who suffers? Why do they suffer? What are the conditions that produce this suffering? How do the consequences of apparently life-affirming ethical choices come to be so monstrously transfigured as to be incommensurate with the choices themselves and to cause pain and anguish? What is it to bear witness and feel the pain of another who is near or far? And what do all these questions signify in a world connected by faster and faster modes of communication, in which a single button can immediately spring on our consciousness – through television, telephone, and screen – the images of precariousness, pain, and suffering that populate the world in which we live? Tragedy encourages us to take these questions seriously, and in doing so also gives us ways of thinking across cultures and times.

Notes

[1] G. Braden, 'Classical Greek Tragedy and Shakespeare', *Classical Receptions Journal*, 9.1 (2017), 103-119 (p. 118).

[2] J. D. Lyons, 'Tragedy and Fear', *The Cambridge Companion to French Literature*, J. D. Lyons (ed.) (Cambridge: Cambridge University Press, 2015), pp. 74-84 (p. 79).

[3] S. Goldhill, 'The Ends of Tragedy: Schelling, Hegel, and Oedipus', *PMLA*, 129.4 (2014), 634-648 (p. 635).

[4] For more on this, see especially J. Billings, *Genealogy of the Tragic: Greek Tragedy and German Philosophy* (Princeton: Princeton University Press, 2014); M. Leonard, *Tragic Modernities* (Cambridge, MA: Harvard University Press, 2015); and J. Young, *The Philosophy of Tragedy: From Plato to Žižek* (Cambridge: Cambridge University Press, 2013).

[5] Most of these examples are taken from and further discussed in E. B. Mee and H. P. Foley, (eds.), *Antigone on the Contemporary World Stage: Classical Presences* (Oxford: Oxford University Press, 2011), pp. 418–419.

[6] J. Nesbø, *Macbeth*, D. Bartlett (trans.) (London and New York: Hogarth, 2018).

[7] E. Suzuki, 'Lost in Translation: Reconsidering Shakespeare's *Macbeth* and Kurosawa's *Throne of Blood*', *Literature/Film Quarterly*, 34.2 (2006), 93-103 (p. 96).

[8] This question is the subject of A. D. Nuttal's *Does Tragedy Give Pleasure?* (Oxford: Oxford University Press, 2010).

[9] For other overviews of tragedy, see R. Williams, *Modern Tragedy* (Peterborough, ON: Broadview Press, 2006); T. Eagleton, *Sweet Violence: The Idea of the Tragic* (Oxford: Wiley-Blackwell, 2002); and J. Wallace, *The Cambridge Introduction to Tragedy* (Cambridge: Cambridge University Press, 2007).

[10] The following description of Aristotle's ethical positions draws predominantly on Martha Nussbaum's writings on the subject. See especially her 'Tragedy and Self-Sufficiency: Plato and Aristotle on Fear and Pity', in A. O. Rorty (ed.), *Essays on Aristotle's Poetics* (Princeton: Princeton University Press, 1992), pp. 261–288; and 'The "Morality of Pity": Sophocles's *Philoctetes*', in R. Felski (ed.), *Rethinking Tragedy* (Baltimore: Johns Hopkins University Press, 2008), pp. 148–169.

[11] Nussbaum, 'Tragedy and Self-Sufficiency', p. 266.

[12] D. Greene and R. Lattimore (eds.), *Greek Tragedies*, Vol. 1 (Chicago: Chicago University Press, 1991), pp. 167–168.

[13] J. Vernant and P. Vidal-Naquet, *Myth and Tragedy in Ancient Greece*, J. Lloyd (trans.) (London: Zone Books, 1990), pp. 29–48, (p. 38).

[14] G. W. F. Hegel argues for this way of understanding the relationship between the tragic hero and his environment in 'Tragedy as Dramatic Art', in J. Drakakis and N. C. Liebler (eds.), *Tragedy* (London: Longman, 1998), pp. 23–52 (p.25).

[15] W. Soyinka, *Death and the King's Horseman* (London: Methuen, 1975). Page numbers for citations are in-text.

[16] Special thanks to Adeleke Adeeko for providing me the Yorùbá language translation of the proverb.

[17] 'Owner of honeyed words' in English.

10

NEIL LAZARUS

The Novel and Consciousness of Labour

Introduction

One aim of this chapter is to elaborate on a template for understanding 'world-literature' in relation to the modern world-system. This might provide the basis for a properly global and comparative approach, which would direct its attention in the first instance not to individual texts, 'which are formally and culturally very different from one another', but to 'the concrete situations from which such texts spring and to which they constitute distinct responses'.[1] Here, the 'concrete situations' that I have in mind are two epochal moments in the 'worlding' of modernity, that are interlinked – indeed, they are both part of the same world-historical process – but nevertheless analytically distinguishable.

The first is an 'inaugural' moment connected to the generalization of commodity production and wage labour across the globe, and often theorized in terms of the type of 'unevenness' discernible in relations between metropole and colony, country and city, one country or region and another, or one sector of production and another. Much celebrated literary writing – Charles Baudelaire is often cited in this context – has dwelt significantly on the moment when commodification achieves sufficient density to become the organizing principle of society and to insinuate itself into the fabric of everyday life, becoming visible as the puzzling substrate of 'common sense'. We might plausibly label this body of work 'modernist' (the understanding generally prevailing among critics today), but only if we stop thinking of it as being geographically or historically discrete in these terms. When modernism is defined in relation to modernity and modernization it is neither originally nor paradigmatically 'Western' in provenance. So we must consider not only metropolitan writers, such as Baudelaire, Edgar Allan Poe, Alfred Döblin, and F. Scott Fitzgerald, but equally (and not secondarily) writers from elsewhere in the world-system, such as Ayi Kwei Armah, Abdul Rahman Munif, Arundhati

Roy, and Wang Anyi, whose generative *situation* is analogous with that of their modernist counterparts in Europe and America.

The second moment to be examined is that governed by the experience of 'globalization' – of capitalist modernization in its phase of consolidation, regularization, and global dispersal. This is often theorized in terms of planetary connectedness, but sometimes also through reference to the deep structures that underlie, determine, and circumscribe social action in all of its myriad forms. Again, there is much celebrated literary writing that has been concerned to find formal means through which to capture and question the experiences corresponding to this phase: an indicative list might include the work of such recent and/or contemporary writers as Yurii Andrukhovych, Roberto Bolaño, Rana Dasgupta, Carlos Fuentes, Jamaica Kincaid, Viktor Pelevin, Pepetela, Thomas Pynchon, and José Saramago, and of their many nineteenth- and early-twentieth-century precursors, such as Pío Baroja, Joseph Conrad, Knut Hamsun, Jaroslav Hašek, James Joyce, Joaquim Maria Machado de Assis, Stéphane Mallarmé, and Upton Sinclair. The two 'moments' sketched here are not merely part of the *geographical* expansion of modernity; they also take place *at the same time*, and introduce a profound sense of unevenness into temporal experience itself.

My project takes as its specific focus the forms assumed by social labour in the context of the 'worlding' of capitalist modernity – a process still in train (and perhaps never-endingly so, for modernization is not something that a society can be imagined as 'achieving' once and for all: it is, rather, an ever-receding and *relational* horizon) – whose origins are often situated around 1850 in the historical and sociological literature. I derive my understanding of such key terms as 'modernity', 'modernism', and 'modernization' from recent scholarship that has attempted to de-link 'modernity' from 'the West' and to link it instead to the capitalist world-system. Immanuel Wallerstein has spoken of the instantiation of capitalism as a world-system around 1500, but it seems clear that it is only in the 'long' nineteenth century, and then as the consequence of European colonialism, that one can speak of the full *worlding* of capital, understood to refer not merely to the socio-spatial *extension* of 'modern' forms of life, but equally to the *intensivities* (or 'intensions') of experience that are engendered as a result. My particular interest lies in examining some of the ways in which, through its *form*, literature has contrived to register these intensivities of experience. So I focus on the category of *work* (or, more technically, *labour*) by way of developing the idea, first postulated by the Brazilian literary theorist Roberto Schwarz, that literary form is 'the abstract of social relations'.[2] By 'form' I mean both (literary) modes of representation and (literary) means of representation – so genre at one end of the chain, style, lexicon, vocabulary, and device at the other, with 'structure of feeling' and 'grammar of identity' somewhere in between the two poles.

A more expansive study might explore the social phenomenology of work as it finds literary representation in different locations across the world-system from the mid-nineteenth century to the present. My focus here, however, will be on the specific characteristics of the literary representation of rural (and particularly *peasant*) labour in the context of capitalist modernization. I hope to establish that a determinative relation exists between changing modes of work, on the one hand, and changes in the forms, genres, and aesthetic strategies of the literary writing that seeks to describe, represent, or bear witness to these social changes, on the other.

In its claim to be able to intervene between '(literary) work' and 'world', my approach to comparative literary scholarship looks beyond those currently established in modernist and postcolonial studies which often assume the incommensurability of 'Western' and 'non-Western' (or 'Third World') cultures and societies. My emphasis on the *comparability* of the generative situations out of which literary productions arise implies, on the contrary, that it is possible to move between 'works' and 'world' without having to restrict oneself (as some in translation studies and comparative literature argue is necessary) either to the languages in which one has fluency or to the local contexts and literary traditions about which one possesses advanced specialist knowledge. It is the deep-structured similarity of the *social situations* out of which literary works from different times and places are produced that makes the development of an authentically global comparative methodology in literary studies a priority today. When we think about literary works in relation to the category of the world-system, we find ourselves able to account for features of their particular formal make-up (topoi, narrative conventions, styles of characterization, etc.) that we have hitherto only been able to identify, but not credibly to explain.

The nameless first-person narrator of Knut Hamsun's *Hunger* (1890) is a young man who arrives in Kristiania (present-day Oslo) from the provinces, hoping to make a living for himself as a writer. *Hunger* charts its protagonist's increasing destitution and despair as he struggles – and fails – to find work, shelter, and sustenance. His creative ambition is progressively stripped away; he is reduced to hoping only that he will be able to sell what he writes so that he can buy food. In one typical passage, we encounter him waking up very early one morning, bursting with ideas.[3] His alertness is half delirium. He hasn't eaten anything for days or had a proper meal for weeks. He takes up a pencil and starts to write. Unusually, the words pour forth. An uncanny happiness floods over him. It is striking that this 'happiness' has scarcely been registered, before it is then described as being mediated by exchange value. His writing takes, for him, the form of saleable goods, whose true measure is monetary.

Hunger is harrowing and unsettling: the longer the narrative proceeds, the more desperate becomes the protagonist's turbulent and desolating search for something – anything – to eat. He is reduced at one point to trying to eat a wood-chip; at another, to chewing a pocket that he has torn from his own jacket; at still another, to sucking a stone. He passes from being in a condition in which he feels hungry ('merely' hungry, as it were) to one in which he knows that he is starving and will die if he doesn't soon eat. Hunger strips him of dignity, judgement, integrity, and social being. To the extent that the narrator retains any sense of self at all under the extreme duress to which he is exposed, he knows himself not as a subject but only as a recalcitrant and starkly objective body in need.

The critical reception of *Hunger* has tended to see it as a 'gateway' to international modernism. The tendency, as Timothy Wientzen explains, has been to abstract from the fact that the narrator is literally starving and to construe his hunger metaphorically as the desire for recognition or self-actualization in the overarching context of an existential struggle for authenticity. In this conventional interpretation, the novel's experimentalism – its radical subjectivism, for instance, its pursuit of the narrator into madness and derangement – is assimilated to the paradigmatic modernist register centred on alienation, anguish, and anomie, and the work itself situated as 'an early example of modernist aesthetics'.[4] Paul Auster, for instance, compares the work to Franz Kafka's parable 'A Hunger Artist' (1922). Far from shedding light on the wellspring of Hamsun's imagination, Wientzen argues, the vaunted literary comparativism of the theorists of 'international' modernism proves to be profoundly decontextualizing. However, Wientzen does not call for a methodological retreat to the incommensurable particular – Hamsun's text is hardly so specific to its own time and place as to be incomparable with writings from other times or places – but, on the contrary, for a *more rigorous and better-grounded* literary comparativism. It is only when we think about *Hunger* in relation to the sociological category of the modern world-system that the particular formal features of the work – its unique aesthetic structure and internal logic – make themselves available. '[T]hough we rarely think of Norway as inhabiting the margins of capitalist development', Wientzen notes, it 'was among Europe's least developed countries in the nineteenth century, a reality that informed the work of some of modernism's earliest painters and writers. In *Hunger* [. . .] Hamsun invoked a history of economic development that endowed the starving body with transnational significance. Restaging the naturalist novel's own approach to hunger, *Hunger* reflects the transnational reconfiguration of economic forms, which depended centrally on the leveraging of bodily needs of entire populations for productive ends.'[5]

Hamsun's formal project in *Hunger* needs to be understood as a registration of Norway's relative peripherality in the world-system at the time of the work's composition. This is less 'international modernism', in other words, than the 'modernism of underdevelopment'.[6] For those, like myself, given to thinking schematically, this conceptualization gives rise to the temptation to conjure up a counter-list of 'modernist' literary works, to set beside the 'international modernist' list to which Auster's conception implicitly refers us. So, with respect to Hamsun, not Joyce, Virginia Woolf, Kafka, etc. – or, at least not *only* them, or not them *in the same way* – but, say: Velimir Khlebnikov, Liam O'Flaherty, Bhabani Bhattacharya, Martin Carter, Kamala Markandaya, Antônio Torres, Dambudzo Marechera, Mohamed El-Bisatie, Liu Zhenyun, Aki Ollikainen, etc.[7] All of these are authors of identifiably 'modernist' works grappling centrally with socially engendered destitution, starvation, or famine and whose formal experimentalism, often misunderstood and disparaged in its own moment, becomes fully intelligible only when it is grasped by the comparative methodology I have been outlining.

There's a striking passage in Ayi Kwei Armah's *The Beautyful Ones Are Not Yet Born* (1968) in which the protagonist (who is nameless, as in Hamsun's novel) leaves the Traffic Control Office in which he works one lunch-time and walks to the harbour. He is very hungry but has no food. His wages are insufficient to keep him and his family from week to week, and his life is therefore pinched and miserable. The novel speaks of 'the mean monthly cycle of debt and borrowing, borrowing and debt': for the protagonist and the many Ghanaians whose material circumstances are similar to his, 'lunchtime was not a time to refresh oneself'.[8] He walks to keep his mind from dwelling on hunger. At first, his thoughts are drawn to the irremediable wretchedness of his life, but then suddenly his desperate and despairing refusal to allow himself to be defined by his hunger gives way to a strange sensation of lucidity and resolution:

> [T]he man followed the line of the hard steel tracks where they curved out and away from inside the loco yard and straightened out ahead for the melancholy piercing push into the interior of the land. On the gravel bed beneath the metal the mixture of fallen ashes and stray lumps of engine coal and steamed grease raised somewhere in the region of his throat the overwarm stench of despair and the defeat of a domestic kitchen well used, its whole atmosphere made up of malingering tongues of the humiliating smoke of all those yesterdays. Out

ahead, however, the tracks drove straight in clean shiny lines and the air above the steel shook with the power of the sun until all the afternoon things seen through the air seemed fluid and not solid anymore. The sourness that had been gathering in his mouth went imperceptibly away until quite suddenly all he was aware of was the exceedingly sharp clarity of vision and the clean taste that comes with the successful defiance of hunger. (p. 22)

The postcolonial world denoted here, and throughout the novel, is defined not by its *lack of development* but by its comprehensive *under-development*. On the one hand, we have the gravel beds, metal, engine coal, grease, and shiny steel tracks; on the other, at the perimeter of the loco yard, the small parcels of barren land on which migrant workers from the north of the country – Tamale, say, or Yendi – now try to grow enough to keep themselves alive. Penetrating deep into the interior of the country, the rail network bespeaks modernization of a kind; not one that facilitates commerce and communication between and among Ghana's own people, but in which goods – bauxite, iron ore, cocoa – are ferried from where they are grown or mined to southern ports, where they can be shipped to the core capitalist zones, subject to a politico-economic logic that Armah understands as neo-colonial. Ghana's integration within the economic world-system has come at the expense of the social well-being of its people. 'So much time has gone by, and still there is no sweetness here' (p. 67). Political *independence* might have come to Ghana, but what little *growth* there is in the novel's world is quantitative only, its fruits jealously hoarded by a kleptocratic elite, and purchased at the cost of the qualitative stagnation or, worse, the undermining or, even, destruction of the wider society.

Stylistically, the passage is notable for staging a 'disconnect' between *word* and *world*. The language (tone, lexicon, register) that Armah uses to describe the reality encountered by his protagonist is compacted, dense, almost cloying. The passage is not easy to read aloud. The sentences are long, intricate, adjectivally saturated and entropic: 'fallen [...] stray [...] steamed [...] overwarm [...] malingering [...] humiliating'. We are led to understand that the reality experienced by the protagonist (the novel refers to him only as 'the man') is so unforgiving and defeating as to threaten even the communicative, inter-subjective aspects of language. In this dimension, too – as in the more solidly material dimensions of social production and reproduction – only a fragile, negative dialectical thread links the degraded present to 'the beautyful ones' of the long future. Language can keep faith with the idea of community only by self-consciously estranging itself from a public discourse that has become contaminated by the prevailing social logic, and is now unuseable.

The first readers of Armah's novel failed to grasp all this. Exactly the same pattern as Wientzen observed in the reception of Hamsun's *Hunger* was evident in the initial reception of *The Beautyful Ones Are Not Yet Born*. But in the African literary context of the late 1960s, concerned above all with the project of cultural decolonization, a stark and reductive opposition was operationalized between 'Afrocentric' and 'Eurocentric' literary discourses, and Armah's novel found itself being read in the terms of this blunt opposition. Just as the tendency of the critical reception of *Hunger* has been to *celebrate* the work as 'an early example of modernist aesthetics', so, *mutatis mutandis*, the tendency of the initial critical reception of *The Beautyful Ones* was to *deplore* it as a belated example of these self-same modernist aesthetics: hence the charge of '*Euro*-modernism' that was often hurled at such African writers as Armah, Wole Soyinka, Christopher Okigbo, and Kofi Awoonor. In his massively influential critique of Armah's novel, for instance, Chinua Achebe wrote that while it was 'a well-written book' – 'Armah's command of language and imagery is of a very high order indeed' – it was all the same 'a sick book':

> Sick, not with the sickness of Ghana but with the sickness of the *human condition*. The hero, pale and passive and nameless – a creation in the best manner of existentialist writing – wanders through the story in an anguished half-sleep, neck-deep in despair and human excrement of which we see rather a lot in the book [. . .] He reminded me very strongly of that man and woman in a Jean-Paul Sartre novel who sit in anguished gloom in a restaurant and then in a sudden excess of nihilistic energy seize table knives and stab their hands right through to the wood.[9]

The force of Achebe's criticism of the false universalism of much Eurocentric theorizing about Africa must freely be conceded. Nevertheless, the fact remains that the understanding of 'modernism' that he betrays in his discussion of *The Beautyful Ones* is drastically attenuated. Confronted with, not to say confounded by, the juxtaposition in Armah's novel of allegorical and realist features, the evident 'compromise' in the work 'between foreign form and local materials',[10] he can conclude only that work's register is alien to Africa, and 'unrecognisable'. What he takes to be Armah's 'modernism' serves to render *The Beautyful Ones* 'un-African' in his eyes.

But it seems to me that the lexicon of Armah's 'modernism' is not that of the pseudo-universalistic 'international modernism' widely affirmed in the critical literature but that of world-literature considered as 'the literature of the world-system'.[11] This is a modernism marked not by any paradigmatic affect ('despair', for instance), interpreted in the light of a lament against an existentially unbearable 'human condition', but rather by its disclosure (whether self-conscious or not) of the complex relations between a local social universe and the wider world. 'Neocolonialism', the term that Armah follows Kwame Nkrumah in reaching for, is a relational concept: it maps unequal social relations between and across town and village, city and province, nation and region, Africa and Europe. When Achebe accused Armah of 'impos[ing] so much foreign metaphor on [...] Ghana that it ceases to be true', and when he concluded that 'Armah is clearly an alienated writer, a modern writer complete with all the symptoms', he was missing the point.[12] It is not a matter of our having, as it were, to 'choose' between 'Africa' and 'the West' – the latter decadent, declining, 'modern' but beginning to lose its monopoly over the definition of the 'now'; the former embattled, emergent, previously held back but now coming forward. We are required, rather, to grasp the terms of the changing relationship between 'Africa' and 'the West' in the historical context of decolonization – an historical watershed, undeniably, but whose *political* and *ideological* significance (the ending of colonial dictatorship) finds little to no *infrastructural* warrant. Far from auguring the dawn of freedom, 'independence' would be better conceptualized as a rationalizing reconstruction of peripherality and clientelism in the world-system. This, of course, is just how Armah *does* conceptualize it. The fiercely compacted form of his novel – with its telescoping of allegorical, parabolic, and realist registers, its forcing together of picaresque, morality play, and critical realism, its blend of 'excrementalism' and quasi-religious puritanism, and so on – then assumes significance (as, arguably, few other formal modes could have done) as both a registration and a critique of the actually existing social landscape of Ghana in the years immediately following decolonization.

One of the central topoi of modern fiction is the young man from the provinces who comes to the city to look for work or, more extravagantly, to seek his fortune. From Peter Abrahams' *Mine Boy* to Émile Zola's *Germinal*, and in works from different times and places which have in common only the structural identity of their *situations*, we are shown the centripetal force exerted by the city. The city's restless, jagged, and unceasing transformation through modernization is overdetermined in these country-to-city literary narratives through being represented under the sign of the shock of the new, as the rural protagonists are made to confront its pace, size, intensity, abruptness, and callous impersonality.

Because the city is so transparently the dominant locus of modernization in the capitalist world-system, there has been a good deal of discussion of literary representations of *urban* labour. Much less critical ink has been spilled in discussion of the literary representation of *rural* work in the contexts of modernity and modernization. If, in the modern era, it is obviously true that the city pulls, it is also the case that the country pushes. Hamsun's narrator and Armah's migrant workers have in common not only the migration to the metropolitan centre but also the desire to get away from rural lives experienced as increasingly harsh and impoverished. In country-to-city fiction, the countryside – the world of land, village, agricultural labour – is typically represented as a depleted and depleting matrix, less and less capable of sustaining life, not only affectively or experientially, but often literally.[13]

Some of the most moving and consequential writing of the modern era has devoted itself, accordingly, to the task of describing the lives of those who remain behind in farm and village when so many fellow villagers, neighbours, friends, and family members leave to look for work in the city. In *The Country and the City*, Raymond Williams identifies three main lines of development in British writing concerned with the increasing residual nature of rural experience: the so-called regional novel; the persistence of 'landscape description and nature poetry' alongside narratives of rural 'relationships and especially of love and desire'; and the proliferation of what, in other contexts, has been called 'salvage ethnography':[14] 'memoirs, observations, accounts of rural life: many of them pervaded by a sense of the vanishing past [...]; but others centred on the uses and abuses of land'. These three lines of development are all complex and contradictory. Indeed, their complexities are such that it is not possible for us to reach any summary judgements.[15]

Published in 1973, *The Country and the City* illuminatingly presages British writing still to come and one can, of course, also use this discussion as a lens onto some of the writing about rural life in the literatures of non-Anglophone Europe since the mid-nineteenth century.[16] However, any discussion of literary representations of rural work in the modern era requires that we give some preliminary thought to two issues. First, there is the dominant popular conception of rural life as being somehow outside, beyond, or beneath modern history, left behind by the forces of modernization and existing within the contemporary world only as a kind of unchanged and unchanging relic. Second, there is the problem of representation: in literary works dealing with rural life, and especially the peasantry, what is the narration's class standpoint? What is the relation between the speaking voice (and the ideology or social consciousness governing it) and the characters, social practices, ideas, and conventions to which it gives expression?

Where the relationship of rural life to modernity is concerned, capitalist development involves (and is only possible on the basis of) a massive, worldwide restructuring of nature, social relations, and built environments. (Accordingly, scholars working under the rubric of 'world-ecology' have demonstrated that the production of capital is also and at the same time the production of nature.)[17] Historians who have been critical of selective European claims to have 'advanced' African or Asian societies in the long years of colonial domination, have sometimes observed acerbically that '[t]he peasant [...] entered colonial rule with a hoe and came out with a hoe'.[18] Their suggestion is not that colonial modernity by-passed the peasant populations and left peasant culture intact, but that it *incorporated and immiserated* the peasantry. Far from being a class left behind in the sweep of time, the global peasantry has been very much part of the story of capitalist modernization. A key corollary here – and we find it being emphasized repeatedly in relevant literary works – is that peasant life in the modern era does not stay the same as it always was, but is subject to ever-changing pressures and demands.

Let us turn now to the question of representation. The object given by literary representation is always situated and relational. It is never that object as it exists in the extra-literary world, but rather is a re-presentation of it as seen from a specific standpoint and mediated through the form of the literary work itself. It has been widely recognized since at least the time of Virgil's *Eclogues* that nearly all of the literary representations of rural labourers are written from across the social division of labour, by writers who are not themselves members of that class. Indeed, the problem of what M. M. Bakhtin and P. N. Medvedev call 'refraction' is nowhere more evident than in the case of the literary representation of the peasantry.[19] Anyone who has read *Piers Plowman* attentively will know that neither its denunciatory depiction of idle 'wasters' – who will not work unless they are paid – nor its celebratory depiction of the honest ploughman, Piers – who 'accepts that it is his duty to produce food for the benefit of the whole of society in exchange for the aristocracy's maintenance of law and order' – is to be taken at face value.[20] When we encounter 'peasants' or 'rural labourers' in a literary work, we are almost always encountering a particular expression of a social relation to these labourers – the 'ideological refraction of a given social type'.[21] Consider the following rather extreme instance drawn from an early work of Ivan Turgenev:

> Give me your hand, dear reader, and come on an outing. The weather is beautiful. The May sky glows a gentle blue. The smooth young leaves of the willow shine as if newly washed. The broad, level road is entirely covered with that short grass with reddish stems which sheep so love to nibble. To left and right, along the long slopes of the low hills green rye quietly ripples. The shadows of small clouds slide across it like globules of moisture. In the distance gleam dark woodlands, ponds glisten and villages shine yellow. Larks rise by the hundreds, sing and fall precipitately and, with small outstretched

necks, are seen conspicuously on small outcrops of soil. Rooks stop on the road, look at you, crouch down to let you pass and, giving a couple of jumps, fly off heavily to one side. On an upland beyond a shallow valley a peasant is ploughing. A dappled foal with short little tail and ruffled mane runs on uncertain legs behind its mother and one can hear its high-pitched neighing ...[22]

Although atypical of Turgenev's work overall, I cite this passage because its reduction of the figure of the peasant to nature, so thoroughgoing as to be almost complete, is often encountered across the wider literary corpus. The ploughman's labour is reckoned to be as little social as that of the rooks and the larks, who indeed command more narrative space. Peasants plough just as larks rise. We cannot read this passage without asking about the standpoint of the narrator who sees things in this way – the word 'standpoint' gesturing not only to a class position but to an ideology, a way of living, and the expression of this class position. The title of the collection, *Sketches from a Hunter's Album*, already points us in this direction.

A very different depiction of peasant labour – and peasant life – is to be found in Wiesław Myśliwski's *Stone upon Stone*, first published in 1999, a vast, sprawling and inexhaustibly rich novel set against the great sweep of Polish history in the twentieth century. Myśliwski's greatest achievement in the work is undoubtedly the creation of his protagonist-narrator, Szymon Pietruszka, whose monologue comprises the novel in its entirety. Named for Simon Peter, the first apostle, Szymek, as almost everyone calls him, shares some of his namesake's attributes and faults: he is stubbornly independent, impulsive, impetuous, courageous, and deeply resistant to social or contextual expectations, qualities which save his life on several occasions, but can also come across as perversity or mulishness. A wordsmith – also like Simon Peter – and possessed of the rare ability to move people with his tales and stories, Szymek's 'typicality' is, however, not that of any stock literary character. Prone to violence, often insensitive, bigoted, and dismissive of women in general, he is unlikeable – indeed, in many respects positively *dislikeable*. He is, evidently, not a virtuous everyman, but he's also too radically singular to serve as the stereotype of a bucolic rascal.

Of the family's four sons, it falls to Szymek to keep up the family farm after his parents die. He is an unlikely traditionalist. He hates the work of farming and the hardscrabble existence it mandates – 'I'd rather sit behind a desk than cart cabbage', he remarks to himself.[23] Growing up, he had thoughts of escaping the farm, but, even before the start of the war, his two younger brothers leave the village for the city, and the murderous violence of the Nazi occupation leaves his older brother, Michał – who, like Szymek, survives the war while working in the underground resistance movement – ungrounded, trapped in a well of silence from which he is never able to escape. (It is worth pausing to dwell on the fact that over a fifth of the total Polish population – some six million or so people – died between 1939 and 1945 as a direct result of the deliberate world-shattering brutality of the occupying German forces.) Szymek is left behind to tend to Michał, the homestead, and the farm and its land as best he can.

But if fate has imposed this burden upon him, this is not to say that he is ever reconciled to it. His accounts of the everyday drudgery of peasant labour – of *routine* work, *routine* hardship, *routine* poverty – are gloriously, untameably, alive with grumbling and complaining (what in Yiddish is called *kvetching*): *this* hurts, *that* is heavy, *this* is a giant waste of time, *that* won't pay, and so on. It would be tautological to describe Szymek's way of thinking as materialist. What else would it be? His approach to life is practical, pragmatic, earth-bound. To which characteristics we must add others, deriving from his own particular temperament: opinionated, impatient, acidulous.

Having survived German Occupation, Sovietization, and the never-ending austerity of peasant life; having worked in a number of different capacities – as a farmer, but also as a tax accountant and wedding registrar – Szymek knows a lot about a lot and has many stories to tell, but then so do many others around him. What makes him unusual is that he is also given to reflection and is determined to put things in context – to grasp them in their particularity, while also understanding their meaning and their significance in the wider frame. Observing that the old road through the village was winding, he adds wryly that 'roads often are. They have to go around one thing or another. A shrine, a pond, a house' (p. 57). 'You took [the road] ... to get to market in town, or to other villages around here', he tells us, 'and whether you were going off to war or headed for the outside world, the road would lead you there just the same' (p. 55). Home-spun philosophy: in Szymek, what is known or has been seen or experienced has become wisdom, however crusty, offbeat, and even counter-intuitive it might be: 'there are some things that nobody has to think up because they're just there. A horsewhip for instance. It's there and you crack it when the horse won't pull. It must have come with the horse. Or the roof on a house, wheels on a cart, soles on boots' (pp. 16–17).

The notion that the horsewhip 'must have come with the horse' is a superb touch: witty, whimsical, both absurd and absurdist – the sort of thing that could be said only by somebody who can enchant people with stories. It opens a sight-line onto another, leavening aspect of Szymek's character: his deep intellectual curiosity about the people and their ways. It would be too strong to describe this interest as 'humane'. It is not really that, and nor of course is it remotely cosmopolitan. But it reveals a subtlety of discernment and even a sensitivity that he evidently prefers not to present too immediately or too often in his regular social intercourse. These qualities are most marked in his achingly sad recollections of his time with Małgorzata, the only woman in his life (other than his mother, perhaps) whom he might be said to have truly loved, but whom he nevertheless loses because of a symptomatic inability to act on his feelings. In one extraordinary passage, Szymek recalls that he often used to go to Małgorzata's house after work when they were both employed by the district administration to set up the new communist government. Once there, she would immediately set to doing housework, and he would watch her. He first describes her 'feeding and watering and washing and cleaning', words that show that he is aware of her work but in a relatively unanchored way. But as his visits continue, the focus of his linguistic reference sharpens considerably:

> As I watched her I could barely recognize myself [...] I sometimes had the sense that the work itself was passing her from hand to hand, that the furniture was moving her around the room. A bucket full of soapsuds is a heavy thing even for a man, but before I'd notice and jump up to help her she'd grab it by the handles and haul it out to the passage [...] Or when she scraped carrots for soup. You'd think carrots were nothing special. But the whole room went red, like the sun was setting red when a high wind's coming. Actually all she needed to do was stand at the range stirring one of the pots with a ladle, even then the whole room was filled with her, every nook and cranny, while the rest of us, her father and mother and me, we were squashed into the tiniest corner. (pp. 385–6)

He does not question the burdens placed upon Małgorzata by the social-sexual division of labour. But he *does* see – and very clearly – how *much* work there is for her to do, and how arduous it is. Although his attentiveness is attributable substantially to sexual desire, it cannot be reduced to this. The warm feeling inside is one thing. We can be arch about this. But the suggestion that as he watched her, he could barely recognize himself, seems to tend in another direction, as does the observation that watching her at work 'took the place of thinking or of words for me'. He notices *everything* that she does: mixing food for the pigs, washing the floor, adding kindling to the stove, rolling dough, slicing dumplings, scraping carrots, feeding the chickens, sewing buttons, sweeping, etc. This is work that she does without remuneration, not for herself, but for others. Indeed, it is the self-sacrificing nature of her housework that particularly moves him: but it also unsettles him. When he says that he 'sometimes had the sense that the work itself was passing her from hand to hand', he sees not only that the work is unending, but also that it is not *quid pro quo*. If it is experienced as a burden (and we are not put in a position to judge this), it is also internalized as an expression of familial love or commitment.

The expressionist register introduced is presumably to be decoded as an objective correlative of the oceanic quality of Małgorzata's love for her family. It is what binds her to her world. But it is precisely this, I think, that gives Szymek pause, leaving him unable to take the step that he longs to take. Małgorzata's acceptance of the given world is not an outlook he can embrace for himself. Something in Szymek interprets Małgorzata's feminine, community-creating love as threatening – not to his masculinity, as such, but to the orneriness, the iconoclastic, anti-social impulsivity, that is so central to how he presents himself to others. He imagines himself dying, rather than living, in Małgorzata's love.

It is not as though Szymek is *not* interested in community. On the contrary, his accounts of the changes that have come to the village, and of the devastating losses that he and others have incurred are imbued with a profound emotional generosity. His language in these passages carries an affective resonance, a product of the gap between the earth-bound – and even earthy – substrate of his consciousness and its transcendental (if insistently secular) conceptualization: 'The moon was like a cow's udder', we read at one point, 'if you'd pulled at its teats we'd have been covered in streams of moonlight' (p. 267).

The attention of readers has understandably been drawn to the final pages of the novel, in which Szymek addresses Michał, sharing his deepest thoughts with him, and imploring him to speak again so that they can face together the experience of getting old, and so, perhaps, retrieve the intimacy they had once felt as brothers. It is to the subject of language that Szymek turns here, casting it as the primary means through which we are made human. But then he surmises that language is also what connects us, not only to those who share the earth with us, but to those who have gone before us and those still to come, binding matter and spirit, earth and hope, together. 'The whole world is one big language', he says.

> If you really listened carefully to it, you might even be able to hear what they were saying a century back, maybe even thousands of years ago. Because words don't know death. They're like see-through birds, once they've spoken they circle over us forever, it's just that we don't hear them [...] Life begins with a word and ends with words. Because death is also just the end of words. Start maybe from the first ones at hand, the ones that are closest to you. Mother, home, earth. Maybe try saying, earth. I mean, you know what earth is. Where do you spit? On the earth. You know, what you walk on, what houses are built on, what you plow. [...] They say that when a person's born, the earth is their

cradle. And all death does is lay you back down in it. And it rocks you and rocks you till you're unborn, unconceived, once again. (pp. 533–34)

If these lines offer consolation, it can only be in the Adornian sense of 'the gaze falling on horror, withstanding it, and in unalleviated consciousness of negativity holding fast to the possibility of what is better'.[24] Szymek's words scan forward as much as backward, constructing a link between the extinction that is the fate of every one of us and the eternity of human striving. Unconception, at one level; a new beginning at another. Springs rising up out of the earth, people's sweat draining back into it. Ashes to ashes, dust to dust: this is how any *individual's* life might be summed up; but it is not how *La Comédie humaine* might be narrated. For *that*, you need Balzac's ninety books; or perhaps just this one of Myśliwski's.

Notes

1. F. Jameson, 'Third-World Literature in the Era of Multinational Capitalism', *Social Text*, 15 (1986), 65–88 (pp. 86–87).
2. R. Schwarz, *Misplaced Ideas: Essays on Brazilian Culture*, J. Gledson (ed.) (London: Verso, 1992), p. 53.
3. K. Hamsun, *Hunger*, R. Bly (trans.), (London: Picador, 1974), p. 48.
4. T. Wientzen, 'The Aesthetics of Hunger: Knut Hamsun, Modernism, and Starvation's Global Frame', *Novel*, 48.2 (2015), p. 208.
5. Wientzen, 'Aesthetics of Hunger', p. 209.
6. M. Berman, *All That Is Solid Melts Into Air: The Experience of Modernity* (London: Verso, 1983).
7. The works that I am thinking of are Khlebnikov's 'Hunger' (1921), O'Flaherty's *Famine* (1937), Bhattacharya's *So Many Hungers!* (1947), Carter's 'University of Hunger' (1954), Markandaya's *Nectar in a Sieve* (1954), Torres's *The Land* (1976), Marechera's *The House of Hunger* (1978), El-Bisatie's *Hunger: An Egyptian Novel* (2008), Liu Zhenyun's *Remembering 1942 and other Chinese Stories* (2012), and Ollikainen's *White Hunger* (2012).
8. A. K. Armah, *The Beautyful Ones Are Not Yet Born* (London: Heinemann, 1988), pp. 21–22. Further references are in-text.
9. C. Achebe, 'Africa and Her Writers', in *Morning Yet on Creation Day: Essays* (London: Heinemann, 1977), p. 25.
10. F. Moretti 'Conjectures on World Literature', *New Left Review*, 1 (2000), p. 60.
11. This is the definition offered in Warwick Research Collective, *Combined and Uneven Development: Towards a New Theory of World-Literature* (Liverpool: Liverpool University Press, 2015), p. 8.
12. Achebe, 'Africa and Her Writers', p. 26.
13. One recalls Jameson's suggestion, with reference to the paintings of Van Gogh, that 'one way of reconstructing the initial situation to which the work is somehow a response is by stressing the raw materials, the initial content, which it confronts and reworks, transforms, and appropriates. In Van Gogh that content, those initial raw materials, are [...] to be grasped simply as the whole object

world of agricultural misery, of stark rural poverty, and the whole rudimentary human world of backbreaking peasant toil, a world reduced to its most brutal and menaced, primitive and marginalized state.' F. Jameson, *Postmodernism, Or the Cultural Logic of Late Capitalism* (Durham: Duke University Press, 1991), p. 7.

14. The *Dictionary of the Social Sciences* defines it as 'the attempt to reconstruct the traditions and practices of cultures that had already suffered radical losses of integrity'. See C. Calhoun (ed.) (Oxford: Oxford University Press, 2002), p. 46.

15. R. Williams, *The Country and the City* (New York: Oxford University Press, 1973), p. 248.

16. John Berger's trilogy *Into Their Labours* (New York: Pantheon, 1991), for instance, deals with the experience of the Alpine peasantry across the span of the twentieth century.

17. Jason Moore has shown that the 'commodity frontiers' of Dutch capital in the long seventeenth century decisively impacted environment and social relations across Holland and the vast sweep of territory that the Dutch traversed in the North and South Atlantic and the Indian and Pacific Oceans. '"Amsterdam is Standing on Norway": Part II: The Global North Atlantic in the Ecological Revolution of the Long Seventeenth Century', *Journal of Agrarian Change*, 10.2 (2010), 188–227.

18. J. Lonsdale, 'Have Tropical Africa's Nationalism Continued Imperialism's World Revolution by Other Means?', *Nations and Nationalism*, 21.4 (2015), 609–629 (p. 614).

19. M. M. Bakhtin and P. N. Medvedev, *The Formal Method in Literary Scholarship: A Critical Introduction to Sociological Poetics*, A. J. Wehrle (trans.) (Cambridge, MA: Harvard University Press, 1985), p. 21.

20. C. Dyer, 'Work Ethics in the Fourteenth Century', in J. Bothwell, P. J. P. Goldberg, and W. M. Ormrod (eds.), *The Problem of Labour in Fourteenth-Century England* (York: York Medieval Press, 2000), pp. 21–42 (p. 29).

21. Bakhtin and Medvedev, *The Formal Method in Literary Scholarship*, p. 21.

22. I. Turgenev, 'Tatyana Borisovna and Her Nephew', in *Sketches from a Hunter's Album*, R. Freeborn (trans.) (London: Penguin, 1990), pp. 204–216 (p. 204).

23. W. Myśliwski, *Stone upon Stone*, B. Johnston (trans.) (New York: Archipelago Books, 2010). References are in-text.

24. T. W. Adorno, *Minima Moralia: Reflections from Damaged Life*, E. F. N. Jephcott (trans.) (London: Verso, 1985), p. 25.

II

CHARLOTTA SALMI

The Worldliness of Graphic Narrative

'This is mad stuff, indeed!' Johann Wolfgang von Goethe reputedly exclaimed when reading Rodolphe Töpffer's experimental picture stories. Despite Goethe's notorious scepticism about caricature, he was so amused by Töpffer's jovial adventures of society gentlemen that he penned an endorsement, published posthumously in his literary journal *Über Kunst und Altertum*. What appeared 'mad' about Töpffer's humorous tales was their novel format: the Swiss artist used a combination of sequential images in panels and text boxes to tell his stories. This mixed medium would later gain word balloons (first used in Richard F. Outcault's strip *Hogan's Alley* in 1896) and grids and gutters (the white spaces between panels) thereby arriving at the form of the modern comic. Töpffer's picture stories were a key influence on the early graphic narrative, contributing to one of the three central national traditions that have shaped its contemporary existence as a world literary form. The graphic narrative, which Scott McCloud glosses as 'juxtaposed pictorial and other images in a deliberate sequence', stems from the crossover and cultural exchange between cartoon cultures in French-speaking Europe, America, and Japan.[1] It includes both comic strips – mostly serialized and commercial picture stories – and the graphic novel, a term coined more recently to denote the 'artistically serious' comic book.

Töpffer's picture stories draw on and contribute to a global literary and visual heritage, and illustrate how graphic narrative came to operate as world literature. The roots of the comic lie partly in early British caricature (associated with eighteenth- and nineteenth-century artists like William Hogarth and George Cruikshank), and in alternative graphic arts like Töpffer's etchings, and Frans Masereel's and Lynd Ward's woodcuts. British caricature was disseminated around the world through satirical magazines such as *Punch*, which travelled with the clerks of empire. These publications, in turn, inspired local versions, like *Japan Punch*, which was central in developing Japanese 'whimsical pictures', or manga, in the early twentieth century. In Europe, the model for longer pictorial narratives developed by artists like Töpffer inspired migrant cartoonists and illustrators who moved to the United States. For example, the model was picked up in Germany by Wilhelm Busch, whose illustrated verse *Max und Moritz* (1865) was adapted by Rudolph Dirks (a German immigrant to America) in *The Katzenjammer Kids* (1896), one of America's earliest and most influential newspaper strips. The Franco-Belgian *bande dessinée* (illustrated strip), Japanese manga, and the American comic thus developed simultaneously, spurred on by various kinds of cultural exchange in the late nineteenth and early twentieth centuries.

This inter-cultural and trans-national history has also fed into the graphic novel, a term first used by the publisher and comics reviewer Richard Kyle in a 1964 piece that called on American comics artists to draw inspiration from their European and Japanese counterparts in order to fulfil the form's potential.[2] 'Serious' graphic narratives of this kind were already being produced by independent publishers in the 1960s, and reached mainstream publishing houses in the 1980s with the serialization of Art Spiegelman's holocaust memoir *Maus*, which won the Pulitzer Prize in 1992 following its publication as a single volume. Loosely speaking, graphic novels are now considered comics that have a more serious content, such as we find in *Maus*, and which typically are aimed at a more adult audience and presented in a single volume, produced by one or two creators. In subject matter, graphic novels tend to take inspiration from the alternative, confessional, and taboo topics of the underground comix scene that sprang out of American counter-culture in the 1960s – *Maus* started its life in Spiegelman's underground magazine *Raw* – while their intermedial style draws on cinema and older visual media, as well as Japanese manga. *Maus*'s contemporaries, Alan Moore's *Watchmen*, and Frank Miller's *The Dark Knight Returns*, both published in 1986, use *eiga teki shuhō* ('cinematic techniques') – close-ups and moving angles – that were popularized by the 'god of comics' in Japan, Osamu Tezuka.[3] The graphic novel's cultural capital has also been acquired by proximity to the prestigious Franco-Belgian *bande dessinée*, from which have emerged several comics auteurs, known for individuated and recognizable aesthetic styles. For example, Hergé (George Remi) is identified with the *ligne claire*, or clear line, a style without shading and cross-hatching, where each line and colour is given equal prominence on the page.

The graphic narrative is therefore a mixed medium in both form and heritage. And though it has become commonplace to cite endorsements by Goethe – who is frequently regarded as the originator of *Weltliteratur* – to claim texts or genres for world literature, the graphic narrative does not require this association with the Sage of Weimar. It belongs to world literature not just as a commodity with a global market (comics have a long history as a US export, while graphic novel sales are growing in Africa, South and East Asia, and the Arab world), but also as a literary form with its own transnational field. If world literature, in its accustomed sense of being a measure of long-standing literary value or recognition, has excluded the graphic narrative as a 'lowbrow' form, the graphic narrative as 'sequential art' (to borrow Will Eisner's term) has all the while been forming its own subset of world literature.

In what follows, I will focus on works from Japan, Iran, and India, in order to think about how the graphic narrative operates as a transnational form, one which challenges the established parameters and definitions of world literature. What we will find is that the contemporary graphic narrative straddles different understandings of the term. Keiji Nakazawa's manga shows how graphic narratives are translated, adapted, and assimilated into different cultural contexts, and how these in turn manifest differently in new contexts, as per David Damrosch's view of world literature. On the other hand, the works of Marjane Satrapi, and S. Anand and Srividya Natarajan demonstrate how the graphic narrative has come to mediate longer histories of cultural and political exchange. They express a 'worldliness' in the sense used by Edward Said: an awareness of geographical specificity and the politics of culture.

Keiji Nakazawa's celebrated cartoon story of Hiroshima, *Barefoot Gen* (*Hadashi no Gen*, 1973) – the first Japanese comic to be translated into English, and to circulate in Europe and North America – set new parameters for both the subject matter of graphic narratives and their global reach. *Barefoot Gen* sprang from a short autobiographical comic that the artist produced in 1972 for *Shōnen Jump*, a magazine for boys, and relates Nakazawa's experiences as an atomic bomb survivor through a fictional protagonist. It was part of a wave of accounts, which started emerging in the 1960s, of the plight of the *Hibakusha* – the 'explosion affected' survivors or radiation sufferers who remained stigmatized in postwar Japan. It was also among the first to use the comic form to warn of the horrors of nuclear warfare.

As an example of Japan's 'Atomic Bomb Literature', *Barefoot Gen* speaks to the survivor's need to testify and the activist's determination to affect future policy. 'I Saw It' – the title of the first avowedly auto-biographical version – attests to the act of witnessing, and through his haunting illustrations of the atomic bomb's infernal after-effects, Nakazawa's readers could imagine for themselves the horrors of nuclear warfare. The work has grown into a series of ten volumes which have been widely translated (most recently into Farsi), often as part of dis-armament campaigns.[4]

Figure 11.1 Keiji Nakazawa's *Barefoot Gen: A Cartoon Story of Hiroshima*.
© Keiji Nakazawa. All rights reserved. Reprinted by permission of the publisher, Last Gasp.

The influence of the series on the scope and subject matter of graphic narratives is linked to the innovative ways in which it makes use of its medium to convey suffering and to enact social critique. Nakazawa's particular mode of *graphiation*, or visual enunciation, transmutes historical evidence through the singularity of his aesthetic style. The drawn line testifies both to what it illustrates and to the presence and perspective of its creator, enabling a synthesis of documentary representation and a self-reflexivity that internalizes what it means to 'materialize history'.[5] Nakazawa's visual grammar renders complex the process of ordering memory and representing history.

Barefoot Gen relates the tragic fate of Gen's parents, who were outspoken critics of the war effort, and uses symbolism to render visible not only the residues of postwar trauma, but the fractures that had existed within Japanese society during imperial rule. In volume one, for instance, Nakazawa contrasts the image of Gen's father holding up a malleable stalk of wheat, a symbol of endurance, with the rising and setting sun of the Japanese Empire, which burns with foreboding on the eve of the bomb. This spherical shape is reflected, in turn, in the faces of servile citizens and punished deserters, indicating a conformity that has been violently imposed.

These contrasts – between violence and rigid conformity, and human endurance and agency – are also transmitted through Nakazawa's style. The gruesome portrayal of the dehumanizing effects of the bomb – molten figures crawl to their deaths, corpses burst in rivers, flesh disintegrates on the walking wounded (see Figure 11.1) – are juxtaposed with Nakazawa's wide-eyed, fluid figures. Bouncing with glee or anger, his characters embody what Thomas LaMarre terms, after Sergei Eisenstein, 'plasticity': a fluidity of movement that captures emotion and agency, rather than maintaining figural integrity.[6] Such 'plasmatic' lines appear to be in the process of dissolution; broken lines or marks express speed or joy in a way that is both gestural and external to the character's body. In *Barefoot Gen* this malleability reflects a form of emotional flexibility or endurance; an ability to heal or recover, literally to bounce back. These visual techniques set the official history of state warfare against individual subjective experiences of trauma and survival.

The domestic dramas that provide the backdrop to the tragic unfolding of events in Nakazawa's work draw in readers, but they also serve the truth that *Barefoot Gen* seeks to communicate. The series conveys the brutal reality of mass death in a form that, as Spiegelman notes in his preface, elicits pleasure through its humour (the violence in the text borders on the slapstick: Gen's father, for example, punches one of Gen's bullying teachers so hard he flies off the walls) – a paradox that complicates the narrative, rather than trivializing it. As Spiegelman notes, the intentionally naïve visualization, like the presentation of Gen's unshaken belief in the triumph of virtue, turns an account of the events of his survival into a reflection on the psychological methods by which he continued to survive. The friendly figures of Nakazawa's Hiroshima reflect the writer's own refusal to lose faith in the goodness of humanity.

Nakazawa has been highly influential on American cartoonists and comics artists. *Barefoot Gen*, which Spiegelman read at the time of creating *Maus*, not only anticipated the thematic of Spiegelman's work on the holocaust (which similarly portrayed family memories of atrocity), but also inspired eye-witness accounts and Western observer-narratives like Joe Sacco's comics journalism on genocide in war-torn Bosnia and the Palestinian territories (*Safe Area Goražde*, 2000; *Palestine*, 2001)[7]. In terms of form, Nakazawa's reach has been still wider. In *Barefoot Gen*, cartoon figures are juxtaposed with realistic backdrops: detailed, architecturally accurate depictions of Hiroshima's cityscapes and surrounding countryside. This combination of simple abstract figures and complex, nearly photo-realistic environments is now so ubiquitous in Japanese comics that the term 'manga', meaning 'comics', has come to be associated globally with this particular aesthetic. This version of manga is now a global phenomenon, embraced by audiences and producers around the world, from Germany and America (occasionally termed 'Euromanga' and 'Amerimanga' respectively) to Brazil and Algeria. This 'global manga' even makes it back to Japan, where 'manga' now encompasses the meanings accrued by the term elsewhere. Graphic novels and narratives from Europe and America that don't follow the style associated with such comics are not sold as manga in Japan, but classified as 'picture books'.[8]

Barefoot Gen's success with readers across the globe has also shaped modes of publication and reception, providing a model for transnational circulation that bypasses established publishing houses. The first translations of *Barefoot Gen*, by Project Gen, a non-profit organization founded in 1976, were initiated by two peace activists, Masahiro Oshima and Yukio Aki, in response to the demand from their American colleagues to make Nakazawa's story more widely available. Volunteer translations continue to contribute to the circulation of comics around the world: manga, in particular, is made freely available to audiences through 'scanlations' – amateur or fan translations scanned and uploaded onto the Internet. These volunteer translations are often driven by socio-political motives. Project Gen sought to reach out to both sides during the Cold War, and many comics today circulate through networks established to achieve similar ends. For example, during the Arab Spring in Egypt in 2011, activists translated and handed out copies of the

Fellowship of Reconciliation's *Martin Luther King and the Montgomery Story* (1953) to spread strategies of civil disobedience.[9]

However, while *Barefoot Gen*'s translation inaugurated the global circulation of manga, its success also raises questions about the ease with which texts can in fact be assimilated into other traditions, or fully understood in translation. In manga, the transition between panels is more often from aspect to aspect (setting the scene or a mood) rather than from action to action and as texts are normally published in *takobon* – thick collections that run to hundreds of pages – they are panel heavy, but text sparse. Such regionally specific systems of graphic representation mean that, although the visual and vernacular grammar of graphic narratives can facilitate or encourage 'the transcendence of limitations' imposed by specific cultures or languages, nuances can nevertheless be lost.[10] The flipping of images or entire pages to meet different directions of reading (left to right in Europe, for example, as opposed to right to left in Japan) can alter facial expressions, situations, and even the perceived narrative progression. Moreover, manga tropes, like the sound effects for blinking and blushing (*piku* and *bo*), often have no equivalent in other languages, raising problems for both the translation of texts and the look of the images, including the visual effect of words – what Jean-Gerald Lapacherie terms *grammatextuality*.[11] Such hurdles expose one of the more prevalent myths about graphic narratives, which is that visual media translate without difficulty across cultures and languages, giving graphic narratives 'a reach that is as democratic as it is immediate'.[12]

We need to remain aware, moreover, that manga is not just a global form of graphic literature, but a globalized one. That is to say, it is now so dominant in the marketplace that some producers perceive regional variance to be at risk. Indeed, Japanese manga and its offshoots have not been universally welcomed by comics artists in other parts of the world. Albert Uderzo's *Asterix and the Falling Sky* (*Le Ciel lui tombe sur la tête*, 2005), for example, pits the Gaul and his fighting companion, Obelix, against alien invaders (nagmas) who try to steal their magic potion. These unwelcome visitors, who take the shape of American superheroes, Walt Disney cartoons, and manga characters, are a clear commentary on the perceived threats to local comics traditions from highly marketized comics genres. The irony, as Mark McKinney points out, is that Uderzo's own series, which follows the Gauls' various acts of resistance against the Roman Empire, was launched at the time of Algeria's War of Independence from France.[13] The irony becomes still greater in view of the fact that, among contemporary Algerian artists, manga offers a medium for telling stories about cultural invasion that does not rely on the artistic legacies of their oppressors: that is to say, the Franco-Belgian tradition of *bande dessinée*. Such national and international cultural battles have long played themselves out in the domain of the graphic narrative. For example, comics regulation in France and America (in the 1940s and 1950s respectively) not only tackled graphic violence and sexually explicit material, but in the former case capped the number of American imports in the comics market.[14]

Barefoot Gen illustrates and has also laid some of the groundwork for some of the ways in which comics circulate and resonate transnationally, occasionally to the detriment of local traditions, whether those in which they originate or those into which they arrive. However, Nakazawa's series has also been an inspiration for the longer historically and politically conscious graphic narratives that followed the establishment of the graphic novel in the 1980s. *Persepolis*, by Marjane Satrapi, and *Bhimayana*, by S. Anand, Srividya Natarajan, and Durgabai and Subhash Vyam, are representative of this trend. From Iran and India respectively, they are, as Edward Said puts it, 'situated in the world and about that world', aware of both the political developments around them and their currency as cultural representations.[15]

Admittedly, this 'worldliness' is not altogether unprecedented, given that contemporary graphic narrative emerged in part out of a satirical cartoon tradition directly shaped by world affairs. One of the two albums by Töpffer that Goethe read, for example, was *Cryptogame*, an imaginative account of a man fleeing his insistent lover only to be swallowed by a whale, captured by Turkish sailors and enslaved by the Algerian sultan. *Cryptogame*, which was first drafted in 1830 during France's initial colonial campaigns in Algeria, reflected the perspectives on the world facilitated by colonial ventures and their associated movements of people and trade. Mr Cryptogame's flight to the ends of the earth (as they appeared to Europeans at the time) set those limits for readers, pre-empting the cartographic impulse that fuelled comics like Hergé's *Adventures of Tintin,* or Marvel's *Captain America.* More recent graphic narratives, however, take to task this impulse and their strategies of representation.

Satrapi's *Persepolis* (published in the original French by L'Association in 2000, and in English translation by Pantheon in 2003) set out to correct the one-sided representation of Iran in global media. As Satrapi explains in her introduction, she wanted to expose her audience to the reality behind the images of fundamentalism, terrorism, and fanaticism that many in the global North associate with the country. In *Persepolis*, she often does this by setting images against text, or by creating visual echoes. For example, in the book's account of the 1979 revolution against the Shah, a text box identifies the revolution as Islamic, but the protesters are represented as rows of identical, two-dimensional citizens, rhyming visually with elements of the pre-Islamic Iranian culture introduced later in her text. The pattern of flattened figures in profile, with their arms raised in identical poses, is reminiscent of the reliefs of subject peoples on the walls of Persepolis, the seat of the ancient Achaemenid Empire. Satrapi's ambivalent imagery thus critiques the Islamic revolution for instilling further conformity and autocracy, and places the protests and her own work in a different regional tradition.

This form of cultural identification is strategic. Contemporary graphic narratives like Satrapi's are in dialogue with their predecessors and the images of the world they popularized. In the early twentieth century, Hergé's illustrations of Tintin, a journalist adventuring around the world with his trusted dog, cemented racist depictions of foreign peoples in Africa, Asia, and the Arab world, while the American government has regularly used comics as propaganda for both military and humanitarian interventions. Most recently, the US military turned to graphic narratives to keep up morale among their forces (collaborating, for example, with Marvel to produce a special edition of *The New Avengers* (2005–2010), a comic for military personnel deployed in Iraq), and to win over foreign populations (soliciting contractors to produce comics targeted at Arab youths during their recent campaigns in Iraq and Afghanistan).[16]

Works such as *Persepolis* are highly conscious of the stereotypes that have been circulated in comics, among other popular media, and in related forms, such as satirical cartoons and caricatures. Having been sent to Austria by her parents to complete her education away from the increasingly restrictive policies of the Islamic regime, Satrapi's protagonist notes that she 'became conscious of the contrast between the official representation of my country and the real life of the people'.[17] The result of this consciousness is a coming-of-age narrative that gives a portrait of Iran and Iranians that turns Western popular assumptions on their heads. As Satrapi has noted in interviews, she especially hoped to reach audiences in the global North, to show that Iran 'has an actual identity, an actual history – and above all, actual people, like me'.[18]

Satrapi uses the easily disseminated and accessible medium of graphic narrative to introduce readers to different, more nuanced perspectives on the world, and she does so through visual strategies that demand her readers pay close attention. *Persepolis* deploys its deceptively simple black and white aesthetic to represent seemingly clear-cut binaries which it then disassembles. This is visible in a panel in which Satrapi uses the black background behind the portrait of a group of stern-faced, bearded men that the narrator suggests is the country's official representation of itself, to bring out the real life that 'went on behind the walls'.[19] Outlines of laughing, dancing, even kissing figures in the black shadows depict an Iran with which her readers might identify.

I REALLY DIDN'T KNOW WHAT TO THINK ABOUT THE VEIL. DEEP DOWN I WAS VERY RELIGIOUS BUT AS A FAMILY WE WERE VERY MODERN AND AVANT-GARDE.

Figure 11.2 **From *Persepolis: The Story of an Iranian Childhood* by Marjane Satrapi published by Jonathan Cape.**

The form of what Gillian Whitlock calls the 'autographic' rests on a kind of objectification that enables artists like Satrapi to explicitly question the systems of exclusion or othering that have marginalized particular voices. All autobiography is constructed, and therefore is about 'the self as another', but the autobiographical 'I' in the graphic narrative, as in cinema, stages this split between the person drawing or directing, and the person represented (in image or by an actor).[20] Comics artists have to view themselves from the outside to create 'self-caricatures'.[21] The autographic therefore invites complicity and scrutiny at the same time. As Charles Hatfield argues, it creates a dialectic where the reader and artist can both occupy the 'I' that narrates from inside through the text boxes and speech bubbles, while having to look at images of the subject from the outside. Satrapi portrays her younger self as split down the middle: her left side a girl with short hair, her right a girl in hijab (see Figure 11.2). These opposing aspects of her identity are projected

189

over different patterns: the objects of scientific measurement (hammers, rulers, etc.), on the one hand, and arabesques, on the other. As such, her portrait plays with the conflicting pressures that bear upon her childhood self and which do not align with the straightforward opposition between reason and culture, freedom and constraint, that her image might initially imply. 'I really didn't know what to think about the veil', the text box notes; 'deep down I was very religious but as a family we were very modern and avant-garde'.[22]

Persepolis continuously performs these sleights of hand, not just with Satrapi's self-portraits but with her family narrative. It juxtaposes seemingly simple images with a wryly self-critical text to reveal more complex and ambiguous realities. For example, while the strict colour code nods visually to the comic *Dialectic Materialism* that Satrapi devours as a child, the text notes her personal struggles to square such Marxist views with her father's Mercedes and the family's maid. In this graphic narrative there are no super-heroes or clear paragons of morality: 'the world is not about Batman and Robin fighting the Joker', Satrapi quips, 'things are more complicated than that'.[23]

In keeping with that complexity, *Persepolis* is not just concerned with critiquing visions of the world that have found currency in a globally domi-nant, Anglophone popular culture; it also works to enhance traditions of cross-cultural dialogue and exchange. The woodcut effect of Satrapi's illus-trations, which critics have likened to both German expressionism and Persian miniatures, balances different aesthetic influences (Satrapi's images reference both Islamic calligraphy and the Christian Pieta), while Satrapi's dark, self-critical humour follows a tradition of confessional comics that first emerged in the American underground (notably with Harvey Pekar, Aline Kominsky-Crumb, and Robert Crumb). If self-caricatures like Satrapi's invite scrutiny from their audiences, they also facilitate identification across differences. In contrast with portraits produced on film or in visual media that aspire to photo-realist accuracy, the simple lines of comics portraits make it easier for readers to place themselves in their protagonist's lives through a process Scott McCloud terms masking. '[We] don't just observe the cartoon', McCloud writes, 'we become it'.[24]

Although Satrapi's autographic uses the familiar tropes of the bildungsro-man or coming-of-age narrative to individualize and humanize her story, depicting childhood adventures and teenage angst, *Persepolis* ultimately has forged its own legacy, diverging from the confessional tradition from which it sprang. It ends with Satrapi and her then husband Reza's project to design a theme park for Tehran, a Disney World using Iranian mythological heroes. While the portrayals of powerful Persian women prevented the project from receiving funding from the Iranian government, these figures lend Satrapi's personal narrative its force. *Persepolis* is an accessible and entertaining work that has both popularized Marji, a rebellious girl in Adidas sneakers and hijab, as a poster child for Iran's youth, and also legitimized the graphic narrative as a platform for otherwise marginalized voices.

A number of Middle Eastern artists subsequently have adopted her signature monochrome style, which likewise helps them to hold cultural contradictions, like pigments, in suspense. Zeina Abirached borrows Satrapi's inky black panels to portray a child's view of the darkness of armed conflict in her memoirs of Beirut's civil war (*A Game For Swallows: To Die, to Leave, to Return* (2012); *I Remember Beirut* (2014)) and Leila Abdelrazaq uses Satrapi's white-on-black reliefs to work the traditional embroideries of her Palestinian heritage into the frames and gutters of *Baddawi* (2015), a work based on her father's memoirs of his youth in a Palestinian refugee camp. As one of the most internationally successful graphic narratives today, Satrapi's work, which has been adapted as an animated film and is the subject of extensive academic study, illustrates the tensions at the heart of a global form which seems to be in many ways more amenable than established literary forms to both commercial and political ends.

If Satrapi's work is an example of a graphic narrative that has been widely translated and disseminated, different insights are available if we consider S. Anand and Srividya Natarajan's *Bhimayana: Experiences of Untouchability – Incidents in the life of Bhimrao Ramji Ambedkar* (2011). *Bhimayana* tells the life-story of the eponymous Dalit reformer and social activist. It does so by drawing on Gond art, which is the traditional art of the Dravidian Dalit communities in central India (the term is derived from 'kond' or 'green mountain').

The book's artists, Durgabai Vyam and Subhash Vyam, belong to these communities, and the book uses Gond art's signature dots and dashes to detail incidents in Ambedkar's life and political activism that have been overshadowed in historical accounts. Its traditional motifs – mainly plant and animal imagery – give Ambedkar's journey to political awakening an almost fabular quality: the train that takes Ambedkar to the city has wheels like snakes, while the speech balloons of the people he encounters are either shaped as doves or scorpions to identify friends or foes. As John Berger comments in his introduction, the earthy colours and tones of the Vyams' palette create a 'conference of corporeal experience' that invites us to enter the body of a community: 'its bloodstream, its organs, its members'.[25]

This is not without some challenges, however. Anand notes that the first version of *Bhimayana* faltered without panels and gutters, the building blocks of comics structure capable of creating the impression of sequential

Figure 11.3 Animal imagery and Gond *digna* in *Bhimayana*.
© Srividya Natarajan, S. Anand, Durgabai Vyam, and Subhash Vyam.
By permission of Navayana.

time. Durgabai and Subhash Vyam therefore turned to Satrapi and Osamu
Tezuka for inspiration, before finding a solution in the traditional *digna*
patterns of their village (see Figure 11.3). The result is a hybrid art form,

which both follows established frameworks of graphic narrative representation and is infused with Pradhan visual codes and customs: *digna* not only echo the shades and patterns found in the village, of *dhan* (grain), *kodo* (mustard seeds), and *moa* grass; they are also traditionally applied to walls and floors in homes, and thus have connotations similar to 'gutters' and 'frames'.

Monika Schmitz-Emans argues that graphic narratives use 'a global language in regionally different dialects'.[26] In Anand and Natarajan's graphic narrative, however, this synthesis is not just a matter of celebrating transculturation, or the blending of traditions. By mixing both art forms and historical accounts of Ambedkar's fight against injustice with clippings from contemporary news about the violence and discrimination Dalits face, the graphic narrative asserts that the unscheduled castes' battle for representation and equal rights remains unfinished. This fusion of a previously neglected regional art form with a commercial and popular narrative framework sharpens both its critique of national culture and its implicit commentary on what constitutes world literature.

Bhimayana challenges nationalist historiography – in particular, the dominant versions of the Indian struggle for independence – and the accepted cultural forms within which such narratives are told. Ambedkar's struggles over water, shelter, and travel in *Bhimayana* are echoed in the forms of discrimination that persist in the present-day cultural sector. For example, one section recounts Ambedkar's march to a public water tank in Mahad (1927) – an act of *satyagraha*, or civil disobedience, to demand equal access for Dalits to water, which predated Gandhi's more famous salt march – while another reflects on the obstacles its artists faced when producing the artwork for the book. The final chapter of *Bhimayana* shows the Gond artists, Durgabai and Subhash Vyam, being turned away by S. Anand's Delhi-based publisher. If the cultural sector has privileged particular narratives over others, graphic narratives are not without their own unequal systems of exchange. Even in comics circles, graphic narratives often have to pass through one of the world centres – America, France, or Japan – to receive global recognition. Moreover, as Anand's afterword indicates, the use of indigenous practices like Gond art can contribute to the commercialization of traditional art forms, where producers like the Vyams are exploited for gains made further down the production chain. Nonetheless, graphic narratives also offer Gond artists a way to earn a living from their skills in a creative process over which they have some control, however indirect.

Bhimayana is much acclaimed abroad, but relatively unknown in India, where its high production value makes it expensive and places limits on its readership. As a consequence, it has been more successful in the global North than in the global South. *Bhimayana* portrays this history of exclusion to reflect on the role of marginal cultures in literary production and canon-formation. It demonstrates how graphic narratives in contemporary world literature can act as an intermedial response to 'high art' or the exclusive parameters within which such categories are determined. *Bhimayana*'s title is a play on the *Ramayana*, the Sanskrit epic poem that tells of the rise and fall of ancient Indian Kingdoms, and which is widely considered to be a paradigmatic instance of 'world literature'. As such, *Bhimayana* joins a number of graphic retellings of the Indian epic (Samhita Arni's *Sita's Ramayana*, Virgin Comics' *Ramayan 3392*, etc.) that challenge the privileging of upper-caste (and, in Arni's case, male) experiences in Indian history and culture. In the case of *Bhimayana*, the reference serves to assert Ambedkar's place in such *itihasas*, or histories, and the place of popular art in national and world literature.

Bhimayana, as the latest expression of a form that started its global life in Nakazawa's translated novel and reached maturity with Satrapi's international bestseller, continues a process of global dialogue and critique. It testifies to cultural interaction and conflict in a form that has itself arisen out of the exchange 'within and not merely between' national cultures and traditions.[27] If we return to Töpffer's picture stories, the history of their appearance in the records of Goethe's remarks are illustrative of the particular role graphic narratives have played in world literature canons and markets. If picture stories were too frivolous to fit with the image of a discerning adjudicator of literary taste that Goethe's associate Eckermann was preserving in his *Conversations* with the writer, Töpffer was unfazed by his exclusion from the first edition of the *Conversations*, and wrote instead a satirical review of one of his albums in the magazine he edited, the *Bibliothèque Universelle de Geneve*. In this mock-review, Töpffer publicized his own work, tongue-in-cheek, by noting Goethe's endorsement. Contemporary graphic narratives continue this tradition of cultural, as well as social, commentary: they both satirize literary texts and establishments, and provide a counter to dominant historical and cultural narratives around the globe. The graphic narrative as world literature thus offers a route for marginal arts as well as marginal voices to receive recognition.

Notes

1. S. McCloud, *Understanding Comics* (New York: HarperPerennial, 1994), p. 9.
2. R. Kyle, 'The Future of "Comics"', *Capa-Alpha, The Comics Amateur Press Association* (November 1964), pp. 3–4.

3. N. O. Power, *God of Comics: Osamu Tezuka and the Creation of Post-War II Manga* (Jackson: University Press of Mississippi, 2009), p. 42.
4. Leonard Rifas from EduComics, the book's English-language publisher, argues that the desire to spread awareness about the dangers of nuclear warfare during the Cold War was a key motivation for publishing the book. Cited in H. E. Jüngst, 'Translating Educational Comics', in F. Zanettin (ed.), *Comics in Translation*, (Manchester, UK and Kinderhook, NY: St. Jerome Publishing, 2008), pp. 172–99 (p. 53).
5. H. Chute, *Disaster Drawn: Visual Witness, Comics, and Documentary Form* (Cambridge, MA: The Belknap Press of Harvard University Press, 2016), p. 26.
6. T. LaMarre, 'Manga Bomb: Between the Lines of Barefoot Gen', in J. Berndt (ed.), *Comics Worlds and the World of Comics* (Kyoto: Kyoto Seika University Press, 2010), pp. 263–307 (p. 282).
7. J. Sacco, *Safe Area Goražde* (Seattle: Fantagraphics Books, 2000); J. Sacco, *Palestine* (London: Jonathan Cape, 2001).
8. J. Berndt, 'Considering Manga Discourse: Location, Ambiguity, Historicity', in M. MacWilliams (ed.), *Japanese Visual Culture: Explorations in the World of Manga and Anime* (Abingdon and New York: Routledge, 2015), pp. 295–310 (p. 299).
9. T. Walker, 'A Graphic History of US Civil Rights – in Comic Book Form', *The Independent* (Sunday 25 January 2015) www.independent.co.uk/arts-entertainment/books/news/a-graphic-history-of-us-civil-rights-in-comic-book-form-10000846.html.
10. D. Stein, S. Denson, and C. Meyer, 'Introducing Transnational Perspectives on Graphic Narratives: Comics at the Crossroads', in D. Stein, S. Denson, and C. Meyer (eds.), *Transnational Perspectives on Graphic Narratives: Comics at the Crossroads* (London: Bloomsbury, 2013), pp. 1–14 (p. 5).
11. J. Baetens and H. Frey discuss Lapacherie's term in *The Graphic Novel: An Introduction* (Cambridge: Cambridge University Press, 2015), pp. 152–153.
12. D. P. Royal, 'Foreword; Or Reading within the Gutter', in F. L. Aldama (ed.), *Multicultural Comics: From Zap to Blue Beetle* (Austin: University of Texas Press, 2010), pp. ix–xi (p. xi).
13. M. McKinney, *History and Politics in French-Language Comics and Graphic Novels* (Jackson: University Press of Mississippi, 2008), p. 17.
14. R. Sabin, *Adult Comics: An Introduction* (London: Routledge, 1993), p. 187.
15. E. Said, 'The Politics of Knowledge', in *Reflections on Exile and Other Literary and Cultural Essays* (London: Granta Books, 2000), pp. 372–385 (p. 375).
16. C. A. Scott, *Comics and Conflict: Patriotism and Propaganda from WWII Through Operation Iraqi Freedom* (Annapolis: Naval Institute Press, 2014), p. 73; and J. Dittmer, *Popular Culture, Geopolitics, and Identity* (Lanham, MD: Rowman and Littlefield Publishers, 2010). Dittmer cites a document from the United States Special Operations Command which comments that 'one effective means of influencing youth [in the Middle East] is through the use of comic books. A series of comic books provides the opportunity for youth to learn lessons, develop role models and improve their education' (p. 2).
17. M. Satrapi, *Persepolis*, A. Singh (trans.) (London: Vintage Books, 2008), p. 304.

18. M. Satrapi, 'How Can One Be Persian?', in L. A. Zanganeh (ed.), *My Sister, Guard Your Veil; My Brother, Guard Your Eyes: Uncensored Iranian Voices* (Boston: Beacon Press, 2006), pp. 20–23 (p. 23).

19. Satrapi, *Persepolis*, p. 304.

20. L. H. Rugg, 'Picturing Oneself as Another', in M. A. Chaney (ed.), *Graphic Subjects: Critical Essays on Autobiography and Graphic Novels* (Madison: University of Wisconsin Press, 2011), pp. 73–75 (p. 74).

21. C. Hatfield, *Alternative Comics: An Emerging Literature* (Jackson: University Press of Mississippi, 2005), p. 114.

22. Satrapi, *Persepolis*, p. 6.

23. J. Bearman, 'Marjane Satrapi: Graphic Novelist', *The Believer* (August 2006) www.believermag.com/issues/200608/?read=interview_satrapi.

24. S. McCloud, *Understanding Comics,* p. 36.

25. J. Berger, 'Foreword', in S. Anand, S. Natarajan, D. Vyam and S. Vyam, *Bhimayana: Incidents in the Life of Bhimrao Ramji Ambedkar* (New Delhi: Navayana Publishing, 2014).

26. M. Schmitz-Emans, 'Graphic Narrative as World Literature', in D. Stein and J. Thon (eds.), *From Comic Strips to Graphic Novels: Contributions to the Theory and History of Graphic Narrative* (Gottingen: Walter De Gruyter, 2013), pp. 385–406 (p. 387).

27. Stein, Denson, Meyer, 'Transnational Perspectives', p. 3.

12

SHITAL PRAVINCHANDRA

Short Story and Peripheral Production

If world literature is the study of literary forms and individual works that travel outside the region in which they were produced, as most recent theorizations would have it, then the short story ought to figure prominently in the field. After all, it is a literary form that is at least as ubiquitous as the novel, and its brevity allows for swift translation and for circulation in a wide range of media, including print magazines, journals, radio, and increasingly, the Internet. Yet, despite its apparent ripeness for inclusion in our discussions of world literature, the short story typically is absent. Franco Moretti famously chooses to make the novel the test-case for his study of literary diffusion, while Pascale Casanova makes room for drama (Shaw, O'Casey, Soyinka) and poetry (Yeats, Darío, Tagore) but focuses overwhelmingly on the novel. David Damrosch organizes the first three chapters of *How to Read World Literature* (2009) explicitly in terms of the genres of lyric poetry, epic, and drama, respectively, while the second half of his book, dedicated to prose fiction, seamlessly moves between discussing novels and short stories without much regard for their generic differences.

Scholars of the short story have long noted that the form is not granted the cultural prestige reserved for other literary genres.[1] A quick glance at the history of the Nobel Prize in Literature, the ultimate means of international literary consecration, suggests that this is true. Before 2013, when Alice Munro won the prize, no Nobel laureate had been recognized for their commitment to the form. (Jorge Luis Borges, perhaps the most widely celebrated of all short story writers, never won it.) We might well conclude, despite the notable and welcome exception of the Caine Prize, to which I will return below, that the exclusion of the short story from discussions of world literature simply reproduces the inattention to the form that is largely in evidence throughout the world republic of letters.[2]

The short story is often regarded, for writers and readers alike, 'as a training or practice genre'; that is, as a launching pad for progression to the longer and (supposedly) more difficult form of the novel.[3] As Mary

Louise Pratt and Lyudmila Parts have pointed out, however, thanks to this reputation, the short story truly comes into its own only in pedagogical settings. The 'classroom-friendly' nature of the short story effectively means that 'a great number of short story collections perform the honourable function of initiating students into the study of literature'.[4] The study of world literature, it seems, is no exception. The short story performs admirably in the pedagogy-oriented anthologies of world literature, where space is tight and there is a need to cover an unprecedented geographical range. Of the nineteen selections housed under the rubric of 'Modernity and Modernism, 1900–1945' in Volume F of *The Norton Anthology of World Literature,* twelve are short stories. Ten of these hail from Asia and Latin America, and have been variously translated from Japanese, Chinese, Korean, Hindi, and Spanish; the remaining two stories are by James Joyce and William Faulkner, both of whom are named in Casanova's study as notable outliers who eventually went on to be consecrated in the metropolitan centres of Paris and London that she analyses. The Norton anthology's main competitor, *The Longman Anthology of World Literature,* also prominently features the short story. Volume F, dedicated to the twentieth century, contains thirty-five short stories, twenty-one of which represent countries in Asia, Africa, South America, or the Caribbean.[5] As far as world literature is concerned, then, the short story's unenviable predicament is to be over-represented in the classroom but overlooked in its critical scholarship.

World literature scholarship is clearly more at ease when genres with greater prestige bear the weighty claims about global literary relations and patterns of literary circulation, whilst being relatively content to task the short story with the burden of regional representation in its textbooks. This reveals the rifts between the texts upon which its theories are based and those through which students see world literature in practice, and could certainly lead to interesting discussions about the problems associated with 'doing' world literature, especially when the purpose of the short story in anthologies seems, at times, to be little more than extending the range of countries included in the overall selection. It would also be worth pondering the fact that it has fallen overwhelmingly to the short story – the least prestigious of genres – to represent the world beyond Europe and North America.[6]

My goal in this chapter, however, is somewhat different. I want to identify certain important questions about world literature that a focus on the short story can raise. My main claim is that, as a world literary genre, the short story speaks not to literary consecration and the consolidation of reputations but, rather, to the *conditions* of literary production, consumption, and distribution that contribute to the creation and perpetuation of the current world literary system, which Moretti rightly characterizes as 'one and unequal'.[7] I begin by examining the brevity or the 'economy' of the short story in relation both to the economic status of its readers and its importance in places where infrastructural shortcomings mean there are few local outlets for the publication of fiction. Looking more closely at the material conditions of literary production and consumption, I suggest, reveals that the short story is an especially important form in some of the 'peripheral' countries included in world literature anthologies, precisely because its brevity can facilitate publication and circulation.

This inevitably leads to the second important subject I consider here: the medium of the magazine or journal. As H. E. Bates has stated, the magazine gave the short story a platform, without which it could never have flourished.[8] As I will also argue, however, in certain non-metropolitan regions, magazines, and the short stories within them, were, and remain, instrumental in shaping national literary canons and traditions. They therefore trouble the questionable if widely held assumption in literary studies that the novel form is synonymous with a properly mature national literature. I dedicate the final portion of the chapter to considering more closely the interesting 'coincidence' between writing in a European language, choosing the novel form, and gaining international recognition. I suggest that, in combination, these factors have much to do with the critical neglect of the short story form, despite the fact that it is such a vital genre in so many literary traditions.

'Novels are read by people who have money, and those who have money also have time. Short stories are written for ordinary people, who have neither money, nor time.' This remarkable pronouncement was made by Premchand, the most famous of all Hindi-Urdu writers, and author of nine novels, more than 150 short stories, and numerous essays, of which several are dedicated to the 'art of the short story'.[9] In line with his commitment to social reform and raising awareness about the plight of the socially disadvantaged, Premchand's writings on the short story identify a fundamental link between socio-economic class and literary genre that is echoed by other materialist critics. Timothy Brennan, for instance, has written that 'under conditions of illiteracy and shortages, and given simply the leisure time required for reading one, the novel has been an elitist and minority form in developing countries'.[10] In a similar vein, Caribbean literature scholar Kenneth Ramchand asserts that 'the preference for the short story is in part a function of living and working conditions'.[11] And, writing about the Caine Prize for African Literature, its director, Lizzy Attree, notes that the short story seems an especially appropriate genre to showcase contemporary African writing, because 'when one considers that Africa is becoming increasingly urbanized, the short story can be used to reflect the experiences of *time-poor* people who work in some of Africa's mega-cities'.[12]

To account for what he sees as the 'disproportionate' number of short stories in the literatures of colonial and postcolonial cultures, Adrian Hunter suggests that it is vital to consider the socio-economic situations of these regions.[13] In areas where publication means are scarce, cheaper-to-produce formats, such as the pamphlet and the magazine, often become especially important venues for fiction publication. 'In cultures with small or non-existent publishing infrastructures', he states, 'the low-capital, low-circulation literary magazine tends to be the main outlet for new writing. Such magazines, for reasons of space and means of production, invariably favour the short story over longer forms of fiction.'[14] Hunter's observations are equally pertinent in today's Internet age. Helon Habila has observed that the Internet has seen a veritable boom of the short story in Africa, adding that 'the Internet, due to its own peculiar restrictions, seems actually to favour stories over novels, thereby reversing the restrictions that traditional publishing had placed on African fiction'.[15] It is precisely in recognition of this state of affairs, Attree explains, that the Caine Prize, which does not accept previously unpublished entries, altered its rules to allow authors to enter stories that had been previously published online.[16]

The Caine Prize, which is a cash award for the best African short story in English (including translations), has certainly increased the visibility of African short stories in first-world metropolitan centres. It has been criticized, however, for inculcating a mentality of dependence. Binyavanga Wainaina, winner of the prize in 2002, recently chided Anglophone Africa's literati for their 'addiction' to the prize. Binyavanga used his prize money to found *Kwani?*, an online literary magazine based in his native Kenya, with the aim of providing a locally based publishing platform, where the short story features prominently. Such initiatives might be 'vastly under-funded and vastly *ungrown*', but are nevertheless 'the ones [to] create the ground that is building these new writers'.[17]

Africa's thriving online short story culture alerts us to the necessity of considering the material conditions of literary production, conditions which are no less pertinent to a study of earlier formats. I turn now to one such, the print magazine, in order to highlight how the short stories published in this format often played an instrumental, if largely unrecognized role in shaping the *national* literatures of so many regions of the non-European world. It is instructive to begin with the example of Edgar Allan Poe, who was not only an early pioneer of the short story, but also one of the first to attempt its definition. What is less often remarked upon, however, is that Poe turned to the short story precisely because it was the only form that would easily allow him to create an independent and distinctly American literary product that was not in direct competition with a European counterpart. 'International copyright law', Martin Scofield explains, 'allowed publishers to pirate British work and print it cheaply, putting original American novels at a disadvantage'.[18] Rather than Moretti's 'law' of formal evolution through dispersal, it was the combination of European cultural prestige and a loophole in copyright law that pushed Poe towards the short story as a vehicle for creating a national literature and readership. This inventiveness fortunately coincided, according to H. E. Bates, with the emergence of the 'Public' and of the magazine.

This vital convergence was also seen elsewhere. In her pioneering study of the rise of the Hindi public sphere in the twenty years between 1920 and 1940, Francesca Orsini, for instance, notes that 'it is hard to overestimate the centrality journals acquired in Hindi literary life in these decades. Most, if not all, of the Hindi literature of the 1920s and 1930s appeared first in journals.'[19] Hindi journals were, of course, also crucial in forging a spirit of anti-colonial nationalism, but equally significant for my purposes is that, as Orsini argues, '[s]hort stories, universally acknowledged to be what made journals sell, were practically created as a genre' by such pioneering Hindi journals as *Madhuri* and *Saraswati*.[20] Similarly, in his self-avowedly 'drastic' argument that 'there are no West Indian novelists, only short story writers in disguise', Kenneth Ramchand focuses on the importance of magazines for West Indian readers. '[E]ven before the emergence of *Bim* (1942), *Kyk-over-al* (1945), *Focus* (1943, 1948, 1956, and 1960), and the BBC's *Caribbean Voices* [radio] program, in all of which the strength of the West Indian short story tradition is obvious', he observes, 'there were, in the 1920s and 1930s, in all the islands, small magazines dedicated to cultivating poetry and the short story'. He notes that the 'exchanges, reprints and reciprocal advertisements' that took place amongst these journals forged the sense of a shared literary heritage across the Anglophone Caribbean, even as the journals were also embedded in distinct Jamaican or Trinidadian traditions.[21]

Bates, Orsini, and Ramchand each highlight the all-important constellation of print, nationalism, and a community of readers, which is, famously, the subject of *Imagined Communities*, Benedict Anderson's canonical and world-encompassing argument about the global rise of nationalism. While Anderson links the emergence of national 'imagined communities' to the birth of print-capitalism, his examples refer continually to the novel and the newspaper. Due to their ability to forge in the individual mind the notion of existing in a community with a shared past and common future, both the newspaper and the novel, Anderson claims, 'provided the technical means for "re-presenting" the *kind* of imagined community that is the nation'.[22] If the importance of the short story and the magazine in the American, the South Asian, and the Caribbean contexts already exposes a gap in

Anderson's argument, two other considerations reveal this omission as even more noteworthy.

First, Anderson's regional area of expertise – Indonesia – has been described by many of its literary scholars as a place where short stories have long been dominant. E. U. Kratz, for example, characterizes Indonesian literature as 'a literature of short stories' and goes on to note that 'in fact, modern Indonesian literature has been called a magazine-literature (sastra majalah) as much of it has been disseminated through magazines and journals'.²³ Anderson's theoretical omission of the short story, however, becomes all the more intriguing when we realize that it is precisely the Indonesian short story that serves as one of his examples of national imagination at work. When drawing on Spanish-language novels by the Filipino writer José Rizal and the Mexican author José Joaquín Fernández de Lizardi, respectively, Anderson is at pains to emphasize the broad pertinence of his argument. He then points to the short stories of the Indonesian nationalist writer Mas Marco Kartodikromo in order to show that his argument applies equally to literary works in non-European languages.²⁴

Anderson's silence about the genre of Marco's fiction serves as another reminder of how the short story is continually overlooked when far-reaching, world-encompassing arguments are at stake. The use of a short story to illustrate the Indonesian context also reinforces my claim that there are some regions where the short story is more culturally necessary than other genres. If the short story has been overlooked in world literature scholarship, this seems to be a symptom mostly of the expectations around what properly constitutes literature. Like the metropolitan consecration of peripheral authors that Casanova analyses, these expectations and assumptions are invariably defined in the metropole. And, typically, these criteria derive from and presume literary systems based on the ready availability of print and its widespread consumption.

For writers who choose the short story genre, this means that their works are highly unlikely to circulate outside of the geographical regions in which they were produced. As a consequence, metropolitan preferences and standards can impinge upon the actual generic choice of writers from the periphery, especially when they are intent on obtaining a metropolitan readership. Ramchand claims that the short story stopped being the preferred mode for West Indian writers only when they began to emigrate to London in the 1950s. He detects in these early West Indian novels 'episodic' qualities that are symptomatic of the émigré writer's greater ease and familiarity with the short story form.²⁵

The global plight of the Caribbean and the Indonesian short story provides an interesting contrast to the Indian situation, to which I shall now turn.

The central point of difference concerns the languages of literary production in all three regions. While the Caribbean presents a paradigmatic case of linguistic colonialism insofar as the region's literary production overwhelmingly occurs in the standard or creolized forms of cosmopolitan imperial languages (English, French, Spanish, and Dutch), Indonesia is a significant exception in the history of European colonialism because, today, Dutch plays little part in its national cultural production. Modern Indonesian literature is mostly written in Bahasa Indonesia, a modernized form of Malay. In neither case is there the same degree of co-existence, within the same national space, of literatures written both in the 'vernaculars' and in a metropolitan language, which is the state of affairs that we confront in the Indian context.

Anglophone South Asian literature's overshadowing of the subcontinent's *bhasha* literatures has often been denounced.[26] That this might have something to do with the fact that the *novel* is Indian Anglophone literature's genre of choice is less often commented upon. As Orsini has observed, Moretti's preoccupation with the novel means that he cannot properly address the South Asian context. The novel simply is not the genre through which the major developments in Indian literature have transpired. On the subcontinent, she continues, 'the major nineteenth- and twentieth-century forms have been poetry, drama and the short story'.[27] Aamir Mufti similarly takes Moretti to task for his focus on the novel, noting that South Asia is one region where this picture is complicated, especially given the fact that in Urdu and Hindi 'the otherwise "minor" form of the short story has long held some of the preeminence associated elsewhere with the "major" form of the novel'.[28]

Evidence for the importance of the short story form in India's *bhasha* languages can be seen everywhere. Entire literary movements in India have hinged on the short story. The genre was central to the reformist and socially committed writings of the pan-Indian Progressive Writers' Movement of the 1930s; the outpouring of short stories in the wake of the subcontinent's partition in 1947 forms an indispensable literary archive with which to study that event; and the formal literary innovations used to express a growing sense of disillusionment with independence were introduced largely through the short story in the *nayi kahāni* (New Short Story) movement of the 1950s and 1960s. Anecdotally, we might also consider Girish Karnad's 2004 play *Broken Images* (*Odakalu Bimba* in Karnad's own translation into Kannada). The work features Manjula Nayak, a Kannada writer who finds sudden, overnight, and global success when she publishes a novel in English. The play examines the resentment that Manjula experiences from those who feel she has 'betrayed' Kannada by switching to English, and has been read as a valuable commentary on the politics of language in India.[29] More significant for my purposes is an aspect that might easily be overlooked: Karnad makes it clear that, before switching to the Anglophone novel, Manjula is primarily known 'as a renowned Kannada short-story writer'.[30]

Scholarship on India's *bhasha* literatures also confirms the ubiquity of the short story. Priyamvada Gopal's *Literary Radicalism in India* (2004) and Toral Gajarawala's *Untouchable Fictions* (2012), rare specimens insofar as they are book-length studies of Indian *bhasha* literatures produced by academics working in Anglo-American university literature departments, also foreground the short story form. Gopal's study of the All-India Progressive Writers' Association notes that an important catalyst for the literary radicalism of 1940s India was an infamous anthology of short stories, *Angārey* (*Live Coals*).[31] Gopal's analysis of the literary movement that flourished in India during the lead-up to independence prominently features the short story, most notably the works of Saadat Hassan Manto and Rashid Jahan. Gajarawala's study of Hindi Dalit fiction makes explicit mention of the importance of the short story form for the Dalit movement.[32] Identifying in certain strands of Hindi Dalit literature 'a willful disinterest in the novel', Gajarawala conjectures that Dalit writers find in the short story tools particularly suited to the Dalit political project.[33] She suggests that the form enables Dalits to embrace the possibilities of realism, which can represent the social workings of caste oppression in order to facilitate critique and transformation, but the genre's intrinsic brevity also allows writers to circumvent the problem of narrative development needed to show the emergence of a Dalit consciousness. In Dalit fiction, claims Gajarawala, Dalit consciousness (*chetnā*) is always an already-existing state of mind.[34]

A short story in Hindi by Dalit writer Ajay Navaria serves as my example of the relevance of the genre in India.[35] Aptly entitled '*Uttarkathā*' (literally, 'A Story in Response'), Navaria's story articulates its pithy reply to the oppression of Dalits with explicit intertextual references that perfectly illustrate the centrality of the short story in Indian *bhasha* literatures. Navaria belongs to the younger generation of Dalit writers in Hindi and his fiction, unlike that of many of his predecessors, centres not on village caste politics but on the negotiation of caste in the city. His characters often speak English as well as Hindi, and their experience of caste often manifests not as a concrete struggle against caste discrimination but as a persistent form of alienation and malaise. Many of these traits are recognizable in '*Uttarkathā*', in which the young narrator's caste origins are left deliberately vague, even though he is obviously sympathetic to the Dalit cause. The main story is framed by an anecdote in which the narrator encounters a man who bears a strong resemblance to Premchand, the socially committed Hindi-Urdu writer whose work features a host of low-caste and 'untouchable' characters.

Upon questioning, the lookalike insists that he is not actually Premchand, but his discomfort suggests that he is deliberately trying to remain anonymous. Looking anxious, he pulls a book out of his bag. 'Whatever else happens in this world, Bhangis will always remain Bhangis', he reads, explaining that this pronouncement is not made by Premchand but by an upper-caste character in Premchand's story '*Dūdh kā Dām*' ('The Price of Milk').[36] Next, the man pulls out some papers from his bag. 'That was the earlier story; this is the story in response', he says, handing the sheets to the narrator.

The bulk of '*Uttarkathā*' comprises the narrator's transcription of the manuscript obtained from the man-who-cannot-admit-to-being-Premchand. Like Premchand's 'The Price of Milk' ('*Dūdh kā Dām*'), it is the story of a young Bhangi boy, Mangal. In that earlier story, Mangal is forced to live off leftovers when, as an infant, his mother becomes the wet-nurse for the male son of an upper-caste family, leaving her with very little milk for her own son. When Mangal grows up, he must survive on the leftovers of this same upper-caste family. At the end of the story, the boy resolves never again to accept the family's leftovers, only to give in when hunger gets the better of him. Navaria's pointed 'story in response', however, envisions a scenario where Premchand himself is compelled to revise his original story to depict Mangal as a man who escapes his supposedly sealed fate as a Bhangi. The new story shows us a Mangal who fulfils his mother's wish for him to do only the kind of work that will bring him respect. Here, Mangal is eventually appointed to the Indian civil service, a feat he accomplishes thanks to help from a community of mentors, relatives, and teachers.

Although 'The Price of Milk' is Navaria's main intertext in '*Uttarkathā*', the informed reader will soon recognize a range of other familiar Premchand characters in the text: Ghisu and Madhav, from Premchand's renowned story '*Kafan*' ('The Shroud'), Jokhu and Gangi, from his '*Ṭhākur kā Kuām̐*' ('The Thakur's Well'), Halku from '*Pūs kī Rāt*' ('January Night'), Pandit Moteram Shastri from '*Paṇḍit Moṭerām Shāstrī kā Satyāgraha*' ('A Moral Victory'), and also the kindly, low-caste character Devidin from Premchand's novel *Gaban* (*Embezzlement*).[37] But Navaria's story offers alternative plotlines for all of Premchand's narratives, rendering the once pitiful 'Bhangi' characters into figures who support Dalit emancipation, and ensuring that the higher-caste characters get their comeuppance. Navaria's story, then, transforms the way in which the reader perceives Premchand's downtrodden protagonists. And here lies the root of the Dalit critique of Premchand. Celebrated as the socially conscious writer who realized the importance of turning his narrative gaze to figures such as the peasant, the 'untouchable' and the prostitute, Premchand is widely credited with bringing a realist, reformist vision to North Indian literature. But, as Gajarawala explains, the Dalit critics of Premchand refuse to be satisfied with mere narrative inclusion. They refuse 'the narrative mode' in which the Dalit is featured, always 'pitiable, downtrodden, insulted'.[38]

I have chosen to focus on this story because it illustrates admirably Gajarawala's claim that 'In Dalit literature, everything is metanarrative'.[39] It also offers a clear example of how much of that intertextual archive consists of short stories, testifying, in its metafictional subversion of Premchand's plots, to the importance of the form in India. In fact, 'Uttarkathā' will make very little sense unless one is acquainted with the representation of Dalits in a range of Hindi/Urdu short stories to which Navaria is explicitly writing back. It is for this reason that Laura Brueck's translation of Navaria's story resorts to rendering its title as 'Hello Premchand!', which gestures to the work's intertextual referents without requiring an explicative paratextual commentary.[40]

The story also reveals that a full appreciation of 'Uttarkathā' and its complex narrative strategy requires that the reader be familiar with a specifically local set of circumstances: caste oppression and a community-wide resolve to radically alter Premchand's towering reputation as a committed and concerned advocate of the oppressed. However, it would be a mistake to see in Dalit literature only a resolutely regional or local set of concerns. To circumscribe Dalit literature's remit in this way would be to ignore that its radical stance against caste discrimination forms part of a much larger network of political literature. As Gajarawala argues:

> Dalit literature is poised between a regionalism that revels in local dialect and the nontransferable specificity of caste conditioning, on the one hand, and *a broad universalism that invokes a certain global paradigm of protest (both politically and culturally)*, on the other. Studies of Dalit literature must thus confront the contradiction between Dalit particularity, specificity, and singularity, and Dalit humanism that opens its ranks to many others.[41]

Scholars have fruitfully compared the political demands and cultural correctives issued by Dalit literature to Latin American *testimonio* narratives and to African-American literature.[42] Dalit narratives themselves invite such comparisons. In a telling incident in Navaria's short story 'Scream' ('*Chīkh*'), for example, the Dalit protagonist's anthropology professor compares him to a black man in order to ridicule him before his classmates.[43] Here, Navaria makes a virtue of the local specificity of Dalit oppression, using it to forge a literary practice through which his work can be likened to the literatures of other communities with long histories of oppression. Focusing on the alternative global patterns of circulation, consumption, and influence that

Navaria explicitly gestures to in a story like 'Scream' gives a very different view of world literature, where the historical and regional specificities of protest do not hinder comprehension but serve instead to facilitate it.

Dalit literature reminds its readers that being anchored in the specificity of the local does not preclude awareness of literary traditions from elsewhere around the globe. In the alternative world literary networks they seek to forge, Dalit authors draw careful attention to their own cultural context, rather than wearing this context 'rather lightly', as Damrosch would have it.[44] By suggesting that cultural context gets in the way of global circulation, Damrosch effectively shuts out certain kinds of political literary texts from the carefully guarded realm of world literature, a consequence that is especially lamentable because it curbs one of the most exciting possibilities of the advent of world literature: 'the potentially radical expansion of the degrees and types of aesthetic value appreciable in metropolitan centres'.[45] Furthermore, as shown by the centrality of the short story to the Dalit literary and political project, to shut out literatures imbued with local cultural content is also to foreclose conversations about *genre*. This becomes especially significant when we consider that the majority of Anglo-American university students who encounter Dalit characters will do so through Arundhati Roy's Anglophone novel *The God of Small Things*, a work often critiqued in Dalit studies for its portrayal of 'untouchables' in a sympathetic but ultimately pitiable light.

This is, perhaps, a fitting point to examine more closely the selection of South Asian stories in Volume F of *The Norton Anthology of World Literature*. The volume contains three short stories from the subcontinent. One is by Premchand; the other two are Saadat Hasan Manto's 'Toba Tek Singh' and Mahasweta Devi's 'Giribala'. Understanding the significance of the presence of Manto's story requires a brief digression to a commemorative anthology of Indian writing compiled by Salman Rushdie and Elizabeth West in celebration of India's fifty years of independence. Today, their selection is best known for its introduction, where Rushdie makes his infamous claim that 'the prose writing – both fiction and non-fiction – created in this period [between 1947 and 1997] by Indian writers in English is proving to be a stronger and more important body of work than most of what has been produced in the eighteen "recognised" languages of India, the so-called "vernacular languages," during the same time'.[46] The sole exception Rushdie makes, however, is to include Manto's Urdu short story 'Toba Tek Singh'. Mahasweta Devi, too, is a name familiar to most (postcolonial) scholars in Western academia thanks to Gayatri Spivak's translations of her short stories, and her theorizations of subalternity that draw on these same translations. The story the Norton includes is, admittedly, not one that

Spivak has discussed, but its selection, like that of 'Toba Tek Singh', never-theless testifies to the fact that inclusion in the canon of world literature continues to require metropolitan approval.

Once we move away from the sphere of world literature anthologies, we start to realize that there is a major distinction to be made between the norms of world literature scholarship and actual world literary *practice*. The former operates according to consolidated metropolitan literary preferences and widely accepted literary-historical narratives, whereas the latter, as I have tried to show, is impinged upon by material conditions, specific cultural practices, and local politics – all issues that world literary scholarship rarely takes into account. Of course, this is hardly the first critique of the logic of metropolitan consecration demanded by world literature, nor is it the first indictment of the market logic that sees world literature include only those works whose 'differences' are easily assimilated. What I have hoped to show by discussing the short story in the world's peripheral regions, however, is that genre – especially the genre-based narrative that links novel to nation – has *everything* to do with the texts that world literature scholarship deems worthy of study, and with which works circulate in the world republic of letters.

Notes

1. See especially M. L. Pratt's excellent article 'The Short Story: The Long and Short of It', in C. E. May (ed.), *The New Short Story Theories* (Athens: Ohio University Press, 1994), pp. 91–114.
2. For specifics about the Caine Prize and its rules, see http://caineprize.com.
3. Pratt, 'The Short Story', p. 97.
4. L. Parts, 'Introduction: The Short Story as the Genre of Cultural Transition', in L. Parts (ed.), *The Russian Twentieth-Century Short Story: A Critical Companion* (Brighton, MA: Academic University Press, 2010), pp. xiii–xxviii (p. xiii).
5. Given that their stories are anthologized in order to offer perspectives from their countries of origin, I have included the stories of emigrant and diasporic writers such as Salman Rushdie and Jamaica Kincaid in this count.
6. Additionally, the Longman anthology chooses the short story to represent the work of authors who belong to 'minority' groups in Western nations. Native Americans are a case in point: the anthology contains several short stories by Gerald Vizenor and Leslie Marmon Silko, for instance.
7. F. Moretti, 'Conjectures on World Literature', *New Left Review*, 1 (2000), 54–68 (p. 56).
8. H. E. Bates, *The Modern Short Story from 1809–1953* (London: Robert Hale Ltd, 1988), p. 31.
9. This series of essays is entitled '*Kahāni Kalā*' ('The Art of the Short Story'). This quote comes from the first of them, '*Kahāni Kalā 1*', translation mine. See Premchand, *Kuch Vichār*, (Delhi/Allahabad: Saraswati Press, 1985), p. 29.

10. T. Brennan, 'The National Longing for Form', in H. K. Bhabha (ed.), *Nation and Narration* (New York: Routledge, 1994), pp. 44–70 (p. 56).

11. K. Ramchand, 'The West Indian Short Story', *Journal of Caribbean Literatures*, 1.1 (1997), 21–33 (p. 23).

12. L. Attree, 'The Caine Prize and Contemporary African Writing', *Research in African Literatures*, 44.2 (2013), 35–47 (p. 43), emphasis added. Attree's focus on urban centres is also meant to dispel the notion that the Caine Prize's attention to the short story posits a (patronizing) link between the short story and African folktale and oral culture.

13. A. Hunter, *The Cambridge Introduction to the Short Story in English* (Cambridge: Cambridge University Press, 2007), p. 138.

14. Hunter, *Introduction*, p. 138.

15. H. Habila, *The Granta Book of the African Short Story* (London: Granta Books, 2011), p. xi.

16. Attree, 'The Caine Prize and Contemporary African Writing', p. 38.

17. See http://thisisafrica.me/lifestyle/must-stop-giving-legitimacy-caine-prize-binyavanga/. *Writivism* is another African-based initiative that awards annual prizes for the best short story, for poetry in translation, and for non-fiction. See https://writivism.org.

18. M. Scofield, *The Cambridge Introduction to the American Short Story* (Cambridge: Cambridge University Press, 2006), p. 6.

19. F. Orsini, *The Hindi Public Sphere, 1920–1940: Language and Literature in the Age of Nationalism* (New Delhi and New York: Oxford University Press, 2002), p. 52.

20. Orsini, *The Hindi Public Sphere*, p. 56.

21. Ramchand, 'The West Indian Short Story', p. 25. See also Lucy Evans's introduction to *The Caribbean Short Story: Critical Perspectives* (Leeds: Peepal Tree Press, 2011), pp. 11–25.

22. B. Anderson, *Imagined Communities* (London: Verso, 1991), p. 25.

23. E. U. Kratz, 'The Indonesian Short Story after 1945', in J. H. C. S. Davidson and H. Cordell (eds.), *The Short Story in South-East Asia: Aspects of a Genre* (London: SOAS Publications, 1982), pp. 139–165 (pp. 139–140).

24. Anderson, *Imagined Communities*, pp. 30–36.

25. Ramchand, 'The West Indian Short Story', p. 22.

26. For a cogent critique of this phenomenon, see A. Ahmad, 'Indian Literature: Notes Towards the Definition of a Category', in *In Theory – Classes, Nations, Literatures* (London: Verso, 1992), pp. 243–287.

27. F. Orsini, 'India in the Mirror of World Fiction', *New Left Review*, 13 (2002), 75–83 (p. 79).

28. A. Mufti, *Forget English! Orientalisms and World Literatures* (Cambridge: Harvard University Press, 2016), p. 131.

29. G. Karnad, *Broken Images*, in *Collected Plays*, Vol. 2 (Oxford: Oxford University Press, 2005), pp. 261–284.

30. *Broken Images*, p. 262.

31. P. Gopal, *Literary Radicalism in India* (Abingdon: Routledge, 2005), p. 15.

32. The term Dalit, meaning 'downtrodden' in Marathi, has a political valence and is deliberately used by the community in place of other words such as 'untouchable' or '*Harijan*' (a term coined by Gandhi). See E. Zelliot, 'Dalit Literature,

Language and Identity', in B. B. Kachru et al. (eds.), *Language in South Asia* (Cambridge: Cambridge University Press, 2008), pp. 450–465.

33. T. Gajarawala, *Untouchable Fictions* (New York: Fordham University Press, 2013), p. 54.

34. For more on Dalit *chetnā*, a complex term in Dalit studies, see Laura Brueck's *Writing Resistance: The Rhetorical Imagination of Hindi Dalit Literature* (New York: Columbia University Press, 2014).

35. Navaria holds a PhD from Jawaharlal Nehru University and teaches in Delhi's Jamia Millia Islamia University's Hindi department. He is the author of a novel, *Udhar ke log* (2008), and two short story collections, *Paṭkathā aur anya Kahāniyāṁ* (2006) and *Yes Sir* (2012).

36. '*Uttarkathā*,' in *Yes Sir* (New Delhi: Samayik Prakashan, 2012), p. 88. All translations from '*Uttarkathā*' are mine. The derogatory term 'Bhangi' refers to sweepers and latrine cleaners.

37. *Gaban* and all of these stories, as well as 'The Price of Milk', are collected, in English translation, in *The Oxford India Premchand* (New Delhi: Oxford University Press, 2004).

38. Gajarawala, *Untouchable Fictions*, p. 8.

39. Gajarawala, *Untouchable Fictions*, p. 1.

40. See A. Navaria, *Unclaimed Terrain*, L. Brueck (trans.) (New Delhi: Navayana Publishing, 2013), pp. 123–155.

41. Gajarawala, *Untouchable Fictions*, p. 3, emphasis added.

42. See P. K. Nayer, 'The Poetics of Postcolonial Atrocity: Dalit Life Writing, *Testimonio* and Human Rights', *Ariel*, 42.3–4 (2012), 237–264; and M. Desai, 'Caste in Black and White: Dalit Identity and the Translation of African American Literature', *Comparative Literature*, 67.1 (2015), 94–113.

43. '*Chīkh*' was first published in 2005 in the Hindi journal *Haṁs*. It later appeared, in a modified version, in *Paṭkathā aur anya Kahāniyāṁ*. 'Scream', the English translation, appears in *Unclaimed Terrain*.

44. 'Works of world literature are best read with an awareness of the work's original cultural context, but they typically wear this context rather lightly.' D. Damrosch, *What is World Literature?* (Princeton: Princeton University Press, 2003), p. 139.

45. T. Brennan, 'The Cuts of Language: The East/West of North/South', *Public Culture*, 13.1 (2001), 39–63 (p. 59).

46. S. Rushdie and E. West (eds.), *The Vintage Book of Indian Writing 1947–97* (London: Vintage, 1997), p. x.

13

KEYA GANGULY

World Cinema, World Literature, and Dialectical Criticism

The Model of the World-System

The topic of world cinema has returned to gather new energy in scholarly discussions. Calling it a return allows me to offer two observations as the starting point of this chapter. First, the idea of world cinema has been around for a long time, as a nominal way to refer to films made outside Hollywood and, in some cases, outside Europe.[1] In this incarnation, 'world cinema' has served as an umbrella term for institutionalizing the even more ambiguous category of 'foreign films', thereby bringing a wider selection of objects into cinemas and classrooms. Promoting a more ecumenical sense of film appreciation, the label here is largely practical rather than conceptual.[2] My second observation relates to the historical consideration that, even if the label has now been dusted off and revived against the backdrop of the discourse of globalization, world cinema was much earlier the object of a different kind of scrutiny. Several decades before the current resurgence of interest, scholars of the political economy of communications systems argued that films (like other mass-mediated forms) played a significant role in the uneven exchange of cultural commodities within the global market. Within such an economic approach, cinema has long been addressed in a global, rather than national-cultural, frame.

This strand of scholarship, based on a broadly Marxian political economy, drew on the conceptual apparatus of 'world-systems' theory developed by Immanuel Wallerstein (and others) that has once again emerged at the forefront of the study of both world literature and world cinema.[3] The contemporary stress on core-periphery relations thus has its antecedents in analyses that have, for over four decades, focused on issues of circulation, influence, and uneven development, all concerns that have now gained critical impetus. But scholars of the political economy of communications (such as Herbert Schiller, Dallas Smythe, and Armand Mattelart) are seldom mentioned these days, perhaps because their macro-social framework is not seen as sufficiently enriching to film and literary criticism.[4] Still, their work attests to the fact that the importation of world-systems analysis into cultural criticism very much follows in the wake of materialist media scholars who were the first to examine how global media industries (film and television, chiefly, but also books, magazines, and other mass-mediated forms) maintain and reproduce the uneven development that is a primary feature of the capitalist system.

While it is important to integrate a materialist understanding of culture under capitalism with an interrogation of art forms such as literature and cinema, the level of generality underlying Wallerstein's theory was then, as it is now, ill-suited to an interpretive enterprise. Both past and present appropriations of world-systems theory fail to account for the negotiations between the experience of modern capitalism, particularly in peripheral contexts, and the precise character of objects such as films (or novels) produced in them. Nonetheless, the present discussion is motivated by the recognition that the question of value – of how cultural objects are embedded within global social relations and, at the same time, express the specificities of their own local time and place – remains paramount for thinking about world cinema. Moreover, Also, the intercalation of global form and local meaning is exactly what has to be unpacked, rather than taken for granted.

In what follows, I will first address the effort of literary scholars to think about the economic determinants of cultural production; my intention is to situate the means by which the concern with individual texts (be they literary or cinematic) has been reoriented to an examination of the global system that conditions their appearance. In the subsequent section, I explore the possibilities for conceptualizing world cinema in dialectical terms. Dialectics leaves behind the positivistic idea that one can think of films, novels, or any other cultural expression as straightforwardly presenting or registering a locale or, more extensively, the world; this is precisely because the pressure of economic determinants requires reckoning with their embeddedness in particular social forms.[5] That is to say, if capitalism promises a false freedom, then it follows that this falsity is also purveyed in forms of culture. Granting this in turn necessitates recognizing that it is not the truth of the world but its *untruth* that is manifest in works of culture, so the task of interpretation rests on an analysis of form – which bears the history of social formations. The final section of this essay proposes a reading that submits the problem of world cinema to these considerations of form and history. While limitations of space prevent a full interpretation, the hope is that aspects of what is at stake in dialectical analysis bring to light something of the stakes of world cinema as well.

From World-System to World Literature

The above intimates that a dialectical conception of the world might improve our understanding of the relationships between cultures of the world and the system of global capitalism into which they are inserted. The And my point of departure for this section is that such a conception is largely missing in the construction of objects with the prefix 'world' attached to them ('world literature', 'world cinema', 'world music', and so on).

Within literary-critical adaptations of the world-systems framework, the most prominent of which is Franco Moretti's 'distant reading', a homology is proposed between the economics of core and periphery, on the one hand, and source and target literatures, on the other. The 'core' (usually understood as the United States, Western Europe, and sometimes Japan) is seen as the source of the global traffic in culture; the periphery and semi-periphery, by contrast, refer to the 'contact-zones' in parts of the world to which the influence of the core extends. While adapting the conception of a world-system for his purposes, Moretti stretches the delineation of core and periphery to such an extent that the import of the economic distinction is negated.[6] Regardless of this slippage, by giving an apparently material cast to the notion of world literature, Moretti raises provocative questions about the differences, as well as the similarities, among literary forms subjected to a law of evolution. This law or evolutionary principle characterizes texts in terms of their divergence from the core of the literary system – so much so that the mode of reading itself is transformed by conceptualizing distance as the new and enabling 'condition of knowledge'. Moretti's ambition has thus been to take a 'wide-angle' look at the ways that novels from around the world always present, as he puts it, a 'compromise between the foreign and the local'.[7]

The bid to trace literary influence from core to periphery – via metaphors of trees, waves, and graphs – allows Moretti to propose what he claims is 'a materialist conception of form'. His points of reference are Wallerstein's world-system, but also Fredric Jameson's important though not unproblematic effort to map the 'geopolitical' consciousness tethering the global experience of capitalism.[8] Garnering wide acclaim as well as a number of emphatic rejections, Moretti's project has of course introduced a new set of terms for comparative analysis; however, it is less clear that he has been able to clarify much about form, let alone along materialist lines. Indeed, the emptying out of form characterizing his proposals about the text and reading has had an idealizing impact on the discussion of world cinema as well – further removing it from the tradition of dialectical thought that has the most to offer an understanding of form.

Alongside Moretti and Jameson, Pascale Casanova has gained attention for her literary sociology of 'the world republic of letters', in which literary 'actors' are seen to manoeuver in a world relatively independent of political borders.[9] She avers that this world constitutes a 'market where non-market values are traded, within a non-economic economy; and measured, as we shall see, by an aesthetic scale of time' (72). A detailed discussion of Casanova's model is undertaken elsewhere in this volume, so I merely want to note that, in her framework too, the specificity of the literary object is rendered abstract. This is because her salutary focus on literature in an 'aesthetic scale' that is *temporally* embedded in various and violent experiences of the 'modern' is not sustained, quickly shifting to spatial considerations; in fact, the shift is self-conscious: 'This conceptual tool is not "world literature" itself – that is, a body of literature expanded to a world scale [...] – but a *space*' (72).

Privileging space over time and, moreover, dissimulating space *as* time in tracing literary networks, results in a telescoping of history. This is visible in the language that Casanova uses to describe her approach. – For example, she admiringly cites Henry James's description of the Persian rug that requires 'the right angle' and the right (Kantian) distance to reveal its intricacy to viewers. But an emphasis on distance as the correct optic for contemplating 'the overall pattern of the designs' is, we should note, one that leaves the specificity of the carpet maker and local user behind. For in this view, the rug's weaver herself would be too close to see 'the carpet as a configuration' – a staggeringly arrogant epistemological stance that eliminates intimacy, familiarity, and, crucially, labour as the basis of understanding both the world we make and the world around us (73). Casanova's project thus provides a cautionary tale. Prioritizing space over time, she focuses on spatial regularities, variations, and repetitions, and thus deprives herself of a perspective that would account for the intensities, duration, and continuities that enfold objects in time *and* place, a complex of relations that resonates more with a Marxist understanding of capitalism's historicity and its interjection of particular ways of experiencing time, both synchronic and non-synchronic. The temporal dimension can hardly be over-emphasized in any reckoning with narrative, cinematic or otherwise, because *it is the propensity of narrative to unfold in time.*

As we can see, taken together or separately, such frameworks founder on the grounds that the 'world' remains strangely inchoate in them, coming into view only when placed in reference to Europe; the result is what Johannes Fabian has called 'allochronic distancing', a dissimulation by means of which 'far from the centre' implies 'further back in time'.[10] Likewise, peripheral forms of cultural expression at the heart of these inquiries can only be understood in pecuniary metaphors of loans and debts to the centre, or in spatial notions of distance and exteriority to the centre's literary system – metaphors that are less conceptual than classificatory, in a reductive sense. For these reasons, the attempt to chart literary influence in terms of abstract models results in the kind of analytic diminution that György Lukács had long ago criticized as the shortcoming of 'mechanical materialism' as opposed to the method of dialectical criticism (which, by contrast, must account for the relay between the textual instance and its abstract determinations). What is more, these models re-inscribe the very logic of difference that the impulse to expand the horizons of literary production had set out to overcome by adopting a global frame. But their individual and collective weaknesses aside, such efforts to account for capitalism's reach into the cultural sphere have at least one valuable outcome: they interrupt belletristic approaches in which the activity of interpreting a text need never contend with the influence of the world market on the production of value.

World Cinema as Form

The treatment of world cinema in film scholarship is no less subject to the weaknesses inhering in literary criticism's attempts to expand the canon and think in world-systemic terms. Accordingly, if world cinema has been studied under headings such as 'transnational film', 'global cinema', 'foreign film', 'non-Western cinema', 'polycentric' cinema, and so forth, this proliferation of labels only reinforces the reified nature of academic knowledge production *in toto*; it also reveals the same lack of engagement with the tradition of materialist aesthetics that, through its attentiveness to questions of form (rather than content narrowly) can account for the 'combined and uneven' experience of modernity.[11]

To embark on a serious engagement with form, we might first think of the disjunction between economic factors and cultural processes as the basis of the antagonisms that structure social relations under capitalism. These are 'social contradictions', to use the terminology of materialist analysis. To discern how these contradictions are manifested in expressive forms such as film, art, and literature, one must recognize that 'the work of art in its totality reflects the full process of life and does not represent in its details reflections of particular phenomena of life which can be related individually to aspects of actual life on which they are modelled'. This is again a statement from 1954, made by Lukács, the most important Marxist philosopher of the twentieth century. Although it has become somewhat routine to associate Lukács with a simplistic notion of realism, in fact his position did not assume transparency between aesthetic forms and reality. Rather, he considered aesthetic forms as 'self-contained' in their structure and relationship to reality – an insight that was more fully developed by his followers in the critical theory of the Frankfurt School. Theodor Adorno, in particular, advanced the idea that social contradictions are *encrypted*, rather than merely reflected, in works of culture, so the relations of cause and effect underlying them cannot simply be read off their surfaces. In a nod to the fundamental principle of mediation in Marxist thought, Lukács had already reminded us that 'non-correspondence [between representation and the real] in this respect is the precondition of the artistic illusion'. And to this end, he also at one point quotes Lenin: 'Art does not demand recognition as *reality*.'[12]

This, then, is the point at which a discussion of any form of culture becomes properly dialectical, insofar as one has to account for the mediations by means of which external realities find refracted expression in the internal dynamics of aesthetic practices. And not every work presents this complexity in the same fashion, just as not every film about revolution is a revolutionary film – a point made by Herbert Marcuse (among Lukács's heirs in the Frankfurt School) in his critique of 'affirmative culture'.[13] For Marcuse, bourgeois culture is affirmative because it offers illusory resolutions to the miseries of existence and deflects attention from the antagonisms of social life, promising empty aesthetic solutions to intractable problems. Cultural works affirm the status quo by affirming the need for consolation and thereby block awareness of the bad reality of the bourgeois world; in this way they serve as the very arena in which the bourgeoisie promotes its expansiveness and inclusivity, all the while reinforcing the inequality between elite and poor, centre and periphery.

Extending into the present context the idea that critical works negate rather than affirm the given world, I submit that not every film from around the world deserves to be considered an exemplar of world cinema; if, that is, the criterion of inclusion is to be more than merely notional or metaphoric, and world cinema is to make a bid for understanding the articulations between cinematic objects and the historical experience of capitalism. For, as the above discussion suggests, these articulations are neither schematic nor self-evidently given in filmic registrations of something called 'the world'. In fact, it could be argued that every film ever made is part of 'world cinema', if only to the nominal extent that from its inception in 1895, cinema has had a world in its sights.

Of course, in the earliest days this world was relatively small, defined largely in terms of the technological exchanges between France, the United States, the United Kingdom, and Germany. Nonetheless, a much larger world came into view almost immediately after the first film screenings in 1895 – with the Lumières taking their *cinématographe* in 1896 to Brussels,

Bombay, Buenos Aires, London, Montreal, and New York City. The response to the medium in these locations was galvanizing and the history of early cinema consequently attests to the history of its existence as a global medium. But especially since world cinema aims to take the measure of films made outside the mainstream cinematic traditions of the West, it is important to understand how films produced in non-metropolitan locations transmit their own negotiations of form and meaning and make their own bid to negate dominant bourgeois understandings of the world.

Time and Plurality

Despite its emergence as a field in its own right, film studies still relies largely on models of understanding proposed in literary criticism (as is evident in the regular citation of major critics such as Fredric Jameson, whose forays into film, architecture, or popular culture do not diminish the fact that his principal identity is as a literary theorist). Such reliance is even more at issue in prominent efforts to conceptualize cinema as a form of peripheral expression. Of course, this is only appropriate since both fields share an interest in addressing why certain texts appear to cross borders and others do not, as well as in exploring what to make of works that give us a deeper understanding of 'the world viewed', as the philosopher Stanley Cavell has put it.[14] But it is exclusively through coordinating the distance between abstract notions of the world (which always leave some of its parts in darkness), and the particular strategies by which that distance is both measured and expressed, that a nuanced conception of world cinema as a *predicament*, rather than merely an archival or pedagogic category, can be advanced.

The film scholar Dudley Andrew is perhaps the most visible representative of recent attempts in cinema studies to rethink world cinema in a substantive manner. While critical engagements with cinema no doubt benefit from 'unthinking' Eurocentric models of film study and 'upgrading', in the words of one of the editors of a recent anthology, 'the geopolitical imaginary of the discipline of film studies to a transnational perspective', Andrew's example is especially noteworthy because it both crosses over into comparative literature and derives its inspiration from literary sources – chiefly, again, Moretti.[15] But whereas Moretti's approach to world literature made its case for a systematic analysis with reference to maps, trees, and graphs, Andrew adapts the language of atlases, phases, and *décalage* (jetlag or time difference), to propose his own historicization of the spatio-temporal arc stretching from the early short films of the aptly named Lumière brothers to the accelerated pace of cinema in the digital age and its offshoots in virtual experience.[16]

As already stated, it is undoubtedly important to consider the element of time in thinking about cinema as a mode that travels from its location of production (be it Hollywood, Shanghai, or Paris) to its reception and exhibition worldwide (be it in movie theatres or film festivals). On this basis, Andrew emphasizes 'world cinema' as a 'phase' that distinguishes it from the present moment of 'global' cinema – in which, as he states, 'images, ideas, and capital' are disseminated across 'a vast but undifferentiated cultural geography' (80). But one should notice here too that, as with Casanova, there is a conflation of time and space in the slippage from the idea of time-lag to the spatial disjunctions involved in talking about cinema in the 'undifferentiated' spaces of capital, whether in Taiwan, Tehran (both premier nodes of contemporary filmmaking), or elsewhere. as if what matters ultimately is the being of films from an 'elsewhere', rather than the relationship of films made anywhere to a coeval and co-present 'now'. The entire problematic becomes one that conceives time-lag as 'our' experience of an 'other' time and, certainly, of other places. Time is both relativized and banalized, an aspect that is also betrayed in Andrew's earlier effort to clear the ground for reconsidering world cinema as a form of travel and a mode of navigation that would 'let us travel where we will so long as every local cinema is examined with an eye to its complex ecology'.[17]

Ecology rather than economy. This is the tellingly abstract and metaphoric emphasis Andrew places on cinema as a system, and it leads him to propose the study of world cinema via the model of an historical atlas:

> [A] course or anthology looking out to world cinema should be neither a gazetteer nor an encyclopaedia, futilely trying to do justice to cinematic life everywhere. Its essays and materials should instead model a set of approaches, just as an atlas of maps opens up a continent to successive views: political, demographic, linguistic, topographical, meteorological, marine, historical.[18]

We can again recognize the imprint of Moretti's thinking, even if figures such as maps and trees are not direct equivalents of their replacements here; moreover, there is no such thing as a marine or meteorological view of cinema (at least until dolphins or cloud formations can make films!). Despite a laudable effort to theorize how the experience of viewing a film articulates with the film's transmission of a particular sense of time as well as its own placement in time, Andrew's avoidance of a dialectical and Marxist vocabulary- in which the problem of temporality has been most compellingly conceptualized ultimately leads to a vacuous engagement with temporal propositions.

Let me say why dialectical thought is better equipped to account for the formal ways that films betoken the relationship of a given time and place to a history that is in the end universal – not in a singular, teleological sense but as a narrative category for the continuity and discontinuity that binds the particular to the general. From this vantage point, the distinction that really matters is that all subjects inhabit the same time under the sign of capital while experiencing it differentially, given specific social and historical circumstances. Belatedness and fashionable contemporaneity are, by this token, two sides of the same coin; and by extension, works of cinema that excel in conjuring this 'simultaneous non-simultaneity', so to speak, are ones that do not just signal the problem of time as a narrative motif or preoccupation but *work out* the relationship to time as internal to their own existence. Such texts may be transportable to a wider circle of viewers and circulated within high-profile metropolitan venues, but their relocation worldwide does not erase their inscription in a particular time and place or their insertion into the complex dynamics of capitalist modernity.

If the above gloss on temporality is a little abstract, we may be helped by returning once more to the source from which much of the discussion of the world-system of cinema and literature has taken its lead: the postulation of a core-periphery problematic by Wallerstein (and others in the tradition of economic history). As already indicated, the problem with thinking of a system of cinematic production in terms of the system of the world economy is not that it is incorrect, but that it is not particularly helpful for understanding works of art and culture. But nor does it help to take umbrage at the idea that the core of the world-system has the upper hand in the production of value – as though one could simply evade the implication of belatedness by declaring it 'Eurocentric' to speak, say, of the Indian social film as borrowing from Italian Neorealism, or of Brazilian *Cinema Novo* as being influenced by Soviet directors such as Sergei Eisenstein. These are facts in the history of world cinema, and denying them has no purchase on critical thinking (quite aside from the inconvenient fact that a large swathe of the former Soviet Union is not in Europe, nor was Italy anything but Europe's internal periphery during the ascendancy of Neorealism's principal auteurs). So, if the core-periphery framework is lacking, this may have more to do with misunderstanding the conceptual parameters on which it is mounted than with its capacity to theorize the workings of capitalism.

Wallerstein, it should be noted, had predicated his own studies of the world-system upon the work of his mentor in the Annales School of social history, Fernand Braudel. The entire edifice of world-systems theory is built on Braudel's study of the *longue durée,* or the long-term structures of social reality. In taking this view of historical unfolding, Braudel's insistence was neither on inexorable processes nor on surface disturbances than on what

Wallerstein adapted as as 'the multiplicity of social times'.[19] Elaborating Braudel's perspective further, Wallerstein makes an observation that is crucial for theorizing world cinema: 'Generalizations about the functioning of such a system thus avoided the trap of seeming to assert timeless, eternal truths. If such systems were not eternal, then it followed that they had beginnings, lives during which they "developed", and terminal transitions.'[20]

The emphasis on development seen as fractured but also structured (rather than linear or progressive) is a key component in Braudel's notion of multiplicity, and it had a great deal of influence on Wallerstein's own take-up of the idea that the capitalist system is structured as an ensemble of changing relations and, importantly, multiple temporalities that are nonetheless part of the same *durée* or stretch of time. But the spatial overtones of a model that highlights distances between core, semi-periphery, and periphery appear to have totally overshadowed the early and abiding emphasis on the concatenation of time *and* space in both Braudel's and Wallerstein's work. I bring it up here as a way to clarify how one might think of world cinema as this kind of intensification of multiple points of view derived from multiple experiences of time within a structure of historical periodization that answers to the term 'modernity'.

The Past in the Present

Let us take an illustrative example of my contention that world cinema is less a category than a predicament. Such a shift in emphasis allows temporality to be taken as a formal proposition on its own, particularly since temporal transitions are the very ground of cinematic narrative; these range from cuts and other mechanisms of editing (for example, montage sequences and flash-back/flash-forward as well as freeze-frames that serve to arrest time or convey its disruption), to the use of slow camera movement to draw attention to a different tempo of life or reinforce the invisible links between 'reel time' and 'real time'. If cinema is the medium best suited to capturing a story and a situation while evoking other stories and situations, then films that successfully conjure the world do so because of their self-conscious investment in exploring what is essentially a here-there relation (a spatial premise) in terms of a now-and-then (a temporal expression).

The film I want to put forward in this regard is not one found in standard discussions of world cinema, though its director, the Indian filmmaker Satyajit Ray (1921–1992), is often included in lists of 'non-Western' or 'Third-World' auteurs. I refer to Ray's 1977 film *Shatranj ke Khilari* ('The Chess Players') for its ability to bring a historical sensibility to life, while drawing the viewer's attention to the distance between the past of the film's story and setting, and a postcolonial present in which viewer,

Figure 13.1 Saeed Jaffrey and Sanjeev Kumar in *Shatranj ke Khilari/The Chess Players*.
By permission of the Satyajit Ray Film and Study Centre.

filmmaker, and critic are collectively bound by their synchronous placement in an uneven set of social relations.[21] In this way, the story plays out a particular episode in the history of India's colonial experience under British rule, though it simultaneously implicates us (which is to say, contemporary viewers) in reckoning with our own time- a time that by no means has seen the last of empire.[22]

Set in nineteenth-century Lucknow, the erstwhile capital of the princely province of Awadh (or Oudh in the British dispensation), *Shatranj ke Khilari* centres on two aristocratic characters frittering away their time, attention, and life in their obsession with playing chess.

Oblivious to the historical changes taking place under their very noses, the nominal protagonists, Mirza Sajjad Ali and Mir Roshan Ali, play their game – one that was originally devised in India, and whose subtlety is tellingly distorted in the changes the British introduce to its rules. The narrative places real historical personages in a fictional scenario, absorbing history and fiction as dual aspects in the narration of time. Nawab Wajid Ali Shah, the last king of Awadh, known in history for his aesthetic tastes rather than political aptitude, is portrayed similarly on screen: totally preoccupied by his pursuit of the sensual pleasures of poetry, music, and dance. Meanwhile, the East India

Company is revealed to have encroached on affairs of all the Indian states, with the British crown imposing direct rule in 1858. Charged with dethroning the king, the British Resident, General Outram (played by Richard Attenborough), places him under surveillance in order to engineer his ouster and annex Awadh. Faced with the prospect of war, Wajid Ali Shah abdicates without resistance and Mughal India disappears into the dust, to be replaced by the sights and sounds of British troops marching into the scene.

Through his painstaking depiction of the principals' disregard of the calamity that surrounds them, Ray obliges the viewer to be more attentive and discerning than his characters. But their inattention or indecision does not negate our sympathy, so our laughter at their follies is in part reflexive: the outcome of a build-up of expectations that is discharged only by acknowledging that the characters' heedlessness is matched by our own. In a metacritical sense, Ray suggests that we too have slept through the lessons of history, its baneful effects continually catching us by surprise. In addition to the frame narrative, the film also allegorizes the period of the Indian Emergency (1975–1977) when, under the cover of national security, India's then prime minister, Indira Gandhi, declared a state of emergency, suspending the rule of law and instituting President's rule instead. A non-violent coup was in the offing, pre-empted by her action to insert back into democratic life the absolute authority of the sovereign. The colonial past is thus articulated in the present of the film, in turn opening out to the present of our moment of viewing.

Exploiting in this way the capacity of allegory both to stretch time as well as render it disjunct (delinking representation from its object), Ray stages his portrait of historical dissolution, collocating the past-present relation that I have suggested is crucial to a film's capacity to evoke a world and even to intervene in it. To this end, *Shatranj* insistently pricks at the viewer to reckon with the image – urging her to *think* with visual means and, obversely, deploying formal elements to convey meanings that might otherwise be missed. To give just one example of Ray's pursuit of this formal dimension via the intricate weaving of dialogue and visual details, let me refer to an incidental scene in which Mirza Sajjad and Mir Roshan, the two chess addicts, visit the elderly lawyer from whom they hope to borrow a chess set. The lawyer's home reveals a space that has undergone a subtle transformation – with Ray's mannerist depiction of a Mughal domain that now shows the influence of an incipient Victorianism. One corner of the drawing room contains the splendid ivory chessboard on which the characters' eyes settle, but the viewer's eye is also drawn to other objects that mark their exoticism, from the tapestry-covered chairs and porcelain vases on pedestals, to the equestrian painting hanging on the wall in the background. The profusion of objects laid out within the frame *almost* distracts us from noticing that this painting is out of place, if not as dramatically as the *memento mori* in baroque art then in the ironic interjection of a picture that is, so to speak, at odds in this picture.

Although – or perhaps because – it is at a tangent from the pictorial styles of Islamic art (in which men on horseback are also a staple subject), the European painting of a rider, against which Sajjad and Roshan are framed, represents a very different staple in the ideology of the image. Its alien provenance here, subtly pointing to the formulaic genre of horseman and hunt in European visual art, serves as a residue of a taken-for-granted repertoire of visual images that John Berger so effectively characterized as a latent aspect of bourgeois 'ways of seeing'.[23] This purely formal detail suggests that, while the larger narrative of *Shatranj* is obviously about British designs on Indian territory, Ray's reflexive camera work proffers a *mise-en-abŷme* for all of the incursions of the distant into the proximate, as well as all of the epistemological encroachments by means of which imperialism accomplishes its goals in expropriating surplus and re-assigning value.

We might then conclude by suggesting that Ray tells a story about colonization while proposing an argument about the colonization of perception

Figure 13.2 Richard Attenborough as General James Outram, Amjad Khan as Wajid Ali Shah, and the Awadh court in *Shatranj ke Khilari/ The Chess Players*.
By permission of the Satyajit Ray Film and Study Centre.

itself: the ways in which our understanding has been muffled, side-tracked, and obscured by the overall reification of consciousness. His indirect references to remaindered time – time that has not been made to fit into the schema of clock and calendar – and his recurrent efforts to convey the remains of the day, have the function of expressing the historical crisis of experience, the universal predicament into which we as modern subjects are everywhere enfolded.[24]

Moreover, his films often propose that the task of limning (that is to say, painting in words or pictures) social contradictions via aesthetic means is best accomplished when one tries *not* to show 'how things really are' but to emphasize instead how they are not. By evoking a mode of existence that is set to disappear in the story-world of *Shatranj*, Ray draws attention to its exteriority to history. It is now only discernible in remnants that intimate other things and ideas that can no longer be recognized for their significance. Nonetheless, the evocation of a life-world on the verge of collapse does not indicate its total eclipse; rather, it retains its hold on the present in the very form of its otherness. Ray is of course not the only director to have exposed the medium's artifice for meta-commentary, but his success in *Shatranj* resides in the extent to which he stitches together an epistemological lesson about how the real has been de-realized with a critique of the ways that the historical experience of capitalism has led to the effacement of sensory regimes that could not be brought into line with its goals.

Notes

1. See, for instance, W. Dissanayake, 'Issues in World Cinema', in J. Hill and P. C. Gibson (eds.), *World Cinema: Critical Approaches* (Oxford: Oxford University Press, 2000), pp. 143–150; and S. Dennison and S. W. Lim (eds.), *Remapping World Cinema: Identity, Culture, and Politics in Film* (New York: Columbia University Press, 2006).
2. This practical, pedagogical imperative is noted in Nataša Ďurovičová's preface to *World Cinemas, Transnational Perspectives*, N. Ďurovičová's and K. Newman (eds.) (New York: Routledge Press, 2010), pp. ix–xv.
3. I. Wallerstein, *The Modern World-System: Capitalist Agriculture and the Origins of the European World-Economy in the Sixteenth Century* (New York: Academic Press, 1976). Other proponents of the world-systems approach include Janet Abu-Lughod and André Gunder Frank.
4. D. W. Smythe, *The Structure and Policy of Electronic Communications* (Champaign-Urbana: University of Illinois Press, 1957); H. Schiller, *Information Inequality* (New York: Routledge, 1995); A. Mattelart, *Mapping World Communication: War, Progress, Culture*, S. Emanuel and J. A. Cohen (trans.) (Minneapolis: University of Minnesota Press, 1994).

5. I have been greatly helped by Silvia L. López's essay 'Dialectical Criticism in the Provinces of the "World Republic of Letters": The Primacy of the Object in the Work of Roberto Schwarz', *A Contracorriente: A Journal on Social History and Literature in Latin America*, 9.1 (2011), 69–88.

6. 'In cultures that belong to the periphery of the literary system (*which means: almost all cultures, inside and outside Europe*) the modern novel first arises not as an autonomous development but as a compromise between a western formal influence (usually French or English) and local materials.' F. Moretti, 'Conjectures on World Literature', *New Left Review*, 1 (2000), 54–68 (p. 58, emphasis mine).

7. Moretti, 'Conjectures', p. 60.

8. F. Jameson, *The Geopolitical Aesthetic: Cinema and Space in the World-System* (Bloomington: Indiana University Press, 1994).

9. P. Casanova, 'Literature as a World', *New Left Review* 31 (2005), 71–90. Page numbers for subsequent citations are included in the text.

10. J. Fabian, *Time and the Other: How Anthropology Makes Its Object* (New York: Columbia University Press, 1983).

11. See anthologies such as L. Nagib, C. Perriam, and R. Dudrah (eds.), *Theorizing World Cinema* (London: I. B. Tauris, 2012), and that of Hill and Gibson, cited above.

12. G. Lukács, 'Art and Objective Truth', in A. Kahn (ed. and trans.), *Writer and Critic: And Other Essays* (London: Merlin Press, 1970), pp. 25–60 (pp. 40–41).

13. H. Marcuse, 'The Affirmative Character of Culture', J. J. Shapiro (trans.) in *Negations: Essays in Critical Theory* (London: MayFly Books, 2009 [1937]), pp. 65–98.

14. S. Cavell, *The World Viewed: Reflections on the Ontology of Film* (Cambridge, MA: Harvard University Press, 1971).

15. Ďurovičová, *World Cinemas*, p. ix. See also E. Shohat and R. Stam, *Unthinking Eurocentrism: Multiculturalism and the Media* (New York: Routledge, 1994).

16. D. Andrew, 'Time Zones and Jetlag: The Flows and Phases of World Cinema', in N. Ďurovičová and K. Newman (eds.), *World Cinemas, Transnational Perspectives* (New York: Routledge Press, 2010), pp. 59–89.

17. D. Andrew, 'An Atlas of World Cinema', *Framework: The Journal of Cinema and Media*, 45.2 (2004), 9–23 (p. 2).

18. Andrew, 'An Atlas of World Cinema', p. 2.

19. I. Wallerstein, *World-Systems Analysis: An Introduction* (Durham, NC: Duke University Press, 2004), p. 3; F. Braudel, 'History and the Social Sciences: The Longue Durée', I. Wallerstein (trans.), *Review*, 1.3/4 (2001), 171–203.

20. Wallerstein, *World-Systems Analysis*, p. 4.

21. For a thematic reading of the film see D. Cooper, 'The Representation of Colonialism in Satyajit Ray's *The Chess Players*', in W. Dissanayake (ed.), *Colonialism and Nationalism in Asian Cinema* (Bloomington: Indiana University Press, 1994), pp. 174–189.

22. At the end of his classic study *Theory of Film*, the eminent film theorist Siegfried Kracauer refers to Ray's film *Aparajito* ('The Unvanquished', 1959), suggesting that Ray had realized cinema's unique ability to evoke a universal contingency anchored in a specific time and place: 'India is in this episode but not only India'. 'What seems remarkable about *Aparajito*', writes a reader of the *New York*

Times to the editor of the film section, 'is that you see this story happening in a remote land and see these faces with their exotic beauty and still feel that the same thing is happening every day somewhere in Manhattan or Brooklyn or the Bronx'. *Theory of Film: The Redemption of Physical Reality* (Princeton: Princeton University Press, 1997 (1960)), p. 311.

23. J. Berger, *Ways of Seeing* (London: Penguin Books (reprint edition), 1990).

24. I pursue the argument about Ray's treatment of temporality at greater length in *Cinema, Emergence, and the Films of Satyajit Ray* (Berkeley: University of California Press, 2010). A broader discussion of cinema and temporality can be found in M. A. Doane, *The Emergence of Cinematic Time: Modernity, Contingency, the Archive* (Cambridge, MA: Harvard University Press, 2002).

14

CHRIS ANDREWS

Publishing, Translating, Worldmaking

The Valves of World Literature

As Stefan Helgesson and Pieter Vermeulen have pointed out, world literature, as an object of study, has to be made; it cannot simply be found.[1] As
readers, students, and teachers of world literature, we construct literary
worlds by discerning relations at a range of scales: between devices, works,
genres, traditions. Like the more general making of symbolic worlds theorized by Nelson Goodman in the wake of Ernst Cassirer, this specific kind
'always starts from worlds already on hand: the making is a remaking'.[2] Our
versions of world literature revise previous versions, often by pointing to
what has been left out and stressing its value. Translation does this implicitly
and prospectively, providing new materials for the remaking of world literature by allowing works to circulate more widely. But that circulation is
channelled and restricted by social, economic, and political forces, which I
will explore in this chapter, drawing in part and implicitly on my practical
experience as a literary translator.

It is a commonplace of translation studies that the English-speaking world
is relatively impermeable to translated literature. The figure of 3 per cent is
often cited: translations are said to account for about 3 per cent of book titles
published in North America and Britain. But if we consider only literary
translations (the distinction is not sharp or simple to make), the figure will
drop. 'The number is actually closer to 0.7 percent', writes Chad Post,
publisher at Open Letter Books and author of *The Three Percent
Problem*.[3] Corresponding figures for the nations of continental Europe,
East Asia, and Latin America are significantly higher.

Extending Abram de Swaan's work on the world-system of languages,
Johan Heilbron formulates a simple principle: 'the more central a language is
in the international translation system, the smaller the proportion of translations into this language'.[4] As de Swaan and others have stressed, English is
not simply a central, but *the* 'hypercentral' language, continuing to displace

others as a second language all around the world. Nevertheless, in recent years, the Anglosphere may have become marginally more permeable to literary works in translation. At the end of this chapter I will mention some indications that this is the case. I would like to begin, however, by pointing out that the quantitative, 3 per cent problem has qualitative corollaries that are less frequently remarked upon.

One is that the proportion of literary to commercial titles is much higher for translations *into* English than for translations *from* English, which are dominated by mass-market fiction. Partly because of this, and partly because literary translation is a financially precarious activity, it is often regarded in the English-speaking world as a form of cultural activism, a noble cause, while in places where it is practised on a larger scale, it has less symbolic prestige. A further corollary of the 3 per cent problem is that the number of people who have a say in deciding which books are translated is relatively small. Publishers or acquisition editors operate the crucial 'valves' that regulate the flow of literary works into English, and although they do not work on their own but belong to gatekeeping networks, along with scouts, literary agents, and translators, those networks are not very populous. Their active and well-connected members have the capacity to leave a lasting mark on the landscape of world literature in English, especially given the vastness and richness of what remains untranslated.

Except in specialist houses set up to publish translations from a particular language, the final decisions on what to translate are often made without the publisher having read the original text. Sometimes a publisher or editor will read a translation of the work into a language other than English. Reliance on trusted opinion is, however, the norm. This opinion is sometimes framed in a reader's report: typically a document of two or three pages discussing the book's plot, characters, and style, and concluding with a frank yes-or-no verdict. As Esther Allen has pointed out, 'The lowly minion who authors [a reader's report] can do something no after-the-fact reviewer, however powerful and unkind, can accomplish: stop the book from being published in the first place'.[5] The reporting reader's positive power is more limited: an enthusiastic recommendation is rarely so decisive; it is more likely to be taken into account when it converges with others, whether they are given in commissioned reports or via informal channels.

A publisher of translations is likely to be swayed by consensus within her group of trusted advisors, but in order to know which books to consult that group about, she needs to be sensitive to rumours circulating in a larger group of industry professionals. She also needs to be alive to a difference explained by John B. Thompson: 'Hype is the talking up of books by those who have an interest in generating excitement about them, like agents; buzz exists when the recipients of hype respond with affirmative talk backed up by money'.[6] This difference has, however, been blurred in recent years by the development of 'buzz marketing', that is, special treatment given to readers who are influential online, such as bloggers and YouTubers. The terms *rumour, hype,* and *buzz* tend to have negative connotations in an academic context, where they are likely to suggest a lack of rigour, but publishers do not have the leisure to engage in the slow and repeated reading of books that they have not acquired, or to pursue lengthy dialogues with their advisors. Specialization in the academic sense is incompatible with their work. If they approached their decisions with the habitus of an academic, they would miss chances to acquire the rights to promising new titles. Publishers have to 'go on their nerve' as Frank O'Hara said of poets. Theorizing explicitly would hobble their practice.

Quick decision making does not entail fickleness, however. A publisher's nerve may dictate persistence in 'heritage publishing', that is, a long-term commitment to an author over a series of books, in the hope of gradually building up an audience, even if individual titles fail to pay their way. This is a practice that has become extremely difficult to maintain in commercial houses where heads of sales and marketing exercise a right of veto over each new acquisition, but even at what Pierre Bourdieu calls the field's 'autonomous pole' – in the smaller, independent publishing houses – heritage publishing cannot be a general policy.[7] The Spanish publisher Jorge Herralde explains why:

> Since a publishing house has a certain more or less fixed number of new titles per year, if the house is to go on welcoming emerging voices, it can't have a policy of publishing 'the complete works' of all its writers, and each time a new author comes on board (whether or not the publisher is aware of this), an old one must be dropped.[8]

The price of openness is having a de facto B-list, composed of authors who are on probation, as it were.

From a purely economic point of view, heritage publishing is imprudent. It must be subsidized while waiting for sales to build. And if sales do build strongly, the original publisher may not be able to secure the rewards for having taken the initial risk. Publishers at the autonomous pole often serve unwillingly as talent scouts for their larger competitors. As the owner of a small independent house said to a member of Bourdieu's team investigating publishing in France: 'We can't make waves, we don't have the means. We are virtuous by obligation.'[9] They are obliged, in other words, to go on prospecting, giving new authors their first chance or foreign authors their first chance in translation, which is why, as Bourdieu writes, they 'play a crucial role in the transformation of the field'.[10]

The Savage Detectives (2007) and *2666* (2008) by the Chilean novelist Roberto Bolaño met with a critical welcome that no Latin American author had enjoyed since Gregory Rabassa's translation of *One Hundred Years of Solitude* (1970) introduced Gabriel García Márquez to the English-speaking world. The phenomenon was not limited to the western hemisphere. The first translations of Bolaño's fiction were into Italian and German, and his signature combination of elegiac themes and energetic style crossed into many other languages and made him a notable influence on new writing from Japan to Iran and beyond. The enthusiastic international reception of Roberto Bolaño's fiction coincided with the expansion of world literature as an academic discipline, and the inclusion of his short story 'Sensini' in the third edition of the *Norton Anthology of World Literature* (2012) testifies to this convergence.

Bolaño's canonization has prompted speculation as to why his work in particular was taken up so quickly and widely. Reasons for his success in translation can certainly be proposed, as I have done elsewhere, but those reasons cannot be credibly weighted without serious sociological fieldwork, and the explanatory power of data gathered by such means would be limited in any case by the uncertainty that is built into cultural markets.[11] Rather than further reconstructing the reception history of Bolaño's work here, I would like to turn to the work itself, which remains an underexploited resource for thinking about the factors that facilitate and impede the circulation of literature beyond its original linguistic domain.

Bolaño's two long novels have been used as examples of a kind of writing that is symptomatic of our age of world or global literature. Alexander Beecroft writes that Bolaño's work in general 'eschews the paradigm of the nation-state altogether', but in the text that I will be focusing on, 'Álvaro Rousselot's Journey', a reaffirmation of that paradigm suggests not withdrawal but a locally particular way of engaging with the literatures of the world.[12] As further examples of that (Argentine) way, I will take Jorge Luis Borges and César Aira, whose fiction and essays show how world literature in practice is always under construction and always answering, as Lawrence Venuti says of translation, to 'contingencies in the receiving situation'.[13]

Paris–Buenos Aires

'Álvaro Rousselot's Journey' condenses and encodes a rich practical knowledge of the processes of translation and diffusion by which world literature is made and remade. The title character is an Argentine writer born in the 1920s. His first and third novels are adapted without permission by a French film director named Guy Morini. Although 'extremely aggrieved', Rousselot opts 'not to act, at least not legally'.[14] The Frenchman's debt is formal as well as thematic. What he has taken from the first novel, *Solitude,* is the device of maintaining uncertainty about whether characters are living or dead: 'Halfway through, it becomes apparent that most of the characters are dead. With only thirty pages left to go, it is suddenly obvious that they are *all* dead, except for one, but the identity of the single living character is never revealed' (79).

The incipient series of appropriations does not continue. Morini's third film has 'nothing in common with any of Rousselot's works' (83). And so the case remains mysteriously open until Rousselot receives an invitation to a literary festival in Frankfurt, from where he proceeds to Paris and attempts to contact Morini. He finally tracks the director down in a hotel in Arromanches on the Normandy coast:

> Morini invited him in. [...] I am Álvaro Rousselot, he said, the author of *Solitude* [...]
>
> It took a few seconds for Morini to react, but then he leaped to his feet, let out a cry of terror, and disappeared down a corridor. Such a spectacular response was the last thing Rousselot had been expecting. He remained seated, lit a cigarette [...]. Then he stood up and started calling Morini. Guy, he called, rather hesitatingly, Guy, Guy, Guy.
>
> Rousselot found him in an attic where the hotel's cleaning equipment was piled. Morini had opened the window and seemed to be hypnotized by the garden that surrounded the building, and by the neighbouring garden, which belonged to a private house, and was visible, in part, through dark latticework. Rousselot walked over and patted him on the back. Morini seemed smaller and more fragile than before. For a while they both stood there looking at one garden, then the other. Then Rousselot wrote the address of his hotel in Paris and the address of the hotel where he was currently staying on a piece of paper and slipped it into the director's trouser pocket.   (98–99)

As Benjamin Loy has pointed out, the relation between Rousselot and Morini echoes an incident from the history of French cinema.[15] When *Last Year in Marienbad* (*L'Année dernière à Marienbad*) was released in 1961, a number of viewers were strongly reminded of Adolfo Bioy Casares's novel *The Invention of Morel* (*La invención de Morel*). In an interview with André Labarthe and Jacques Rivette, the scriptwriter, Alain Robbe-Grillet, did not deny familiarity with Bioy Casares's novel (which he had reviewed for *Critique* in 1953), and even described it as 'an amazing book', but rather than acknowledging an influence, albeit unconscious, he went on to make a dubious generalization about the artist being directly nourished by reality and interested in artworks only in so far as they contain 'things that one wanted to do as a result of emotions caused solely by the real world'.[16]

Given this background, one might have expected 'Álvaro Rousselot's Journey' to be a vindication of the wronged Argentine, a writing back from the periphery to a centre of cultural power, but to read it as such would be reductive. The story presents Morini's films as building on, rather than simply pillaging, their literary models: *Lost Voices* is 'clearly a *clever* adaptation' of *Solitude* (79, my emphasis), while *The Shape of the Day* improves Rousselot's third novel: 'It was exactly like *Life of a Newlywed* but better' (82). Morini's method of compressing the 'trunk' of the story, expanding the beginning and ending, and giving more importance to secondary characters (93) seems to produce a more sophisticated narrative, but Morini's sophistication is parasitic on Rousselot's invention. For a time, it might be said, the Argentine and the Frenchman formed an artistically successful dyad, characterized by asymmetrical but mutual dependence: Morini needed Rousselot's narrative ideas and Rousselot needed Morini to refine them. It is tempting to see here a colonial scheme of raw material extraction transposed to the intellectual plane, but as I pointed out above, form as well as materials have been appropriated, and a postcolonial reading should not obscure Rousselot's equanimity: he is neither moved by resentment nor cowed by Morini's positional prestige.

When Morini's films stop resembling Rousselot's books, the writer feels that he has lost something: 'After relief came sadness. For a few days Rousselot was even preoccupied by the thought that he had lost his best reader, the reader for whom he had really been writing, the only one who was capable of fully responding to his work' (84). What brings Rousselot to Paris is not the desire to reclaim a renown that is rightfully his, but 'the mystery awaiting him there' (85). At the heart of this mystery lies the question: why did Morini *stop* adapting Rousselot's work? Why has he 'broken off communication' (84)? Communication is what Rousselot seems to be attempting to renew when he slips his addresses into Morini's pocket in Arromanches, after a curious moment of joint attention.

At its very end, the story leaves questions of property and communication in suspense and turns, surprisingly, to identity: 'For the rest of the day Rousselot felt that he really was an Argentine writer, something that he had begun to doubt over the previous days, or perhaps the previous years, partly because he was unsure of himself, but also because he was unsure about the possibility of an Argentine literature' (100). Far from dissolving his national literary identity, Rousselot's drift in Paris has confirmed it. Why? Perhaps Rousselot feels like an Argentine writer not because of what he has written but because of what has happened to him: the uncanny final encounter with a 'vaguely familiar' Morini in an old hotel that contains 'a zone infiltrated by mist' (98) attaches the story to a tradition of gothic and fantastic short fiction that has flourished in the Río de la Plata region from the late nineteenth century to the present day. It is Rousselot's exemplary destiny to lose and find himself in a mystery that might have been invented by one of his compatriots.

Averroes's Predicament

If we read 'Álvaro Rousselot's Journey' as a parable about the circulation of literature, it offers three lessons. The first is obvious: in circulating, works are exposed to the risk of expropriation. The second two lessons invite further reflection: formal innovation can travel from periphery to centre; and the affirmation of a literary nationality is not necessarily a nostalgic or parochial gesture.

For Benjamin Loy, 'Álvaro Rousselot's Journey' and the relation between *The Invention of Morel* and *Last Year at Marienbad* show that models presupposing a unique 'Greenwich meridian of literature' or waves of innovation propagated outward from a centre towards the periphery do not respond to the realities of cultural exchange since the Second World War.[17] The validity of such models in earlier periods may be challenged as well. In '"Considering Coldly ... "' Efraín Kristal mounts a powerful argument to show that Franco Moretti's conjecture that writers in the periphery invariably respond to Western forms with compromise solutions cannot account for late-nineteenth-century Spanish American *modernismo*, whose leading proponent, Rubén Darío, was 'as far away in the periphery as it is possible to be: he was born an illegitimate child in a Nicaraguan village'.[18] More generally, Kristal argues against Moretti's postulation of a homology between the inequalities of the world economic and literary systems.

Moretti ends his 'Conjectures on World Literature' by proposing two cognitive metaphors for the spread of literary forms: 'trees and waves are both metaphors – but except for this, they have absolutely nothing in common'.[19] Both metaphors, however, imply that new forms originate in one place. This is precisely what Kristal disputes, producing a range of Spanish American counter-examples. An advantage of network metaphors, as an alternative to trees and waves, is that they allow for the emergence of new forms in a number of places, under influences converging from various directions.[20]

Network metaphors may, however, be misleading if they are taken to imply isotropy, uniform connectivity, and general robustness. The network of world literature is clearly not isotropic: it does not allow for equal ease of flow in all directions. Moretti makes this point in response to Kristal: 'Yes, forms *can* move in several directions. But *do* they?'[21] Singular counter-examples invalidate an invariable law, but not a statistical tendency. Moreover, not all nodes of the network are equal: there may not be a single meridian, but there are hubs with an exceptionally high degree of connectivity. It was by living and working in the Latin American hubs of Santiago de Chile and Buenos Aires that Rubén Darío was able to establish a continental reputation before moving to Paris and Madrid: *modernismo* was not launched and directed from his hometown of Metapa.[22] Finally, many of the network's links are fragile, notably those established by translation, which, although modestly remunerated in general, is nevertheless an additional cost for a publisher, and thus an obstacle to circulation.

The constant making of new links in the network of international publishing is accompanied by the failure of old ones: communication is broken off, as between Rousselot and Morini. To switch to the labyrinth metaphor, circulating works often reach a dead end. As the fiction of Jorge Luis Borges reminds us insistently, the labyrinth entraps as well as connects; it is both barrier and passage. And even where a connection is established in good faith via translation, incomprehension may continue to isolate those who receive foreign texts. This is the lesson of Borges's story 'Averroes' Search', which throws a sceptical light on the notion of a world literature without frontiers.[23] At the end of the story, the twelfth-century Islamic scholar Averroes (Ibn Rushd), initially puzzled by the terms *tragedy* and *comedy* in Aristotle's *Poetics*, suddenly feels that he has grasped their meaning: '*Aristu [Aristotle] gives the name "tragedy" to panegyrics and the name "comedy" to satires and anathemas*'.[24] He has mistakenly aligned the rhetorical opposition of praise to blame with the generic opposition of tragedy to comedy. This is not an invitation to disdain the great scholar, but a parable about the boundedness of cultural understanding, as the reflexive coda indicates: 'I felt that Averroes, trying to imagine what a play is without ever having suspected what a theatre is, was no more absurd than I, trying to imagine Averroes yet with no more material than a few snatches from Renan, Lane and Asín Palacios'.[25] Borges's search fails like that of his character (the original title, '*La busca de Averroes*', 'The Search of / for Averroes', refers to both).

The Argentine writer had the advantage of a far richer store of scholarly works to consult, but the mere accumulation of those works does not automatically reduce a cultural and historical distance, for they still have to be read, and a reader can reconstruct only a small number of contexts with the degree of detail that might have assuaged Borges's doubts. Nevertheless, he completed and published his story, drawing on what he modestly called *snatches* (the word used in the original is *adarmes*, derived from the Arabic word *dirham*, itself derived from the Greek *drakhme*, referring to a small unit of currency and weight). Borges's response to the formidable difficulties of context reconstruction (which also beset the study and teaching of world literature) is not to retreat to a firmer home ground, but to license his partially informed imagination while signalling its fallibility. This is consistent with the cosmopolitan programme espoused in 'The Argentine Writer and Tradition': 'we must believe that the universe is our birthright and try out every subject'.[26]

Borges is not denying that the location from which the universe is explored makes a difference. On the contrary, he says that there is a characteristically Argentine way of trying out every subject: 'without superstition, with an irreverence which can have, and already has had, fortunate consequences'.[27] This, he thinks, is analogous to the Irish and Jewish ways of engaging with and contributing to European literature from a non-central position. As Beatriz Sarlo has remarked, *las orillas,* the edges, is a key term in his work, but it is often to be understood as a limit between two entities rather than a far extremity: between the city and the pampa, between the old world and the new, between popular and high culture.[28] Buenos Aires in the mid-twentieth century occupied a liminal, rather than a truly marginal position in world literature. During Franco's dictatorship in Spain (1939–1975), it was, along with Mexico City, the primary centre for publishing in, and translation into, Spanish.[29] This position, and the achievement of Borges and his contemporaries (such as Roberto Arlt, Leopoldo Marechal, and Silvina Ocampo), has contributed to the confidence of Argentine writing as a whole, which remains undented by the nation's cumulative economic woes. As the critic Martín Schifino has written, contemporary Argentine literature is characterized by an absolute lack of inhibition.[30]

Under Construction

A particularly uninhibited heir to Borges's liminal position is César Aira, whose work has recently benefited from heritage publishing in the United States. Aira cheerfully accepts the predicament of Averroes:

> books move in space, they leave the neighbourhood, the city, the society that produced them, and end up in other languages, other worlds, in an endless voyage towards the incomprehensible. The ship that transports them is misunderstanding.[31]

Aira accepts the misunderstanding built into circulation as a happy fault or fortunate fall (*felix culpa*), and his irreverent way of trying out a range of subjects answers to the contingencies of his particular situation. For many years he earned his living as a translator of bestsellers from English. Although he opposes the bestseller to true literature, there are indirect connections between the work that he did to boil the pot and his original writing, as shown by the cover copy that he wrote for his novel *Ema, the Captive* (*Ema, la cautiva*):

> Some years ago [...] I was able to earn enough to pay my analyst and go on vacation by translating long novels of the variety known as 'gothic' [...]. Naturally, I enjoyed those books, but over time I came to feel that there were too many passions, cancelling each other out like air freshener. No sooner had the thought occurred to me than I came up with the eminently sportive idea of writing a 'simplified' gothic novel. [...] I resorted to the Eternal Return. I renounced Being, became Sei Shonagon, Scheherezade, plus the animals. The 'anecdotes of destiny'.[32]

Ema, the Captive responds to Esteban Echeverría's canonical poem 'The Captive' ('*La Cautiva*', 1837), in which a white couple escapes from Indian captors into a second, paradoxical captivity constituted by the vast and inhospitable spaces of the pampa. When Aira's Ema, who has been transported to the frontier as a convict, is kidnapped, she enters a fabulous realm of exquisite refinement, in which she circulates far more freely than she was able to among the soldiers and settlers. The indigenous captors in Echeverría's poem are animalized; in Aira's novel, by contrast, they are portrayed as dandies and aesthetes. They live in paper houses and sleep on rush mats. They celebrate a Monkey Festival (75–76) and build snow-gardens (165). Their serving girls are referred to by the Japanese term *kamuros* (71). In their territory, the *hototogisu* bird sings at night (90), and shogun-pheasants roam (154). These displaced Japanese features are remnants of a project that Aira signalled in an interview with Graciela Speranza: the idea behind *Ema* was, he said in 1993, to rewrite *The Pillow Book* of Sei Shonagon, who served as a lady-in-waiting to the Empress Sadako in the last decade of the tenth century CE.[33]

If Aira 'became' Sei Shonagon (or Scheherezade or indeed the Isak Dinesen of *Anecdotes of Destiny*), it was not by means of meticulous scholarly context-reconstruction, but by taking a few elements from her work and resignifying them, putting those dirhams into circulation in his utopic economy. These becomings are processes rather than states: unfinished, sometimes barely begun. The aim, in this ongoing project, is not to end up being someone else, but to draw on foreign models in order to become who or, as Nietzsche put it, *what* one is.[34] The identity thus affirmed is a work in progress, as Aira explains in his essay on exoticism:

> literature is the means by which a Brazilian becomes Brazilian, an Argentine, Argentine [...].

And I'm not talking about coming to be a *true*, genuine Brazilian or Argentine. Authenticity is not a value that is given beforehand, waiting for the individual to come along and occupy it. On the contrary, it is a construction, like destiny, or style. It's not just a matter of being an Argentine or a Brazilian, but of inventing a system [*dispositivo*] to make that identity worth having, and living with.[35]

Nationality is seen here both as a given and as a goad to invention. For Aira, the system that makes it worth being Argentine cannot be merely inherited; it must also be reinvented by each new writer. The Aira system is neither nostalgic nor parochial. It draws on the literatures of the world through translation and adventurous reading, but does so in response to the contingencies of a local writing situation: as Sandra Contreras has argued, Aira's exoticism provided a way to break with the 'literature of exile', influentially theorized by Juan José Saer and Ricardo Piglia.[36]

Disconcerting in its deliberate frivolity, Aira's work divides the reading public in Argentina, where it has become the centre of a counter-canon. In translation, it has gradually found what seem to be sustainable niches in a wide range of languages, including Turkish and Chinese. *Ema, the Captive* was originally published in 1981; the French translation appeared in 1994, the German in 2004, the English in 2016. Aira's case reminds us that although some novels by very famous authors are now 'born translated', with translations appearing at the same time as, or even before, the book in the original language, this acceleration has not been generalized.[37] Literary works still can and do circulate slowly via translation.

The vectors of slow and delayed circulation are generally smaller publishers, which do not have the means to compete in bidding wars for titles surrounded by international buzz. 'Virtuous by obligation', they must look to the overlooked. If they multiply, so do the potential routes of circulation and the niches for authors who appeal strongly to a scattered rather than a mass readership, since a smaller house can break even on a title with fewer sales.

The following publishers, established since 2007, many on a non-profit basis, have considerably enriched the supply of literary translations into English: Open Letter Books, Contra Mundum, Jantar Publishing, Stockholm Text, And Other Stories, Hispabooks, New Vessel Press, Two Lines Press, Restless Books, Deep Vellum, Phoneme Media, Fitzcarraldo Editions, and Tilted Axis (this list is not exhaustive). According to the Three Per Cent database of translations published in the United States, the number of translated literary titles has risen significantly, if in a somewhat jagged manner, from 360 in 2008 to 579 in 2016.

This is good news for the academic field of world literature, whose rapid growth may already be stimulating the publication of translations. But disciplines do not grow or shrink in isolation; they compete for students and funding. One of the reasons for the rise of world literature is that it provides an administratively attractive solution to the problem of dwindling enrolments in literary subjects offered by programmes in comparative literature and languages. World literature can, at least on paper, replace a range of those subjects and allow for economies of scale. But where this happens, the institutions concerned are training fewer students to read fluently in languages other than English. World literature instructors who studied in a language programme may feel that they are collaborating in the impoverishment of the linguistic ecosystem, and that their students are not benefiting from the specialized training that they themselves received.

Translators into English, for their part, may suspect that they are contributing to the process of standardization that Erich Auerbach envisaged with some trepidation in 1952, when he imagined the number of literary languages shrinking to one.[38] But three points can be made in response. The first is obvious but easy to forget: translation adds to the sum of worthwhile experiences that are possible in the world. Before 2016 it was not possible to read Bei Tong's novel *Beijing Comrades* or a substantial collection of Hasan Sijzi's poetry in English. Now it is. The second point is that translation into English facilitates translation into other languages and thereby more fluid circulation of literary works in general. For better *and* worse, publishers in Tehran and Tokyo watch the review pages of the English-language press, and although a book is often translated into other languages first, the appearance of a translation into English can have a powerful knock-on effect.

Finally, it is worth remembering that an important, if numerically minor, function of translation is to prompt readers to learn the source languages of works that have fascinated them. When this happens, the reader eventually has access not only to the initiatory work in the original language but is equipped to explore the literature in which it emerged with a new degree of freedom, prospecting beyond the narrow limits of what is selected for translation. Additionally, such a reader may contribute to the expansion of those limits by participating in the practical internationalism advocated by Pierre Bourdieu at the end of 'A Conservative Revolution in Publishing', which is not the work of a community to come, but of communities that exist already, often in the form of widely flung networks: translators, publishers, critics, scholars, booksellers, bloggers, and others collaborating to enlarge and enrich what world literature can be.[39]

Notes

1. S. Helgesson and P. Vermeulen, 'World Literature in the Making', in S. Helgesson and P. Vermeulen (eds.), *Institutions of World Literature* (New York: Routledge, 2015), p. 1.
2. N. Goodman, *Ways of Worldmaking* (Indianapolis: Hackett, 1978), p. 6.
3. See 'About Three Percent', www.rochester.edu/College/translation/threepercent/index.php?s=about.
4. J. Heilbron, 'Towards a Sociology of Translation: Book Translations as a Cultural World-System', *European Journal of Social Theory*, 2.4 (1999), 429–444 (p. 439).
5. E. Allen, 'Literature's Invisible Arbiters', *The Guardian*, November 20, 2007.
6. J. B. Thompson, *Merchants of Culture: The Publishing Business in the Twenty-First Century* (Cambridge: Polity, 2010), p. 193.
7. See P. Bourdieu, 'A Conservative Revolution in Publishing', R. Fraser (trans.), *Translation Studies*, 1.2 (2008), 123–153.
8. J. Herralde, *Opiniones mohicanas* (Barcelona: El Acantilado, 2001), p. 31. Unless otherwise indicated, the translations are my own.
9. Bourdieu, 'A Conservative Revolution in Publishing', p. 135.
10. Ibid.
11. C. Andrews, *Roberto Bolaño's Fiction: An Expanding Universe* (New York: Columbia University Press, 2014), pp. 1–32.
12. A. Beecroft, *An Ecology of World Literature* (London: Verso, 2015), p. 289.
13. L. Venuti, *Translation Changes Everything: Theory and Practice* (New York: Routledge, 2013), p. 194.
14. R. Bolaño, *The Insufferable Gaucho*, C. Andrews (trans.) (New York: New Directions, 2006), p. 82. Further references to this book will be given in parentheses in the text.
15. B. Loy, '*Deseos de mundo. Roberto Bolaño y la (no tan nueva) literatura mundial*', in G. Müller and D. Gras (eds.), *América Latina y la literatura mundial: Mercado editorial, redes globales y la invención de un continente* (Madrid/Frankfurt: Vervuert, 2015), pp. 273–293 (pp. 282–290).
16. See A. S. Labarthe and J. Rivette, '*Entretien avec Resnais et Robbe-Grillet*', *Cahiers du Cinéma*, 123 (1961), 1–33 (pp. 14–15).
17. The notion of a 'Greenwich Meridian of literature' was proposed by Pascale Casanova in *The World Republic of Letters*, M. B. DeBevoise (trans.) (Cambridge, MA: Harvard University Press, 2004), pp. 87–91.
18. E. Kristal, '"Considering Coldly …": A Response to Franco Moretti', *New Left Review*, 15 (2002), 61–74 (p. 65).
19. F. Moretti, 'Conjectures on World Literature', *New Left Review*, 1 (2000), 54–68 (p. 67).
20. Loy, '*Deseos de mundo*', p. 280; V. Cooppan, 'Codes for World Literature: Network Theory and the Field Imaginary', in J. Küpper (ed.), *Approaches to World Literature* (Berlin: Akademie-Verlag, 2013), pp. 103–121.
21. F. Moretti, 'More Conjectures', *New Left Review*, 20 (2003), 73–81 (p. 75).
22. See B. Matamoro, *Rubén Darío* (Madrid: Espasa, 2002), pp. 47–101.

23. See C. Pradeau, '*Un Drakkar sur le lac Léman*', in C. Pradeau and T. Samoyault (eds.), *Où est la littérature mondiale?* (Paris: Presses Universitaires de Vincennes, 2005), pp. 65–81 (pp. 73–75).
24. J. L. Borges, *Collected Fictions*, A. Hurley (trans.) (New York: Penguin, 1998), p. 241.
25. Borges, *Collected Fictions*, p. 241.
26. J. L. Borges, 'The Argentine Writer and Tradition', E. Allen (trans.), in E. Weinberger (ed.), *Selected Non-Fictions* (New York: Penguin, 2000), pp. 420–426 (p. 427).
27. Borges, 'The Argentine Writer and Tradition', p. 426.
28. B. Sarlo, *Jorge Luis Borges: A Writer on the Edge*, John King (ed.), (London: Verso, 1993), pp. 20–33.
29. G. Adamo, 'Argentina', in E. Allen (ed.), *To Be Translated or Not to Be: PEN / IRL Report on the International Situation of Literary Translation* (Barcelona: Institut Ramón Llul, 2007), pp. 53–58 (p. 53).
30. M. Schifino, '*Rutas argentinas*', *Revista de libros*, 166, October 2010, 40–43.
31. C. Aira, '*Lo incomprensible*', *ABC Cultural*, February 26, 2000.
32. C. Aira, *Ema, the Captive*, C. Andrews (trans.) (New York: New Directions, 2016), pp. 231–232. Further references to this book will be given in parentheses in the text.
33. G. Speranza, *Primera Persona: Conversaciones con quince narradores argentinos* (Santafé de Bogotá: Norma, 1995), p. 205.
34. F. Nietzsche, *Ecce Homo: How to Become What You Are*, D. Large (trans.) (Oxford: Oxford University Press, 2007), p. 31.
35. C. Aira, '*Exotismo*', *Boletín del Centro de Estudios de Teoría y Crítica Literaria (Rosario)*, 3 (1993), 313–317 (p. 317).
36. S. Contreras, *Las vueltas de César Aira* (Rosario: Beatriz Viterbo, 2002), pp. 71–72.
37. See R. Walkowitz, *Born Translated: The Contemporary Novel in an Age of World Literature* (New York: Columbia University Press, 2015), pp. 2–3.
38. E. Auerbach, 'Philology and *Weltliteratur*', M. Said and E. Said (trans.), *The Centennial Review*, 13.1 (1969), 1–17 (p. 3).
39. Bourdieu, 'A Conservative Revolution in Publishing', p. 151.

FURTHER READING

Contemporary Theories of World Literature

Apter, Emily, *Against World Literature: On the Politics of Untranslatability* (London: Verso, 2013).

Beecroft, Alexander, *An Ecology of World Literature: From Antiquity to the Present Day* (London: Verso, 2015).

Casanova, Pascale, *The World Republic of Letters*, M. B. DeBevoise (trans.) (Cambridge, MA: Harvard University Press, 2004).

Cheah, Pheng, *What Is a World? On Postcolonial Literature as World Literature* (Durham: Duke University Press, 2016).

Damrosch, David, *What Is World Literature?* (Princeton: Princeton University Press, 2003).

—(ed.), *World Literature in Theory* (Oxford: Wiley Blackwell, 2014).

D'haen, Theo, *The Routledge Concise History of World Literature* (London: Abingdon, 2012).

D'haen, Theo, Iannis Goerlandt, and Roger D. Sell (eds.), *Major Versus Minor? Languages and Literatures in a Globalized World* (Amsterdam: John Benjamins, 2015).

Friedman, Susan, 'World Modernisms, World Literature, and Comparativity', in Mark Wollaeger and Matt Eatough (eds.), *The Oxford Handbook of Global Modernisms* (Oxford: Oxford University Press, 2012), pp. 499–525.

Hayot, Eric, *On Literary Worlds* (Oxford: Oxford University Press, 2012).

Helgesson, Stefan, 'Postcolonialism and World Literature: Rethinking the Boundaries', *Interventions*, 16.4 (2014), 483–500.

Helgesson, Stefan and Pieter Vermeulen (eds.), *Institutions of World Literature: Writing, Translation, Markets* (Abingdon: Routledge, 2016).

Hitchcock, Peter, *The Long Space: Transnationalism and Postcolonial Form* (Stanford: Stanford University Press, 2010).

Kristal, Efraín, '"Considering Coldly . . .": A Response to Franco Moretti', *New Left Review*, 15 (2002), 61–74.

Kumar, Amitava (ed.), *World Bank Literature* (Minneapolis: University of Minnesota Press, 2003).

Moretti, Franco, 'Conjectures on World Literature', *New Left Review*, 1 (2000), 54–68.

Mufti, Aamir, *Forget English! Orientalisms and World Literatures* (Cambridge, MA: Harvard University Press, 2016).

Pizer, John, *The Idea of World Literature: History and Pedagogical Practice* (Baton Rouge: Louisiana State University Press, 2006).

Pollock, Sheldon, Benjamin A. Elman, and Ku-ming Kevin Chang (eds.), *World Philology* (Cambridge, MA: Harvard University Press, 2015).

Prawer, S. S., *Karl Marx and World Literature* (Oxford: Oxford University Press, 1976).

Prendergast, Christopher (ed.), *Debating World Literature* (London: Verso, 2004).

Said, Edward W., *Humanism and Democratic Criticism* (New York: Columbia University Press, 2004).

Thomsen, Mads Rosendahl, *Mapping World Literature: International Canonization and Transnational Literatures* (London: Continuum, 2008).

WReC (Warwick Research Collective), *Combined and Uneven Development: Towards a New Theory of World-Literature* (Liverpool: Liverpool University Press, 2015).

Cosmopolitanism

Bernheimer, Charles (ed.), *Comparative Literature in the Age of Multiculturalism* (Baltimore: Johns Hopkins University Press, 1995).

Brennan, Timothy, 'The Critic and the Public: Edward Said and World Literature', in Adel Iskander and Hakem Rustom (eds.), *Edward Said: A Legacy of Emancipation and Representation* (Berkeley and Los Angeles: University of California Press, 2010), pp. 102–120.

Lazarus, Neil, 'Cosmopolitanism and the Specificity of the Local in World Literature', *The Journal of Commonwealth Literature*, 46.1 (2011), 119–137.

Noyes, John K., *Herder: Aesthetics Against Imperialism* (Toronto: University of Toronto Press, 2015).

Paik, Nak-chung, *The Division System in Crisis: Essays on Contemporary Korea*, Kim Myung-hwan, Sol June-kyu, Song Seung-cheol, and Ryu Young-joo (trans.) (Berkeley and Los Angeles: University of California Press, 2011).

Parry, Benita, 'A Departure from Modernism: Stylistic Strategies in Modern Peripheral Literatures as Symptom, Mediation and Critique of Modernity', in Ulrika Maude and Mark Nixon (eds.), *The Bloomsbury Companion to Modernist Literature* (London: Bloomsbury Academic, 2018).

Tihanov, Galin, 'Narratives of Exile: Cosmopolitanism beyond the Liberal Imagination', in Nina Glick Schiller and Andrew Irving (eds.), *Whose Cosmopolitanism? Critical Perspectives, Relationalities, and Discontents* (Oxford: Berghahn, 2014), pp. 141–159.

Nation and Transnationalism

Bernard, Anna, *Rhetorics of Belonging: Nation, Narration, and Israel/Palestine* (Liverpool: Liverpool University Press, 2013).

Bartolovich, Crystal, 'Global Capital and Transnationalism', in Henry Schwarz and Sangeeta Ray (eds.), *A Companion to Postcolonial Studies* (Oxford: Wiley-Blackwell, 2000), pp. 126–161.

Brennan, Timothy, 'The Case against Irony', *Journal of Commonwealth Literature*, 49.3 (2014), 379–394.

Featherstone, David, *Solidarity: Hidden Histories and Geographies of Internationalism* (London: Zed Books, 2012).

Harlow, Barbara, *Resistance Literature* (London: Methuen, 1987).

Prashad, Vijay, *The Darker Nations: A People's History of the Third World* (New York: The New Press, 2007).

Scale and System

Auerbach, Erich, *Time, History, and Literature: Selected Essays of Erich Auerbach*, James I. Porter (ed.), Jane O. Newman (trans.) (Princeton: Princeton University Press, 2014).

Even-Zohar, Itamar, 'Polysystem Studies', *Poetics Today*, 11.1 (1990), 1–270.

Kliger, Ilya and Boris Maslov (eds.), *Persistent Forms: Explorations in Historical Poetics* (New York: Fordham University Press, 2016).

Moretti, Franco, *Graphs, Maps, Trees: Abstract Models for a Literary History* (London: Verso, 2005).

Orsini, Francesca, 'The Multilingual Local in World Literature', *Comparative Literature*, 67. 4 (2015), 345–374

Palumbo-Liu, David, Bruce Robbins, and Nirvana Tanoukhi (eds.), *Immanuel Wallerstein and the Problem of the World: System, Scale, Culture* (Durham, NC: Duke University Press, 2011).

Fields

Born, Georgina, 'The Social and the Aesthetic: For a Post-Bourdieuian Theory of Cultural Production', *Cultural Sociology*, 4.2 (2010), 171–208.

Bourdieu, Pierre, *The Field of Cultural Production: Essays on Art and Literature*, Randal Johnson (ed.) (Cambridge: Polity Press, 1993).

Bush, Ruth, *Publishing Africa in French: Literary Institutions and Decolonization, 1945–1967* (Liverpool: Liverpool University Press, 2016).

Dalleo, Raphael (ed.), *Bourdieu and Postcolonial Studies* (Liverpool: Liverpool University Press, 2016).

English, James F., *The Economy of Prestige: Prizes, Awards, and the Circulation of Cultural Value* (Cambridge, MA: Harvard University Press, 2005).

Helgesson, Stefan, *Transnationalism in Southern African Literature: Modernists, Realists, and the Inequality of Print Culture* (New York: Routledge, 2009).

McDonald, Peter D., *Artefacts of Writing: Ideas of the State and Communities of Letters from Matthew Arnold to Xu Bing* (Oxford: Oxford University Press, 2017).

McKenzie, D. F., *Bibliography and the Sociology of Texts* (Cambridge: Cambridge University Press, 1999).

Sapiro, Gisèle, 'Autonomy Revisited: The Question of Mediations and its Methodological Implications', *Paragraph*, 35.1 (2012), 30–48.

Translation and Publishing

Allen, Esther, 'Translation, Globalization, and English', in Esther Allen (ed.), *To Be Translated or Not to Be: PEN / IRL Report on the International Situation of Literary Translation* (Barcelona: Institut Ramón Llul, 2007), pp. 17–33.

Bourdieu, Pierre 'A Conservative Revolution in Publishing', Ryan Fraser (trans.), *Translation Studies*, 1.2 (2008), 123–153.

Brouillette, Sarah, *Postcolonial Writers in the Global Literary Marketplace* (New York: Palgrave Macmillan, 2007).

Heilbron, Johan, 'Towards a Sociology of Translation: Book Translations as a Cultural World-System', *European Journal of Social Theory*, 2.4 (1999) 429–444.

Hermans, Theo, *The Conference of the Tongues* (Manchester: St Jerome, 2007).

Lindberg-Wada, Gunilla (ed.), *Studying Transcultural Literary History* (Berlin: Walter de Gruyter, 2006).

Munday, Jeremy, *Introducing Translation Studies: Theories and Applications*, 4th ed. (Abington: Routledge, 2012).

Sapiro, Gisèle, 'Translation and the Field of Publishing', *Translation Studies*, 1.2 (2008), 154–166.

Venuti, Lawrence, 'Translation Studies and World Literature', in Lawrence Venuti, *Translation Changes Everything: Theory and Practice* (New York: Routledge, 2013), pp. 193–208.

Walkowitz, Rebecca L., *Born Translated: The Contemporary Novel in an Age of World Literature* (New York: Columbia University Press, 2015).

Script

Coulmas, Florian, *The Writing Systems of the World* (Oxford: Blackwell, 1989).

Dehaene, Stanislas, *Reading in the Brain: The New Science of How We Read* (London: Penguin, 2009).

Morison, Stanley, *Politics and Script: Aspects of Authority and Freedom in the Development of Graeco-Latin Script from the Sixth Century B.C. to the Twentieth Century A.D.* (Oxford: Clarendon Press, 1972).

Park, Sowon S. (ed.), *The Chinese Scriptworld and World Literature*, a special issue of the *Journal of World Literature*, 1.2 (2016).

Pollock, Sheldon, *The Language of the Gods in the World of Men: Sanskrit, Culture, and Power in Premodern India* (Berkeley and Los Angeles: University of California Press, 2006).

Young, Robert J. C., 'That Which Is Casually Called a Language', *PMLA*, 131.5 (2016), 1207–1221.

Orality

Austen, Ralph A. (ed.), *In Search of Sunjata: The Mande Oral Epic as History, Literature and Performance* (Bloomington: Indiana University Press, 1999).

Barber, Karin, 'African Histories of Textuality', in Gunilla Lindberg-Wada (ed.), *Studying Transcultural Literary History* (Berlin: Walter de Gruyter, 2006), pp. 66–75.

Bauman, Richard, 'Verbal Art as Performance', *American Anthropologist*, 77.2 (1975) 290–311.

Finnegan, Ruth, *Oral Literature in Africa* (Oxford: Clarendon Press, 1970).

Furniss, Graham and Liz Gunner (eds.), *Power, Marginality and African Oral Literature* (Cambridge: Cambridge University Press, 1995).

Nagy, Gregory, *Poetry as Performance: Homer and Beyond* (Cambridge: Cambridge University Press, 1996).

Hale, Thomas A., *Griots and Griottes: Masters of Words and Music* (Bloomington: Indiana University Press, 1998).

Okpewho, Isidore, *The Epic in Africa: Towards a Poetics of the Oral Performance* (New York: Columbia University Press, 1979).

Lord, Albert B., *The Singer of Tales*, 3rd edn., David F. Elmer (ed.) (Cambridge, MA: Harvard University Press, 2019).

Lyric

Fabb, Nigel, *Linguistics and Literature: Language in the Verbal Arts of the World* (Malden, MA: Blackwell, 1997).

Gasparov, M. L., *A History of European Versification*, G. S. Smith and Marina Tarlinskaja (trans.), G. S. Smith with L. Holford-Strevens (eds.) (Oxford: Clarendon Press, 1996).

Jakobson, Roman, 'Linguistics and Poetics', in *Language in Literature*, Krystyna Pomorska and Stephen Rudy (eds.) (Cambridge, MA: The Belknap Press of Harvard University Press, 1987 [1960]), pp. 62–94.

Maslov, Boris, 'Comparative Literature and Revolution, or the Many Arts of (Mis)reading Alexander Veselovsky', *Compar(a)ison*, 2 (2008), 101–129.

Tynianov, Yuri, 'The Ode as an Oratorical Genre', Ann Shukman (trans.), *New Literary History*, 34.3 (2003 [1922–1928]), 565–596.

Von Hallberg, Robert, *Lyric Powers* (Chicago: University of Chicago Press, 2008).

Ziolkowski, Theodore, *The Classical German Elegy, 1795–1950* (Princeton: Princeton University Press, 1980).

Tragedy

Bushnell, Rebecca (ed.), *A Companion to Tragedy* (Malden, MA: Blackwell, 2005).

Felski, Rita (ed.), *Rethinking Tragedy* (Baltimore: Johns Hopkins University Press, 2008).

Foley, Helene P., *Female Acts in Greek Tragedy* (Princeton: Princeton University Press, 2001).

Kelly, Henry A., *Ideas and Forms of Tragedy: From Aristotle to the Middle Ages* (Cambridge: Cambridge University Press, 1993).

Kerrigan, John, *Revenge Tragedy: Aeschylus to Armageddon* (Oxford: Clarendon Press, 1996).

Poole, Adrian, *Tragedy: A Very Short Introduction* (Oxford: Oxford University Press, 2005).

Williams, Bernard, *Shame and Necessity* (Berkeley and Los Angeles: University of California Press, 1993).

Zhang, Longxi, *From Comparison to World Literature* (Albany: State University of New York Press, 2015).

Novel

Bower, Rachel, *Epistolarity and World Literature, 1980–2010* (London: Palgrave Macmillan, 2017).

Cleary, Joe, Jed Esty, and Colleen Lye (eds.), 'Peripheral Realisms', a special issue of *Modern Language Quarterly*, 73.3 (2012).

Esty, Jed, *Unseasonable Youth: Modernism, Colonialism, and the Fiction of Development* (Oxford: Oxford University Press, 2006).

Moretti, Franco (ed.), *The Novel*, Vols 1 and 2 (Princeton: Princeton University Press, 2006).

Jameson, Fredric 'Third-World Literature in the Era of Multinational Capitalism', *Social Text*, 15 (1986), 65–88.

Lazarus, Neil, 'The Fetish of "the West" in Postcolonial Theory', in Crystal Bartolovich (ed.), *Marxism, Modernity and Postcolonial Studies* (Cambridge: Cambridge University Press, 2002), pp. 43–64.

Schwarz, Roberto, *Misplaced Ideas: Essays on Brazilian Culture*, John Gledson (ed.) (London: Verso, 1992).

Siskind, Mariano, 'The Globalization of the Novel and the Novelization of the Global. A Critique of World Literature', *Comparative Literature*, 62.4 (2010), 336–360.

Graphic Fiction

Baetens, Jan and Hugo Frey, *The Graphic Novel: An Introduction* (Cambridge: Cambridge University Press, 2015).

Chute, Hillary L., *Disaster Drawn: Visual Witness, Comics, and Documentary Form* (Cambridge, MA: The Belknap Press of Harvard University Press, 2016).

Denson, Shane, Christina Meyer, and Daniel Stein (eds.), *Transnational Perspectives on Graphic Narratives: Comics at the Crossroads* (London: Bloomsbury, 2013).

Groensteen, Thierry, *The System of Comics*, Bart Beaty and Nick Nguyen (trans.) (Jackson: University Press of Mississippi, 2007).

MacWilliams, Mark W. (ed.), *Japanese Visual Culture: Explorations in the World of Manga and Anime* (New York: Routledge, 2015).

McKinney, Mark (ed.), *History and Politics in French-Language Comics and Graphic Novels* (Jackson: University Press of Mississippi, 2008).

Sabin, Roger, *Comics, Comix & Graphic Novels: A History of Comic Art* (London: Phaidon, 2008).

Stein, Daniel, and Jan-Noël Thon (eds.), *From Comic Strips to Graphic Novels: Contributions to the Theory and History of Graphic Narrative* (Berlin: Walter De Gruyter, 2013).

Short Story

Balogun, Fidelis Odun, *Tradition and Modernity in the African Short Story: An Introduction to a Literature in Search of Critics* (Westport: Greenwood Press, 1991).

Brueck, Laura R., *Writing Resistance: The Rhetorical Imagination of Hindi Dalit Literature* (New York: Columbia University Press, 2014).

Gajarawala, Toral Jatin, *Untouchable Fictions: Literary Realism and the Crisis of Caste* (New York: Fordham University Press, 2013).

Hunter, Adrian, *The Cambridge Introduction to the Short Story in English* (Cambridge: Cambridge University Press, 2007).

May, Charles E. (ed.), *The New Short Story Theories* (Athens: Ohio University Press, 1994).

Orsini, Francesca, 'India in the Mirror of World Fiction', *New Left Review*, 13 (2002), 75–88.

Pravinchandra, Shital, 'Not Just Prose', *Interventions*, 16.3 (2013), 424–444.

Cinema

Adorno, Theodor W., 'Transparencies on Film', Thomas Y. Levin (trans.), *New German Critique*, 24/25 (1981/1982), 199–205.

Doane, Mary Ann, *The Emergence of Cinematic Time: Modernity, Contingency, the Archive* (Cambridge, MA: Harvard University Press, 2002).

Jameson, Fredric, *The Geopolitical Aesthetic: Cinema and Space in the World System* (Bloomington: Indiana University Press, 1992).

Kracauer, Siegfried, *Theory of Film: The Redemption of Physical Reality* (Princeton: Princeton University Press, 1997).

Dennison, Stephanie, and Song Hwee Lim (eds.), *Remapping World Cinema: Identity, Culture, and Politics in Film* (London: Wallflower Press, 2006).

López, Silvia L., 'Dialectical Criticism in the Provinces of the "World-Republic of Letters": The Primacy of the Object in the Work of Roberto Schwarz', *A Contracorriente: A Journal on Social History and Literature in Latin America*, 9.1 (2011), 69–88.

Marcuse, Herbert, 'A Note on Dialectic', in *The Essential Frankfurt School Reader*, Andrew Arato and Eike Gebhardt (eds.) (New York: Continuum, 1988), pp. 444–451.

INDEX

Cambridge Companions to ...

AUTHORS

Edward Albee edited by Stephen J. Bottoms

Margaret Atwood edited by Coral Ann Howells

W. H. Auden edited by Stan Smith

Jane Austen edited by Edward Copeland and Juliet McMaster (second edition)

Balzac edited by Owen Heathcote and Andrew Watts

Beckett edited by John Pilling

Bede edited by Scott DeGregorio

Aphra Behn edited by Derek Hughes and Janet Todd

Walter Benjamin edited by David S. Ferris

William Blake edited by Morris Eaves

Boccaccio edited by Guyda Armstrong, Rhiannon Daniels, and Stephen J. Milner

Jorge Luis Borges edited by Edwin Williamson

Brecht edited by Peter Thomson and Glendyr Sacks (second edition)

The Brontës edited by Heather Glen

Bunyan edited by Anne Dunan-Page

Frances Burney edited by Peter Sabor

Byron edited by Drummond Bone

Albert Camus edited by Edward J. Hughes

Willa Cather edited by Marilee Lindemann

Cervantes edited by Anthony J. Cascardi

Chaucer edited by Piero Boitani and Jill Mann (second edition)

Chekhov edited by Vera Gottlieb and Paul Allain

Kate Chopin edited by Janet Beer

Caryl Churchill edited by Elaine Aston and Elin Diamond

Cicero edited by Catherine Steel

Coleridge edited by Lucy Newlyn

Wilkie Collins edited by Jenny Bourne Taylor

Joseph Conrad edited by J. H. Stape

H. D. edited by Nephie J. Christodoulides and Polina Mackay

Dante edited by Rachel Jacoff (second edition)

Daniel Defoe edited by John Richetti

Don DeLillo edited by John N. Duvall

Charles Dickens edited by John O. Jordan

Emily Dickinson edited by Wendy Martin

John Donne edited by Achsah Guibbory

Dostoevskii edited by W. J. Leatherbarrow

Theodore Dreiser edited by Leonard Cassuto and Claire Virginia Eby

John Dryden edited by Steven N. Zwicker

W. E. B. Du Bois edited by Shamoon Zamir

George Eliot edited by George Levine

T. S. Eliot edited by A. David Moody

Ralph Ellison edited by Ross Posnock

Ralph Waldo Emerson edited by Joel Porte and Saundra Morris

William Faulkner edited by Philip M. Weinstein

Henry Fielding edited by Claude Rawson

F. Scott Fitzgerald edited by Ruth Prigozy

Flaubert edited by Timothy Unwin

E. M. Forster edited by David Bradshaw

Benjamin Franklin edited by Carla Mulford

Brian Friel edited by Anthony Roche

Robert Frost edited by Robert Faggen

Gabriel García Márquez edited by Philip Swanson

Elizabeth Gaskell edited by Jill L. Matus

Edward Gibbon edited by Karen O'Brien and Brian Young

Goethe edited by Lesley Sharpe

Günter Grass edited by Stuart Taberner

Thomas Hardy edited by Dale Kramer

David Hare edited by Richard Boon

Nathaniel Hawthorne edited by Richard Millington

Seamus Heaney edited by Bernard O'Donoghue

Ernest Hemingway edited by Scott Donaldson

Homer edited by Robert Fowler

Horace edited by Stephen Harrison

Ted Hughes edited by Terry Gifford

Ibsen edited by James McFarlane

Henry James edited by Jonathan Freedman

Samuel Johnson edited by Greg Clingham

Ben Jonson edited by Richard Harp and Stanley Stewart

James Joyce edited by Derek Attridge (second edition)

Kafka edited by Julian Preece

Keats edited by Susan J. Wolfson

Rudyard Kipling edited by Howard J. Booth

Lacan edited by Jean-Michel Rabaté

Virginia Woolf edited by Susan Sellers (second edition)

Wordsworth edited by Stephen Gill

W. B. Yeats edited by Marjorie Howes and John Kelly

Xenophon edited by Michael A. Flower

Zola edited by Brian Nelson

TOPICS

The Actress edited by Maggie B. Gale and John Stokes

The African American Novel edited by Maryemma Graham

The African American Slave Narrative edited by Audrey A. Fisch

Theatre History by David Wiles and Christine Dymkowski

African American Theatre by Harvey Young

Allegory edited by Rita Copeland and Peter Struck

American Crime Fiction edited by Catherine Ross Nickerson

American Gothic edited by Jeffrey Andrew Weinstock

American Modernism edited by Walter Kalaidjian

American Poetry Since 1945 edited by Jennifer Ashton

American Realism and Naturalism edited by Donald Pizer

American Travel Writing edited by Alfred Bendixen and Judith Hamera

American Women Playwrights edited by Brenda Murphy

Ancient Rhetoric edited by Erik Gunderson

Arthurian Legend edited by Elizabeth Archibald and Ad Putter

Australian Literature edited by Elizabeth Webby

The Beats edited by Stephen Belletto

British Black and Asian Literature (1945–2010) edited by Deirdre Osborne

British Literature of the French Revolution edited by Pamela Clemit

British Romanticism edited by Stuart Curran (second edition)

British Romantic Poetry edited by James Chandler and Maureen N. McLane

British Theatre, 1730–1830, edited by Jane Moody and Daniel O'Quinn

Canadian Literature edited by Eva-Marie Kröller (second edition)

Children's Literature edited by M. O. Grenby and Andrea Immel

The Classic Russian Novel edited by Malcolm V. Jones and Robin Feuer Miller

Contemporary Irish Poetry edited by Matthew Campbell

Creative Writing edited by David Morley and Philip Neilsen

Crime Fiction edited by Martin Priestman

Dracula edited by Roger Luckhurst

Early Modern Women's Writing edited by Laura Lunger Knoppers

The Eighteenth-Century Novel edited by John Richetti

Eighteenth-Century Poetry edited by John Sitter

Emma edited by Peter Sabor

English Literature, 1500–1600 edited by Arthur F. Kinney

English Literature, 1650–1740 edited by Steven N. Zwicker

English Literature, 1740–1830 edited by Thomas Keymer and Jon Mee

English Literature, 1830–1914 edited by Joanne Shattock

English Novelists edited by Adrian Poole

English Poetry, Donne to Marvell edited by Thomas N. Corns

English Poets edited by Claude Rawson

English Renaissance Drama, second edition edited by A. R. Braunmuller and Michael Hattaway

English Renaissance Tragedy edited by Emma Smith and Garrett A. Sullivan Jr.

English Restoration Theatre edited by Deborah C. Payne Fisk

The Epic edited by Catherine Bates

Erotic Literature edited by Bradford Mudge

European Modernism edited by Pericles Lewis

European Novelists edited by Michael Bell

Fairy Tales edited by Maria Tatar

Fantasy Literature edited by Edward James and Farah Mendlesohn

Feminist Literary Theory edited by Ellen Rooney

Fiction in the Romantic Period edited by Richard Maxwell and Katie Trumpener

For EU product safety concerns, contact us at Calle de José Abascal, 56–1°,
28003 Madrid, Spain or eugpsr@cambridge.org.

www.ingramcontent.com/pod-product-compliance
Ingram Content Group UK Ltd.
Pitfield, Milton Keynes, MK11 3LW, UK
UKHW020356140625
459647UK00020B/2502